QUALITATIVE RESEARCH

MARKET RESEARCH IN PRACTICE SERIES

Published in association with The Market Research Society
Consultant Editors: David Barr and Robin J Birn

Kogan Page has joined forces with The Market Research Society (MRS) to publish this unique series of books designed to cover the latest developments in market research thinking and practice.

The series provides up-to-date knowledge on the techniques of market research and customer insight and best practice in implementing them. It also shows the contribution market research and customer information management techniques can make to helping organizations of all kinds in shaping their strategy, structure, customer focus and value creation.

The series consists of several essential guides that focus on the core skills developed in the MRS training and qualifications programmes (www.mrs.org.uk). It provides practical advice and case studies on how to plan, use, act on and follow up research, and on how to combine it with other sources of information to develop deep insights into customers.

Fully international in scope of content, its readership is also from all over the world. The series is designed not only for specialist market researchers, but also for all those involved in developing and using deeper insights into their customers – marketers in all disciplines, including planning, communications, brand management, and interactive marketers.

Other titles in the series:

Business to Business Market Research, Ruth McNeil
Consumer Insight, Merlin Stone
The Effective Use of Market Research, Robin J Birn
Market Intelligence: How and why organizations use market research, Martin Callingham
Market Research in Practice: A guide to the basics, Paul Hague, Nick Hague and Carol-Ann Morgan
Questionnaire Design, Ian Brace
Researching Customer Satisfaction and Loyalty, Paul Szwarc

Kogan Page Ltd
120 Pentonville Road
London N1 9JN
Tel: 020 7278 0433
www.koganpage.com

QUALITATIVE RESEARCH

GOOD DECISION MAKING THROUGH UNDERSTANDING PEOPLE, CULTURES AND MARKETS

SHEILA KEEGAN

KOGAN
PAGE

London & Philadelphia

Publisher's note

Every possible effort has been made to ensure that the information contained in this book is accurate at the time of going to press, and the publishers and author cannot accept responsibility for any errors or omissions, however caused. No responsibility for loss or damage occasioned to any person acting, or refraining from action, as a result of the material in this publication can be accepted by the editor, the publisher or the author.

First published in Great Britain and the United States in 2009 by Kogan Page Limited

120 Pentonville Road
London N1 9JN
United Kingdom
www.koganpage.com

525 South 4th Street, #24
Philadelphia PA 19147
USA

ISBN 978 0 7494 5464 7   7047828

British Library Cataloguing-in-Publication Data

A CIP record for this book is available from the British Library.

Library of Congress Cataloging-in-Publication Data

Keegan, Sheila.
  Qualitative research : good decision making through understanding people, cultures and markets / Sheila Keegan.
      p. cm.
Includes bibliographical references and index.
  ISBN 978-0-7494-5464-7
  1. Marketing research. 2. Qualitative research. I. Title.
  HF5415.2.K36 2009
  658.8'3—dc22   2009019016

Typeset by Saxon Graphics Ltd, Derby
Printed and bound in India by Replika Press Pvt Ltd

Contents

About MRS

- With members in more than 70 countries, MRS is the world's largest association serving all those with professional equity in provision or use of market, social and opinion research, and in business intelligence, market analysis, customer insight and consultancy.
- MRS has a diverse membership of *individuals* at all levels of experience and seniority within agencies, consultancies, support services, client-side organizations, the public sector and the academic community.
- It also serves MRS Company Partners agencies, suppliers of support services, buyers and end-users – of all types and scale who are committed throughout their *organizations* to supporting the core MRS values of professionalism, research excellence and business effectiveness.
- In consultation with its individual members and Company Partners, MRS supports best practice by setting and enforcing industry standards. The commitment to uphold the MRS *Code of Conduct* is supported by the Codeline service and a wide range of specialist guidelines.
- MRS contributes significantly to the enhancement of skills and knowledge by offering various qualifications and membership grades, as well as training and professional development resources.
- MRS enables its members and Company Partners to be very well-informed through the provision of a wide range of publications, information services and conferences.
- MRS offers many opportunities for meeting, communicating and networking across sectors and disciplines, as well as within specialisms.
- As 'the voice of market research', MRS defends and promotes research in its advocacy and representational efforts.
- Through its media relations and public affairs activities, MRS aims to create the widest possible understanding of the process and value of market, social and opinion research, and to achieve the most favourable climate of opinion and legislative environment for research.

The editorial board

SERIES EDITORS

David Barr has been Director General of the Market Research Society since July 1997. He previously spent over 25 years in business information services and publishing. He has held management positions with Xerox Publishing Group, the British Tourist Authority and Reed International plc. His experience of market research is therefore all on the client side, having commissioned many projects for NPD and M&A purposes. A graduate of Glasgow and Sheffield Universities, David Barr is a Member of the Chartered Management Institute and a Fellow of The Royal Society of Arts.

Robin J Birn has been a marketing and market research practitioner for over 25 years. In 1985 Robin set up Strategy, Research and Action Ltd, which is now the largest international market research company for the map, atlas and travel guide sector, and the book industry. He is a Fellow of the Market Research Society and is also the editor of *The International Handbook of Market Research Techniques*. He is currently Marketing Training Developer at Imparta Ltd.

ADVISORY MEMBERS

Martin Callingham was formerly Group Market Research Director at Whitbread, where he ran the Market Research department for 20 years and was a non-executive director of the company's German restaurant chain for more than 10 years. Martin has also played his part in the market research world. Apart from being on many committees of the MRS, of which he is a Fellow, he was Chairman of the Association of Users of Research Agencies (AURA), has been a council member of ESOMAR, and has presented widely, winning the David Winton Award in 2001 at the MRS Conference.

Nigel Culkin is a Fellow of the Market Research Society and member of its Professional Advisory Board. He has been a full member since 1982. He has been in academia since 1991 and is currently Deputy Director, Commercial Development at the University of Hertfordshire, where he is responsible for activities that develop a culture of entrepreneurism and innovation among staff and students. He is Chair of the University's Film Industry Research Group (FiRG), supervisor to a number of research students and regular contributor to the media on the creative industries.

Professor Merlin Stone is Business Research Leader with IBM's Business Consulting Services, where he works on business research, consulting and marketing with IBM's clients, partners and universities. He runs the IBM Marketing Transformation Group, a network of clients, marketing agencies, consultancies and business partners, focusing on changing marketing. He is a director of QCi Ltd, an Ogilvy One company. Merlin is IBM Professor of Relationship Marketing at Bristol Business School. He has written many articles and 25 books on marketing and customer service, including *Up Close and Personal: CRM @ Work, Customer Relationship Marketing, Successful Customer Relationship Marketing, CRM in Financial Services* and *The Customer Management Scorecard*, all published by Kogan Page, and *The Definitive Guide to Direct and Interactive Marketing*, published by Financial Times-Pitman. He is a Founder Fellow of the Institute of Direct Marketing and a Fellow of the Chartered Institute of Marketing.

Paul Szwarc began his career as a market researcher at the Co-operative Wholesale Society (CWS) Ltd in Manchester in 1975. Since then he has worked at Burke Market Research (Canada), American Express Europe, IPSOS RSL, International Masters Publishers Ltd and PSI Global prior to joining the Network Research board as a director in October 2000. Over the past few years Paul has specialized on the consumer financial sector, directing multi-country projects on customer loyalty and retention, new product/service development, and employee satisfaction in the UK, European and North American markets. Paul is a full member of the Market Research Society. He has presented papers at a number of MRS and ESOMAR seminars and training courses.

Acknowledgements

I feel very blessed to have spent my working life in the company of qualitative researchers. I think they are the most interesting, creative, intellectually challenging and entertaining group of colleagues I could ever have hoped for. They are also very generous of their time. Although in theory we are all 'competitors', in my experience qualitative researchers have always been willing to help out with their time or wisdom, whatever the problem. This view has been borne out during the writing of this book.

I would particularly like to thank Rosie Campbell, my business partner at Campbell Keegan for over 25 years. She gamely kept the business going as I burrowed away in my office for months on end – and then dutifully commented on each chapter as it emerged. I also greatly appreciate the contributions from a number of experienced qualitative researchers: Sarah Davies from The Futures Company, Fiona Jack from Green Light International, Jim Ryan from IMS Health and Pat Sabena from Patricia Sabena Qualitative Research Services.

Many thanks, also, to Rose Molloy and Angela Webb from the Association for Qualitative Research who were instrumental in getting together a team of qualitative researchers who are new to the industry, to read sections of this book. The team was fantastic in pointing out areas that needed clarification, omissions, errors – and my dreadful grammar. Many thanks to them all: Naomi Boal, Lydia Fellows, Lucy Beesley, Jess Francis, Amy Jo Lewis and Julie McNair.

I would also like to thank those researchers and their clients who have generously contributed case studies to bring the book to life: Susan Stancombe of Stancombe Research & Planning (Australia), Coby Dykstra and John Attfield of Attfield Dykstra & Partners (Germany), Pat Sabena of Patricia Sabena Qualitative Research Services (USA), Vicki Arbes of Open Mind Research Group (Australia), Piyul Mukherjee of Proact Research & Consultancy Private Ltd (India), Laura Mitchelson from Amber Insights (China) and Vicki Kateley from Bounty (UK).

Thank you also to Steve Hastings and Tony Solomon from isobel advertising, who kindly allowed me to include their mood board, concept boards and final advertising.

I give my special thanks to Chris, for keeping the home fires burning and for endlessly cooking supper. Last, but not least, I want to thank Carrie, who has survived and thrived in a qualitative home and has paid me back by going into marketing and becoming a potential client!

Introduction

This book is an attempt to weave together three elements: practical 'how to' advice for qualitative researchers who are new to the business, together with a preliminary grounding in the theory of qualitative research and – essentially – how these two aspects feed off one another. The third aspect is maverick, but unavoidable. It is my personal perspective on qualitative research. It is impossible for me to write about this subject 'objectively', for reasons that will become clear throughout the book. It is my belief that qualitative research – or rather qualitative thinking – is a way of seeing the world, and it is impossible for us, as researchers, to 'stand outside' our research. However, this does not excuse us from trying our best to be as aware as possible of potential biases. We need to develop our personal skills in awareness, questioning and reflecting on our thinking, and we need to aim for impartiality in the analysis and interpretation of our research.

This is an exciting time to be involved in qualitative research. There is a move towards thinking about research in more collaborative ways: clients and researchers working together on research issues, rather than the traditional model of the researcher as expert, interviewing research participants and reporting back to the client. Technology is opening doors to new types of research, carried out in different ways amongst different groups of people for example online focus groups, groups on Second Life and blogs. Similarly, research in some areas has become an explicitly *consultative* process, such as *deliberative research* in which participants are educated in a specific area, which enables them to more effectively evaluate potential initiatives. Over the last 20 years, qualitative research has infiltrated parts of society we could never have imagined possible; it is now embedded in virtually all areas of commercial and public sector thinking.

However, my personal concern about some of these developments is that we may move towards a situation in which qualitative research becomes more to do with performance than rigorous analysis. By this I mean, that simply *doing* or *watching* the research *becomes* the research. To get the most use out of qualitative research, and for it to really show its worth, I believe that it is important that the research data is analysed and interpreted thoroughly and with an understanding of the underlying theory that supports this way of working. For this reason, I have tried to ground the 'How to' advice in this book in strong theory, and I have also spent considerable time expanding on qualitative analyses and interpretation and discussing how our research outcomes can be communicated in ways that make them most useful to our clients.

The structure of the book mirrors these areas. The first two chapters provide an introduction to market research in general and the position of qualitative research within it. Chapter 3 gives an overview of different philosophies of qualitative research and how they impinge on practice. However, the purpose of commercial qualitative research is ultimately concerned with helping create effective organizational strategies. Chapter 4 therefore discusses qualitative research from the client's perspective. Before dealing with the nuts and bolts of conducting qualitative research, Chapter 5 looks at the type of research issues that qualitative research can be useful for and includes a number of case studies as illustration. Chapters 6–9 cover the real meat of qualitative research, the methodologies employed, developing skills in these methodologies and how research stimuli and projective techniques can be used to aid understanding and help develop strategic guidance for clients. Chapter 10 looks at the ways in which qualitative research can be used for the generation and development of new ideas. Then, having covered the hard-core areas of qualitative practice, we return, in Chapters 11 and 12 to examine how we can use this knowledge in terms of writing a research proposal and managing a research project.

Chapters 13 and 14 are, arguably, the most important chapters in that they deal with the ways in which qualitative research data can be analysed and presented to clients. Finally, in Chapter 15 we look at multi-country studies.

1 Market research: the big picture

THE PURPOSE OF MARKET RESEARCH

Market research has become part and parcel of consumer culture. Many of us, at some time, have been stopped by street interviewers, recruited for a telephone survey or asked to attend a focus group. But what is the real purpose of market research, beyond the obvious fact of gathering data? How is this data interpreted and used? In what ways can it help organizations to gain a better understanding of the people for whom they are providing products and services? In the following chapters we will be addressing these key questions.

Given the diversity that exists within the market research industry and the different models that researchers adopt, it is difficult to give a precise definition of market research that all practitioners would agree with. Market research often spills over into consultancy, idea generation or problem solving. Good research often includes all these elements. This is also a time of change for the market research industry and it is therefore difficult to define its borders clearly.

Throughout this book we will discuss different approaches to market research and the ways in which the boundaries of market research, and of qualitative research in particular, are becoming less clear, and we will address the benefits and drawbacks of this evolution.

We are all researchers

As individuals, we all spend much of our time 'conducting research': choosing between different brands of toothpaste, deciding which holiday to take or even which country to live in. We are constantly weighing up the pros and cons of these decisions. We seek information and use our past experience to help us make the 'right' choice. Some of this decision making is conscious and rational, but much of it is based on gut feeling, habit or other unconscious influences. Gerald Zaltman, a professor of marketing at Harvard Business School claims that 'at least 95 per cent of all cognition occurs below awareness' (Zaltman, 2003: 50). If this is true, it challenges the widely held belief in self-determination and throws down an interesting gauntlet for market research.

Why organizations use research

It would be easy for organizations to assume that they know what their customers or clients need and want and how their products and services are perceived. However this could be dangerous, especially if the organization is trying to communicate with a group of people, such as their customers or competitor's customers, who may have quite diverse values and beliefs. Organizations could become inward looking and complacent. They could make assumptions about consumers, adopt a certain tone of voice, or develop products or services that they think are appropriate, without properly checking these out.

Market research enables companies to keep abreast of their customers. Finding out what customers (past, current or potential) want lies at the heart of market research. Research deepens organizational understanding of, and raises questions about, the assumptions organizations make in relation to their customers. It provides a dispassionate and structured perspective that enables organizations to understand their customers better.

Organizations go through much the same processes in conducting research as we each do individually, although perhaps in a more structured way. In order to make appropriate decisions, organizational teams need to gather information and develop understanding about the people to whom they are trying to sell products or provide services, and to understand the priorities, needs and aspirations of their current and potential customers or clients. In particular, they must get to grips with the way in which their organization, brands, products or services might usefully fit into or enhance people's lives. As a result, organizations are better equipped to develop products and services that more closely match consumer needs.

Changing markets

At the same time, consumer attitudes and behaviours are not static. They are continually evolving so that communications and ways of communicating that might have been effective last year may no longer be appropriate. The market itself is also evolving, as competitors launch new brands, products or advertising. The relationship between organizations and the people they are targeting is always dynamic.

Any organization, when it is interacting with the general public or with other businesses – and especially with its own staff – needs to be constantly vigilant. It must be on the look out for the changing needs and expectations of all its stakeholders (people who have a vested interest in the organization, eg current or potential customers/clients, different groups of employees, suppliers, advertising agencies and professional bodies). Market research enables organizations to gather, analyse and interpret data about a particular market and the products, brands or services within that market. This helps the organization make better tactical and strategic decisions and to reduce its risk, especially when venturing into uncharted territory.

Market information and understanding obtained from market research are fed into a broad pool of data which includes sales and economic data, trends and predictions, which is gathered from a variety of sources. This information pool is used by marketers or strategists within the organization to help develop corporate strategy and consumer communications. Market research is not a substitute for experience and judgement, but it can help clients to make more informed business decisions.

THE GROWTH OF MARKETING AND MARKET RESEARCH

The techniques and approaches that fall within the broad field of market research developed when marketing emerged in the 1930s. Marketing started from the broad premise that giving people what they wanted or needed would be a more commercially advantageous approach than trying to persuade them to buy what you wanted to sell them. This meant that companies had to talk to people, to find out what they wanted and to test their responses to potential products.

Large corporations in the United States, keen to beat off their competitors, sought to understand the needs and buying habits of their customers. Direct questioning was distrusted. How could you be sure that what people said was actually what they did? Observing consumers' behaviour was thought to provide a more accurate reflection of their motivations than simply asking them what they thought. Buying patterns were monitored. Cans of baked beans on a supermarket shelf were counted at the beginning and end of a set period, and in this way audits were born. Market research companies such as Nielsen and Audits of

Great Britain emerged and, for the first time, managers had accurate data on sales, market size and trends (Hague, Hague and Morgan, 2004: 2–3).

Since then, market research has become mainstream in the developed world and it is continuing to grow worldwide, especially in emerging markets. In 2007, net research rates in Lithuania grew 23 per cent, in Latvia 22 per cent and in the Middle East and Africa 18 per cent (Esomar, 2008). Multi-country studies, in which one country coordinates parallel studies across a range of countries, are now common (see Chapter 15).

THE SPREAD OF MARKET RESEARCH TECHNIQUES

Market research techniques are extremely flexible and, over time, have been adopted in 'non-marketing' contexts. In fact, the term 'market research' has become something of a misnomer. The techniques and approaches originally developed for marketing have proved equally useful for research in central and local government, arts organizations, business marketing, not-for-profit organizations, change management programmes and many more areas. The basic methodologies are the same, although the way they are used in these different areas is modified to fit the context.

Consumer research

This is the area that is most familiar to the general public, the one they are most likely to encounter. Research is carried out extensively by large organizations that deal with the public, on all aspects of their customer offering. New consumer products or services are researched regularly in the process of their development, generally through a mixture of qualitative and quantitative approaches (see Chapter 2). Similarly, advertising research is typically carried out at various stages in the development of the advertising campaign, from the initial ideas, through the rough executions to the finished advertising campaign. Packaging, promotions, products, the interface between the company and its customers, as well as future corporate developments may all be researched at some stage.

Business-to-business research

Businesses may sell exclusively to other businesses rather than direct to the general public. It is therefore important that they understand the attitudes, needs, protocols and procedures of these businesses. Although the principles of business-to-business research are similar to those applied in a consumer market, the practices need to be adapted to fit business customers. For instance, issues of business confidentiality, technical knowledge and the best way to interview research participants (by phone, face to face, online) need to be considered.

Social research

Market research techniques have been adapted for use by not-for-profit organizations, central and local government (especially in the UK), charities, monitoring bodies that track government initiatives, and in a wide variety of social arenas. There are, of course, multitudes of opinion polls that aim to predict voting choices, to monitor social attitudes and so on. Focus groups have also become familiar, as a way in which governments can listen to public opinion and obtain feedback on new policies. This has sometimes led to accusations of 'government by focus groups'.

However, social research has also been used in less obvious ways, for example, to develop public awareness through advertising in such diverse areas as teenage road safety and campaigns to educate the public about health risks (eg of flu, sexually transmitted diseases and the importance of child immunization). Equally it has been used to help shape policies, for example on the regulation of public bodies or educational reforms.

Organizational change research

As well as using research to understand outside groups of people, organizations may also use it with their own employees. Such internal research can help reveal staff attitudes, beliefs and concerns, as input to organizational change strategies. Where a company is undergoing a major restructuring, it is useful to pinpoint departments or groups of people who feel particularly vulnerable or who need support during the change process. Equally, it is essential to identify those people within the organization who are very supportive of change and who can help facilitate the changes throughout the organization.

When an organization is launching a new customer initiative such as a new train service or a new bank account, staff who deal with customers are especially important. They have a direct and ongoing relationship with customers and can provide feedback about how people are likely to react to the initiatives and, once launched, how they actually react in practice.

Employee research may also provide guidance on how to develop more effective internal employee communications or how an organization can communicate more effectively with its shareholders or the media (Goudge, 2006: 63–80).

For the sake of simplicity, the term 'market research' is used throughout the book to mean the spectrum of uses listed above, unless otherwise specified.

USING MARKET RESEARCH TO GENERATE IDEAS

Nowadays, market research is not just about market information and data gathering. It is often used to help identify opportunities for the future (this is sometimes referred to as 'marketing research' to differentiate it from 'data gathering'). Market research can be invaluable in the creative process of developing new products, services, brands or advertising. Research participants, particularly in qualitative research, are viewed as active in the research process rather than simply as passive sources of information and they can generate ideas and concepts that help clients to develop their markets. They work with the researcher, and sometimes directly with client organizations, to generate and build on ideas, or to help shape the embryonic ideas developed by the client (see Chapter 10).

RESEARCH SPECIALISTS

Some research agencies specialize in specific markets or groups of people. For instance, there are research agencies – or departments within agencies – that specialize in research with children or with ethnic communities, the youth market, the elderly and so on. Equally some agencies will specialize by sector, for example the drinks market, IT, social research or media research. Agencies may also be split by methodology; some specialize in qualitative research, others in quantitative research, while large agencies cover both types. The differences between these two types of research is discussed in detail in the next chapter but, to give a quick definition, quantitative research is concerned with proportions and statistical measurement (how many, when), whereas qualitative research is concerned with understanding relationships (why and how).

WHAT IS A TYPICAL MARKET RESEARCH PROJECT?

No research project is truly typical, in that each project will vary in terms of its research objectives, the people to be researched, the scale of the project and so on. Essentially, however, a market research project, in very simplified form, involves the following elements:

■ An organization (the client) identifies a need for information, understanding and/or evaluation of ideas from a specific group (the target audience), such as its current and potential customers, users of a particular product or service or a group of employees. The data will be gathered by interviewing or other data-gathering methods.

■ A researcher or team of researchers, usually specialists from an outside research agency, is invited by the client to discuss the research issues with the client team at a briefing meeting. The project is debated and the research objectives are defined. A project design will then be drawn up by the research team and agreed with the client. This will include details of the basis on which research participants are selected (the research sample), the way in which the research will be carried out (the research methodology), the costs and a schedule.

■ In interview-based research (the dominant methodology in commercial research), the research agency will arrange for the appropriate research participants to be recruited. The way this is done will differ between qualitative and quantitative research. For qualitative research, participants are usually pre-recruited for interviews. For quantitative research they may be recruited and interviewed at the same time, as in street interviews. There are many other forms of research, which will be covered later on in this book. All of these activities are known as fieldwork.

■ Often, in interview-based qualitative work, researchers will use a topic guide outlining the key areas that need to be covered. This acts as an *aide-mémoire*. The researcher will amend and refine the questions as the research process develops, with the aim of exploring and understanding the relevant areas. For quantitative work a structured questionnaire is generally used. The questions are strictly adhered to so that the answers can be aggregated and analysed according to different age groups, product usage and so on.

■ For qualitative research, the materials that are produced from the research – audio tapes, videos, notes, drawings and so on (the data) – are then analysed and interpreted. This involves the researchers working with the data in order to draw out overall meaning and highlight its relevance to the concerns of the client. This is quite different from quantitative research, in which the completed questionnaires are subject to statistical and numerical measurements, and are usually presented as charts, graphs, tables, diagrams, frameworks and text.

■ The researchers then present the findings, conclusions and recommendations to the client in a presentation or debrief, sometimes followed by a written report.

■ The project may be followed up with workshops within the organization, in order to disseminate the findings and encourage different interest groups to draw out the implications of the research for their own work.

MARKET RESEARCH ORGANIZATIONS

Most sizable countries have a professional market research organization (sometimes more than one), which promotes the interests of its members, encourages good practice, and usually has a code of conduct that members must adhere to; examples include the AMSRS in Australia, the AMA in the United States, the MRS in the UK and the MRS in Sri Lanka.

In some countries there is an organization specifically for qualitative researchers, such as the AQR in the UK, the QRCA in the US and the AUAQR in Australia.

2 How 'qualitative' fits within the wider world of research

QUALITATIVE RESEARCH IN RELATION TO QUANTITATIVE RESEARCH

Market research encompasses a broad and varied field of activity. Many different research methodologies are employed, in many different contexts. Methodologies tend, nevertheless, to fall into two distinct categories: quantitative or qualitative.

Quantitative research measures the proportion of a population who think or behave in a particular way. This is achieved by counting the number of people who buy certain brands or agree with certain statements, and producing statistics to show the proportions of the population that fall into specific categories, such as users of brand X and of brand Y. Because quantitative research focuses on precise numerical measurements of consumer attitudes and behaviour – how many or how much – it is relatively easy to understand conceptually. The practicalities of conducting and analysing such research, however, are a good deal more complex.

Qualitative research is less easy to define. It explores questions such as what, why and how, rather than how many or how much; it is primarily concerned with meaning rather than measuring. Understanding why individuals and groups think and behave as they do lies at the heart of qualitative research. It is sometimes described as cultural research because the focus is on the relationships between people and / or between people and products, services or brands within a specific cultural context.

Qualitative and quantitative research can each be characterized in the ways outlined below.

Quantitative research

- It generally involves large numbers of people, including specific sub-groups, grouped for example by age, social class, marital status or brand usage.
- It usually involves the administration of a pre-prepared question-naire, agreed with the client, containing standard questions that are asked of all respondents within the sample (or sub-sample), in the same way throughout the survey.
- It captures an aggregate of individual responses. Each respondent is taken through the questionnaire, without reference to other research participants, and their individual responses are collated.
- The questions are more likely to tap rational, more surface beliefs, atti-tudes and behaviours, partly because of the nature of the question-and-answer format and partly because the interviewer is not trained in in-depth interviewing.
- It involves statistical and numerical measurement of the raw data captured in the questionnaires.
- The results can be used as a benchmark; the survey can be repeated in the future using the same questions, and the results can be compared.
- The questionnaire, once designed, can be administered by interview-ers who are trained to administer quantitative questionnaires. This calls for very different skills from those required for skilled qualitative interviewing.

Qualitative research

- This usually involves small samples of people, who may be represen-tative of the population as a whole or who may represent a small sub-section of the general population, such as those who buy a certain brand of cough medicine or who care for an elderly relative.
- It is person-centred, in that it starts with an attempt to understand the world of the individuals being researched: to gain some understand-ing of what is important to them, how they view the world, and the context within which they will evaluate the idea, product or service that may be presented to them. The emphasis is on the depth of understanding and relationships that the individual has, for example,

with particular brands, or how different brands are perceived as relating to one another.

■ The interaction between researcher and research participant/s is informal, rather like normal conversation; it is fluid, open-ended, dynamic and (to a degree) spontaneous and creative.

■ The aim is to understand people holistically, to see for instance what they think and feel, and to get beneath their 'top of mind' responses: to tap their emotional and intuitive knowledge. Research participants are also encouraged to respond to ideas that are presented to them and to generate their own ideas.

■ This may involve a wide range of techniques (eg drawing, visualization, diary keeping), in order to build up an understanding of the research participant and his or her relationship with the topic that is being researched.

■ Although we may refer to the outcomes of qualitative research as data, they are not data in the sense of being facts or statistics. They refer to behaviour, thoughts, opinions, meaning and the like.

■ It involves a high level of interpretation and synthesis of data by the researcher throughout the research process, both in the interaction with research participants and in the analysis and presentation of the research outcomes. As such, qualitative researchers need to be highly skilled and competent in all stages of the research process.

Case study

A (hypothetical) research project has been commissioned to gather data on teenage smoking. It has two objectives:

1. To map the demographic profile of under-age smokers.
2. To understand current attitudes and behaviour in relation to smoking and possible routes to encourage smoking cessation.

The first objective would probably require a quantitative approach, in that we need to know the proportion of under-16s who smoke and then break this down into sub-sets: age bands, gender, region and so on.

The second objective would probably need qualitative research to explore why young people are smoking, why they continue and the smoking 'context', in order to identify how to encourage them to stop.

THE INTERPLAY OF QUALITATIVE AND QUANTITATIVE METHODOLOGIES

Until relatively recently, qualitative and quantitative market research were regarded as more or less separate entities. Researchers tended to be either qualitative or quantitative; the research approaches and language differed and there was a degree of suspicion on both sides. Many qualitative researchers regarded quantitative research as boring and unable to answer essential questions about the meaning of human behaviour. Meanwhile, many quantitative researchers regarded qualitative research as subjective, overly influenced by the views of the researcher, weak on reliability and validity, too small scale to inspire confidence and not to be trusted as a basis for making important decisions. By contrast, they regarded quantitative research as 'objective', more 'scientific' and therefore a sounder basis for decision making. These differences eventually led to the formation of qualitative research associations, such as AQR, QRCA and AUAQR discussed in the previous chapter, which catered specifically for the qualitative research community.

Nonetheless, in spite of these differences in perspective, there was a – sometimes begrudging – acknowledgement from both 'qual' and 'quant' communities that each approach had its role. Small-scale qualitative research was often employed in the initial stages of a project. For example, it was used to explore people's attitudes, behaviour or language in a particular market, and this understanding was used to help refine the research topics, or to develop questions for the main quantified research stage.

Alternatively, either a quantitative or a qualitative approach was used. In theory the choice of approach would depend on the nature of the research problem. In reality, it was often dependent on the views of the commissioning client, with those who were 'pro-quant' choosing quantitative methodologies and those who were 'pro-qual' choosing qualitative ones.

As a result, quantitative research was sometimes used in situations where qualitative research would have provided more insight and useful direction. However, quantitative research, whilst providing data based on large sample sizes and so offering breadth of coverage, cannot provide the depth of psychological understanding offered by qualitative research. It cannot enable marketers to 'get inside the heads' of their customers.

Can we trust qualitative research?

Times have changed and qualitative research is now accepted on its own terms. Martin Callingham, formally a Group Market Research director, discusses the work that has been done within the UK qualitative community to explore the extent to which qualitative studies are reliable (Is the data collected repeatable?) and valid (Is the data meaningful?) in relation to quantitative studies. He concludes that qualitative and quantitative research operate in different paradigms and cannot be compared on a point-by-point basis. He suggests that, instead of comparing the two, 'A better question to ask is "Does qualitative research help decision making in a company?", and it seems certain that it does' (Callingham, 2004: 106).

Scientific objectivity may be an inappropriate benchmark for measuring the behaviour, attitudes, needs and emotions of human beings, because we are often contradictory, illogical and irrational in our thinking. However there do need to be quality standards and methods of evaluation in order for qualitative research findings to be regarded as legitimate and, therefore, a source of knowledge that the client can trust and act upon. This is an area that we will repeatedly return to throughout this book.

A HEALTHY TRUCE

With growing understanding of the different contributions made by qualitative and quantitative research, it eventually became obvious that the 'qual versus quant' debate was misguided and futile. The two research approaches have come of age and commercial researchers across the board generally acknowledge the value of each. Nowadays they are viewed as offering different perspectives rather than as opposing approaches vying for superiority. They can provide complementary understanding: two sides of the same coin. Sometimes a qualitative approach is more appropriate for given research objectives. Sometimes, quantitative research can provide the more useful input. In practice, with complex research projects, mixed or hybrid methodologies that include both qualitative and quantitative elements are common.

In fact, there are signs that the traditional division between qual and quant is becoming increasingly blurred. A more pragmatic approach, of 'informed eclecticism' (Nancarrow, Spackman and Barker, 2001: 3–28) is gaining ground, in which qual and quant approaches are mixed and matched as needed.

The myth of objectivity

The debate about whether quantitative is 'better' than qualitative – or vice versa – was misguided. It was based on the simplistic assumptions that quantitative research is 'objective' and qualitative is 'subjective' – and that objective research is more trustworthy and therefore superior. The underlying assumption was that truly 'objective' research – in the sense that an objective reality exists and can be increasingly known through the accumulation of more complete information – is possible. However, objectivity is a principle that breaks down in practice.

In any research study, we are selecting and processing and making sense of the data. The research objectives, which are defined by the client, flow from the particular assumptions and priorities within the client organization; they are not 'objective'. In the research process, we select those elements of research participants' responses that are relevant to answering the research questions. Equally, the research conclusions and recommendations need to be crafted to answer the objectives of the research. This is true in both quantitative and qualitative research.

It was often claimed that quantitative research was more objective than qualitative research, because there was less human involvement; questions were standardized and statistically analysed. However, in quantitative research, the questions are chosen and phrased by human beings in a certain way that cannot but influence the response; there is no such thing as a neutral question. Similarly, the way in which the question is asked – the emphasis and tone of voice – as well as the person asking it – all influence the outcome.

For instance:

Why do you need to go shopping?

has quite a different meaning from:

Why do *you* need to go shopping?

Whether a particular question is asked at the beginning of the questionnaire or at the end – the order effect – influences the response. So too does the mood of the research participant; is he or she in a rush? Upset? Tired? Distracted?

Then we must consider the way in which the researcher or client chooses to interpret the responses to the individual questions in the questionnaire. Perhaps it would be most useful to separate the research findings from those people who use the product and compare them with those that don't? This will give a different picture than separating findings from those who buy on price from those who buy on quality.

Quantitative research can easily be interpreted as 'objective' when it is presented as tables and charts that divorce the data from the real human beings at its source. It is easy to forget the ambiguity, guesswork and indifference that the respondents may have felt in answering the questions, and to see only the neatly defined attitudes and behaviours presented in the charts.

Both quantitative and qualitative researchers prioritize their findings by structuring their presentations to be most useful for the client – to answer the questions that he or she has defined as important.

With qualitative research, there is often a conversational style of interaction between the researcher and the researched, in which interpretation plays a large part in developing the outcomes of the research. It is obvious, up front, that the research cannot be 'objective' in a scientific sense, in the same way that everyday conversation does not purport to be scientific. The researcher is arguably the most important research tool in qualitative research and his or her past experience, training and personality will inevitably colour the outcomes.

But, if we cannot achieve objectivity, what is there? The aim of most researchers, both qualitative and quantitative, is to be impartial in the way in which we carry out the research and interpret the research data. We need to be ever conscious of unintended biases. Sometimes bias comes from external sources such as the location in which the research takes place or the style of the research. Often bias comes from ourselves. Being aware of own behaviour, reflecting on and questioning our assumptions, and seeing things from a different perspective are essential research skills that we will repeatedly address throughout this book.

3 The nature of qualitative research

IN THE BEGINNING

Qualitative research as we know it was born after the Second World War. The burgeoning economies of the 1950s and mass communications – television and general interest magazines – fuelled the development of consumer culture (Mariampolski, 2001: 10). This coincided with the re-birth of Freudian psychology, and 'motivational research', as it was then called, was closely linked to psychoanalytical theory.

Over the next decade, with the growth of marketing and a new pragmatism, the re-named 'qualitative research' began to focus more on research data; it became closely aligned with business, and the commercial arm of qualitative research became established.

Hy Mariampolski (2001: 14–21), an eminent US qualitative researcher, provides a good overview of the intellectual heritage of qualitative research from the mid-17th century to the present day. Although many of the influences he refers to are still embedded within commercial practice, contemporary qualitative research has become largely divorced from its academic roots. As Wendy Gordon (1999: 18), an equally eminent UK researcher, describes it:

> qualitative marketing research, as applied to contemporary commercial and social problems, exists like a goldfish in an empty glass bowl, separated from its impressive academic heritage, credentials and authority, and therefore vulnerable to challenge.

COMMERCIAL RESEARCH AND ACADEMIC RESEARCH

Commercial qualitative research (research carried out as a business), in which the research agency works with the client's problem in order to find a solution, is very different from academic qualitative research (usually based in universities) in which researchers generally define the issues they wish to work on, without the absolute requirement to find a usable solution. These two issues, ownership of the problem and the focus on knowledge versus a solution, are the two key differences between commercial and academic research.

Amongst commercial researchers, success in their careers is achieved through helping clients to make good business decisions – and the client endorsement that follows. Their skills are pragmatic and they are judged in terms of how useful their input is. Theory is important, but only in so far as it helps them to help the client. Commercial qualitative research is still essentially a craft, a skills-based activity that is learnt through apprenticeship and experience. As a consequence, until the last decade or so there was less emphasis on formalized training or publishing educational texts, and more on 'on-the-job' training. Nowadays, a combination of formal training and apprenticeship is increasingly the norm.

Commercial research also differs from academic research in terms of project size and timescale. A commercial project may, in some cases, be quite small scale and completed in a month or two – and researchers may be involved in 10 or more projects over the course of a year. An academic study is more likely to be extensive in scope and to take much longer than an equivalent commercial study, not least because procuring funding for the study can be a time-consuming exercise. Very broadly, the distinctions between the approaches of academic and commercial research can be summarized as shown in the box on the next page.

However, commercial researchers are increasingly exploring outside their existing frame of reference. Qualitative research is widening in application and scope and there is a need to develop theories that make sense of new ways of practising. At the moment, it is only through the rare 'honeybees' (Nancarrow and Tinson, 2006: 9–12) who flit between the two communities that ideas are exchanged. In the future, perhaps both sides will see the benefits that come with closer collaboration.

DOING QUALITATIVE RESEARCH

Different qualitative researchers describe what they do in different terms, and the practice of qualitative research can vary from practitioner to practitioner, making it difficult to agree on a simple definition.

Academic research	Commercial research
emphasis on methodology	emphasis on end benefit
theory informs practice	practice and theory are an iterative process
wide range of methods	qualitative 'thinking' privileged over methods (ideally)
long timescales	intensive, fast turn around
prioritize validity/reliability	prioritize understanding, experience, direction
cerebral	holistic (mind/body/emotion)
largely verbal	sensory, esp visual/emotional
judged by academic rigour	judged by usefulness

The emphasis, in recent years, on formal training has helped new researchers to become proficient more quickly, but there is no substitute for learning from an experienced qualitative researcher who acts as a mentor, observing the apprentice researcher at work, talking through the process, the thinking and the way in which the presentation is put together. Then comes the process of learning through trial and error under the guidance of the mentor. The advantage of this way of learning is that it enables qualitative research – or, more accurately, qualitative thinking – to seep into the bones. Qualitative research becomes part of the researcher's self, involving his or her intuition, emotion and physical responses, as well as intellect. In practice this means that, in a research situation, experienced qualitative researchers may initiate or respond to a situation physically without necessarily being conscious of why they are acting in this way – at least until afterwards; they will just 'know', in the sense of knowing how to drive a car. It's a bit like improvizational jazz, which is a whole body experience, not just involving the conscious mind. As with jazz, this 'knowing' in qualitative research is honed by years of hard work and experience.

Martin Callingham (2004: 109), a former 'client research buyer', describes the stereotypical qualitative researcher as having:

> an unusual mix within their temperament, many aspects of which could be seen as contradictory. They are intelligent, curious and passionate about the truth, and validate the veracity of the truth through their own conviction of interpretation of evidence that they have personally collected. They are independent minded and able to synthesize original approaches on the basis of their intellect and through actively listening. They are prepared to stand by their findings, which are ultimately grounded in the field-work they have done, and they enjoy 'selling' their findings and changing the

way others think about the world, but they are not bombastic or bullying. Indeed they are the reverse, being sensitive to their environment and generally liberal minded, and achieve their end through persuasion. As a group they are very responsive to delivering findings that the clients believes and they like to be liked; but the truth still comes first.

It is a stereotype that rings true – perhaps because it is flattering! It also encompasses the broad range of skills and personal qualities that are necessary for good qualitative research.

You often hear the view expressed that 'anyone' can do qualitative research: it's just a matter of going out and talking to people. On one level this is true. Clients who talk – and more importantly, listen – to their customers will learn a great deal. But there is a world of difference between chatting with customers and conducting skilled, professional qualitative research, which involves active listening, observation, intuition, understanding, analysing, interpreting, contextual experience, structuring and communicating useful outcomes. It's the difference between dancing round your bedroom singing into a hairbrush and becoming a professional opera singer. Good qualitative research is a form of alchemy in which data is transmuted into understanding and knowledge. At best, it is 'gold dust' to the client. Is qualitative research an art or a science? Good 'qual' is both: a duet of intellectual rigour and analysis flavoured with creativity and innovative thinking.

In the following chapters, I will attempt to illustrate this dance and the transformation of research data into inspiring and pragmatic understanding and client recommendations.

QUALITATIVE THEORIES OF PRACTICE

Good qualitative research practice is based on a combination of practical skill and theory (either implicit or explicit). Practice and theory feed one another so that they become more than the sum of their parts; neither is 'superior' to the other. Researchers who are not aware of the theoretical basis of the way in which they are working can become confused and lose direction, especially if their clients are working from a different theoretical basis.

In this section I give a brief overview of relevant qualitative theories, pulling out the main approaches and highlighting the areas of conflict. This is not a comprehensive discussion, as this book is essentially a practical guide to commercial research. For those who are interested in pursuing the philosophy of research, I would suggest reading Clive Seale (1998: 1–82) or Carla Willig (2001: 1–13).

Logical positivism versus interpretivism

There are several different theoretical positions from which to understand qualitative research. These can be clustered into two camps: positivist and interpretivist approaches. I have given simple definitions below, although these rather undersell the complexity of the area.

Logical positivism, as a philosophy of classical science, emphasizes two fundamental commitments: to empiricism (ie there is knowledge only from experience) and to logical analysis, by means of which philosophical problems and paradoxes would be resolved and the structure of scientific theory made clear (Paley, 2008: 646–50). Positivism is modelled on the natural sciences, and its aim when applied to human beings is to discover 'laws' of society that act in a similar manner to the laws of the natural sciences. It is a model of research that tends to treat social facts as existing independently of the activities of both research participants and researchers; in other words, it often assumes there is an absolute truth to be discovered.

Interpretivist approaches challenge the view that conventional knowledge is based upon objective, unbiased observation of the world, that there is a truth out there to be found. There are a variety of interpretivist approaches, including postmodernism and symbolic interactionism (Mead, 1962: 78) but the common theme is that they assume that all knowledge is provisional and relative: that is to say that the views of research participants – and research outcomes themselves – are interpretations of the world. There is no absolute truth. There are many different interpretivist approaches, each with a different emphasis.

One of the best-known interpretivist approaches is social constructionism, which describes knowledge as a social process of 'negotiated understanding': that is, human beings are essentially social and we create meaning together (Burr, 1995: 4–5). From a social constructionist perspective, we construct our world, rather than perceiving reality, by interpreting the world in terms of our past experience and the context we are in.

There are other descriptors for these two stances that have a similar, if more applied, meaning. Imms and Ereaut (2002: 26) quote veteran qualitative researcher Mary Goodyear, who distinguishes between cognitive style, in which research participants' comments are taken at face value and can be classified, summarized and reported, and conative style, which emphasizes meaning and interpretation, in relation to the clients' research objectives. They also cite researchers such as Smith and Fletcher, who differentiate between rational/non-participatory and emotional/participatory, and Wendy Gordon, who defines dependent and psychodynamic stances.

Although these stances might initially seem quite abstract positions that bear little relationship to the craft of qualitative research, they do have practical implications for qualitative practice. It is possible to carry out good – but different – qualitative projects when working from within either philosophical position. Very often, a qualitative project will borrow from both traditions. In this case, it is important that the researcher is clear about which way of thinking is being employed, for what reason and at what stage.

Positivism, interpretivism and qualitative research

In 1986, qualitative researcher Gerald de Groot (1986) attacked the subjectivity of qualitative research, its lack of validity and over-reliance on projective techniques (see Chapter 9) that had 'no scientific grounding'. Many qualitative researchers at the time dubbed de Groot a positivist for attempting to judge qualitative research by strict scientific principles that were simply not relevant. Qualitative research embodies the messiness, contradiction and partial truths that are inherent in all human communication. By definition, they argued, an interpretivist approach was needed.

Nowadays, most qualitative researchers simply accept the ambiguous position of qualitative research in relation to classical science, but the issue of positivism in qualitative research will not quite die. Paul Paley still asks, 'Can qualitative research be positivist?' (2008: 648). Not surprisingly, there is no simple answer. He suggests that, if qualitative research is regarded as a way of experiencing the world, then positivism is precluded. On the other hand, if qualitative research is regarded as a set of tools or techniques that are independent of philosophical basis, then positivist qualitative research is possible. This debate will run and run. Suffice to say, reports of the death of positivism in qualitative research are greatly exaggerated.

However, although interpretivism can seem more fluid and forgiving than positivism, it does not imply a lack of research discipline and rigour. In fact, as we shall see in Chapter 7, it can be argued that it requires more discipline.

DIFFERENT MINDSETS IN PRACTICE

The best way to illustrate how these different philosophical approaches translate into practice is to examine how a group discussion is conducted on the basis of a (broadly) positivist approach compared with one run on a (broadly) interpretivist basis (acknowledging that, in reality, groups will incorporate elements of each).

Wendy Gordon (1999: 111–14), in her excellent and very readable book *Good Thinking*, describes the dependent group and the psycho-dynamic group, which can loosely be interpreted as coming from a positivist and interpretivist position respectively. To avoid confusion – and without, I hope, corrupting Gordon's meaning – I will refer to them as positivist and interpretivist styles.

The positivist group

This operates on the basis of rational, informational dialogue exchanged between the researcher and the research participants. The participants, through either explicit or implicit reinforcement, answer questions that the researcher poses to each of them in turn. As Gordon (1999: 112) explains:

> This group experience is like eight simultaneous depth interviews orchestrated by the group moderator who separates him/herself, psychologically, from the group and who appears to be in control. This kind of group is parental or authoritarian in nature and is based on the belief that anarchy (or childish misbehaviour) will take place unless discipline is imposed from the start.

Gordon lists the assumptions underlying a positivist group:

■ A group discussion is a rational form of debate.
■ Participants have information that the moderator can extract by asking questions.
■ What people say in group situations is what they mean.
■ The moderator is in control of the process.
■ People are able to articulate feelings and emotions when asked to talk about them.
■ There is a truth (about the market, the brand, behaviour or opinions) that can be found through following an agenda of questions set by the client or research coordinator.

The positivist group is likely to be little fun; it is an earnest attempt to extract supposedly factual, rational information, with the onus on the moderator to direct, control and collate the research findings.

The interpretivist group

By contrast, this is an altogether livelier affair. It starts from the assumption that people's attitudes and behaviours have a strong cultural component. Participants are encouraged to interact with one another in a fluid, improvizational manner that involves emotions and bodily gestures; it is not just a rational exchange. The moderator is, and cannot but be, part of the group. From the outside, the interpretivist group may look messy and chaotic, as research participants interact naturally in animated conversation. However, at the same time, the group moderator is monitoring, encouraging, steering, homing in on and developing important comments, analysing the verbal content, watching body language for emotional cues and starting to develop embryonic hypotheses related to the research objectives. What is apparently a very relaxed and casual process requires, at the same time, a highly skilled moderator, in order to get the most out of the group.

Again, Gordon lists the assumptions underlying an interpretivist group:

- What people say may or may not be what they really think, do or mean.
- Socially acceptable, politically correct and conformist attitudes will be expressed unless the group is encouraged to share more heartfelt feelings and beliefs.
- While direct questions are necessary, it is equally important to ask questions in an indirect and less confrontational way, using projective questioning and enabling techniques (see Chapter 9).
- There is no objective truth that can be extracted from a group of people – all of the contributions are subjective and even when participants agree with one another, this does not mean that their agreement makes the content factually correct.
- People who attend group discussions are neither stupid nor intellectually inferior. If they are puzzled by the material shown or seem to have difficulty understanding the questions or what is required, it is the fault of the moderator or the client for not having designed the material well enough or for having presented it in an inappropriate manner.

As you might imagine, the positivist and interpretivist approaches will deliver quite different outcomes, will be analysed in different ways and presented differently to the client.

Individual researchers tend to prioritize one way of working over the other. It will probably be obvious by this stage that, personally, I tend towards the interpretivist camp, and this will inevitably colour the way in which I write this book. I believe it is the most useful approach to qualitative research when the aim is to understand research participants, how they think and behave within a certain context, at a particular moment in time. This can help us to predict, with some degree of success, how consumers might think and behave in the future. This belief is based on more than 30 years working as a qualitative researcher and on my training as a psychologist, but it is also, in a sense, a lifestyle choice. I get a great deal more personal and creative satisfaction when I approach qualitative research with this frame of mind.

4 The business of qualitative research

A CAMEL WITH TWO HUMPS

In the last chapter we talked about the nature of commercial qualitative research: the skills required, the way of thinking and the different theories of practice. However, none of these would exist if it was not for the business of commercial qualitative research. The nature and the business of qualitative research are interdependent, like the two humps of a camel. They are separate from one another, in the sense that they each serve a different function; research is primarily concerned with analytical rigour and with generating understanding and knowledge, whereas business is, essentially, about generating revenue. This difference sometimes leads to conflict, for example, when client time constraints cut across the requirements for good research. Equally however, within a commercial research context the two 'humps' are inextricably bound together because they share the same ultimate goal of producing effective business strategy.

It is perhaps a little early to talk about the business of research when we have not yet talked about methodology and research skills. However, it is important to emphasize that commercial qualitative research exists within a business framework. Understanding this framework will help make sense of the methodologies and research decisions discussed in later chapters. This chapter, therefore, describes the basic structure of a qualitative research project. Projects will vary considerably, but most will, very broadly, follow the format below.

WHO COMMISSIONS QUALITATIVE RESEARCH?

It is important to understand how qualitative research fits within the broader business picture:

■ How does a qualitative research project come about?
■ Who within the organization commissions it?
■ How do they decide which research agency to use?
■ How long does the project take?
■ In what form does the researcher or agency present the findings back to the client?

The need for research can arise at any level – and in virtually any department – in an organization. In larger organizations, there is generally a dedicated research department. In this case, the research needs of different departments will be channelled via the research team, who will generally commission the research study through an external research agency. In the last few years, many research departments have been renamed insight departments or teams, to reflect the shift in emphasis from research as passive data collection to the active design and use of research as a guide to problem solving.

Commercial qualitative research, regardless of the research issues, is primarily about understanding sub-groups of the population – gaining insight into the way in which they make sense of their world – and helping to develop products, services or communications targeted at these sub-groups. The aim is to effect change in their attitudes, beliefs or behaviour.

This overarching aim applies equally to those organizations that are trying to sell toothpaste, those that are trying to prevent young people being killed on the roads through road safety campaigns and those that are trying to instil cultural change amongst their employees.

Many different types of organization commission qualitative research. They generally fall within the four categories outlined in Chapter 1, and expanded below.

Customer-facing companies, which sell to the general public

Large, fast-moving consumer goods (FMCG) companies such as Coca-Cola, Procter & Gamble and L'Oréal were the first on the market research scene in the 1960s and 1970s, and large manufacturing companies are still the biggest spenders. Consumer research generated 83 per cent of worldwide industry turnover in 2007 (Esomar, 2008: 14), much of it qualitative.

There is enormous variety in the type of qualitative projects carried out. The bulk of research commissioned is concerned with the development of new products or services, re-launching existing products, branding, product changes, advertising development, packaging and promotion. However, research is also used to explore 'corporate issues' with consumers, including the company's social responsibility, green issues, development of shareholder communications and so on.

Companies that sell to other businesses

Business-to-business (B2B) research is similar to business-to-consumer research in principle, but less so in practice. It may be commissioned by a business supplier that wants to find out more about its client's future plans, how it evaluates its suppliers or whether it would be receptive to a new service the supplier is about to launch (see case history, Chapter 5). Equally, a client might want to survey its suppliers, to understand more about its resources and future intentions.

Government research

In some countries, central and local government are key buyers of commercial qualitative research (for instance in the UK, public sector clients provided 15 per cent of research turnover in 2007) (Esomar, 2008: 12). Research is commissioned for a variety of reasons, for example:

■ to inform social policy making, such as the development of educational services; to gauge attitudes towards smoking or immigration; to explore how science can be better promoted in schools; to examine how teenagers can be encouraged to eat more healthily;
■ to heighten public awareness of health and social issues, such as benefit fraud, drink-drive campaigns, the importance of child immunization; to promote flu immunization; to encourage people to practice 'safe sex';
■ to develop recruitment campaigns, such as those for the army or NHS; to encourage blood doning.

Some qualitative research agencies specialize in public sector research.

Conducting research within organizations

In recent decades, there has been growing interest in organizational change, with the introduction of a number of management initiatives such as total quality management (TQM), bottom-up knowledge capture and employee empowerment that aimed to improve the effectiveness, efficiency or creativity of organizations. Often these initiatives require re-structuring of the organization and/or a change in 'mind-set' of employ-ees at all levels.

Qualitative research with employees, including senior management, can provide guidance on how these changes can be brought about, the implications of the changes for different work groups, what the resist-ances to change might be and how they might be overcome.

Other users of qualitative research

There are many, diverse, organizations that also use qualitative research: not-for-profit organizations, charities, professional bodies, design or communications companies, universities, schools, management consult-ants, accountancy, law firms and many more. The adaptability of qualita-tive research techniques means that they can be easily adapted for use in virtually any context.

DECIDING ON THE NEED FOR RESEARCH

Research projects may be discussed and planned within the client organi-zation for many weeks or even months before they crystallize into a research brief. This is particularly likely if the research is part of a new product or service launch, or a strategic review in which research is slotted into an ongoing development programme. Typically, many parties are involved in developing the project to the point where it can be taken into research. These may include the marketing team (eg brand manager, marketing director), the research and development department, research or insight teams, advertising planners, design, communications, PR and others. All of these people, either individually or collectively, may be known as 'the client'. Often different departments, or different indi-viduals within the organization, will have different needs and expecta-tions of the research and it is important that these are taken into account by the research agency when it is designing the project.

Alternatively research may be 'spontaneous', triggered by some exter-nal factor such as the launch of a competitive brand or some other change in the marketplace, so that the client company needs to know how chang-ing market conditions may impact on its brand. This type of research often requires fast turnaround.

Large organizations usually commission an external research agency to carry out the research because agencies have the necessary experience, expertise and infrastructure to handle the project. The researchers can look at the issues freshly, with a different perspective from the development team's. Having an outside researcher can also help to smooth any differences of opinion within the organization; the researcher has no axe to grind. The impartiality of the researcher is important, especially in relation to public sector work which needs to be – and be seen to be – non partisan.

CHOOSING THE AGENCY OR RESEARCHER TO DO THE WORK

Clients decide on which research company to use by a variety of methods, and are not necessarily consistent in how they make their choices. For instance, clients that normally ask for a proposal from more than one agency may dispense with this stage if there are time pressures, or if they want an agency that worked on Stage One to continue with Stage Two. Qualitative research is very much a 'people' business. Clients put a lot of trust in the research team to carry out the research process thoroughly, to be meticulous and insightful in their analyses and to present the findings clearly, eloquently and authoritatively. A poorly executed or presented piece of research reflects badly on the commissioning client and, not unnaturally, people want to be sure that the researchers they use will not let them down. It is a truism that a qualitative researcher is only as good as his or her last job. The main methods of commissioning research are outlined below.

The client adopts a formal tendering process

Large organizations and government departments are more likely to use a tendering process. The MRS Code of Conduct recommends that no more than three agencies should be asked to submit a research proposal for a specific job, and they should all be informed that it is a competitive pitch. This is good practice as well as being good manners. Writing a proposal is time consuming – it may take a day or more to write. If the agency's proposal is unsuccessful, then it is a day of lost time and this costs money. Agencies have a right to be able to make an informed choice about whether or not it is in their interests to invest in writing a proposal.

In a competitive pitch, the client will send a written brief to all the agencies that are pitching. This may be an extensive document, including substantial background data, with input from the various individuals and departments that are involved in the project. Each of the competing agencies will be asked to prepare a proposal outlining its suggestions for addressing the research issues, within the client's budget and to be delivered by a specified date (see Chapter 11).

Selected agencies on the client's existing roster are invited to pitch

Agencies may have been previously assessed and selected to be on the client's roster. Being on the roster does not necessarily mean that the agency will get work from the client but simply that, from time to time, it may be selected as a suitable agency to carry out, or pitch for, a particular project. The client will update its roster periodically, which allows new agencies to be included. Getting on the roster is often a complicated and time-consuming process, as the agency has to provide a great deal of information.

An agency is chosen on the basis of prior experience

The client may have worked with an agency or an individual on a previous project, or a researcher may have been recommended by another client. The researchers might have particular experience that the client is seeking.

The choice is idiosyncratic

A research agency having offices close by, a chance meeting, or an individual with whom the client feels comfortable may influence the choice of researcher or agency. Clients may, very sensibly, choose a researcher whom they feel will 'get on' with their senior management. Often it is the researcher rather than the agency that is selected. There are many senior qualitative researchers working on a freelance basis who are avidly sought by clients.

THE CLIENT BRIEF

The research agency will receive the client briefing document either before being chosen, if there is a competitive pitch, or after the project is confirmed if there is no pitch. However, once the agency has been chosen, the client must fully brief the researchers face to face on the background and objectives of the study and discuss the practicalities of the research programme.

If there was no competitive pitch, then a full briefing document may not have been prepared. Briefing documents vary from very comprehensive documents to one-page outlines. Some clients even dispense with a written document altogether and prefer a meeting where the research agenda is thrashed out between researchers and client. The researchers will then confirm what has been agreed in writing, and this acts as the briefing document. The level of formality depends on the client, the size and complexity of the job, and the organizational politics involved. However succinct the briefing document is, it will usually include the sections discussed below.

The background to the project

This section discusses why the research is needed, why it is needed now and, most importantly, what the research outcomes will be used for. Usually it will include details of any previous research that the organization has conducted in this area, and possibly the key findings from this research. Sometimes copies of previous research may be attached. This is useful, as it can help prevent the new agency from 're-inventing the wheel'.

The research objectives

This is the most important section of the brief. What, in broad terms, does the organization want to get out of the research? Often the objectives are prioritized, from the broadest to the most specific or vice versa. For instance, the research objectives for a project on the re-launch of a yoghurt drink would look something like the example in the box below.

Primary objectives:

1. To identity the optimum positioning for Brand A within the yoghurt-drinks market.

Secondary objectives:

2. To explore attitudes and behaviour in the yoghurt-based-drinks market, within the context of other non-alcoholic drinks.
3. To examine brand awareness and imagery within the yoghurt-drinks market and how the overall market is segmented.
4. To understand current brand imagery, characteristics and positioning of Brand A within the above, and the potential for re-positioning the brand.

As this example illustrates, the main client focus (primary objective) is to seek guidance on how the company can develop Brand A (the company's brand), and boost its success in the yoghurt-drinks market. The secondary objectives help to provide a framework for the primary objective; the researcher needs to provide understanding of how the overall drinks market 'works', where yoghurt drinks fit within this market, how Brand A is perceived within this context, and how it might be changed in order to improve its position in the market so that, hopefully, the brand will improve its market share.

It is common in a research project such as this to 'start broad' (the overall market) in order to provide context and then to home in on the specific brands or areas that are of particular interest. However, this is not invariably true. There are times when it is more appropriate to move from specific to general objectives.

It is worth pointing out that the research objectives will be different from the business objectives, which define the broader commercial aims.

The target audience

The target audience is the specific sector or sectors of the general population that the client wants to address with its advertising, product or service. For instance, the target audience for children's clothes is likely to be mothers of school-age children, whereas the target audience for technical toys is more likely to be men and boys. Defining target audiences is often quite a sophisticated process and there may be several different target audiences to be considered. Depending on the nature of the project, the client may define the parameters of its target audience quite finely, to include socio-economic variables – age, gender, social class – as well as variables such as attitudes, behaviour, propensity to take risks or to be opinion leaders.

Often the client will define its target audiences and the research agency will be invited to recommend how they might best be covered in the research sample. If appropriate, an agency might suggest refinements to the client's defined target audience, for example if it could broaden the understanding gained from the research.

The research sample

The research sample – the research participants to be included in the project – will reflect the objectives of the research as well as the target audience. It will represent the people that the client and researchers consider important to include within the study. For instance, if the objective is to develop advertising aimed at encouraging non-users of Brand X to try the drink, then the primary focus within the research will be on people who do not use it. In this instance the research sample will not represent the current usership, but potential future users.

In other projects, the research sample might reflect the current target audience for the product/service. For example, if the objective is to increase usage of Brand X amongst heavy users, then 'heavy' users of Brand X may be over-represented in the sample and 'light' users less so. The research sample thus reflects the sub-sample of the population that the client wants to influence.

Methodology

Most clients, by the time they have produced the research brief, will have a pretty clear idea about whether they need quantitative or qualitative research or a mixture of the two. Occasionally, if the client is not a researcher buyer, they may want to discuss these areas.

Some clients will suggest a specific qualitative approach, such as group discussions, depth interviews or an ethnographic type approach (see Chapter 6). This may be on the basis of past experience and/or their informed opinion. Other clients will encourage the research agency to recommend a research approach. Most clients will be receptive to suggestions from the agency as to methodology – as well as other structural aspects such as research sample, location and stimuli.

Timing

Key timing elements of the client's brief will be:

- the date when a proposal (if required) needs to be delivered to the client;
- the date when the stimulus materials (see Chapter 8) will be ready to go into research;
- the date when the verbal presentation (if appropriate) is required and/or when the written report must be delivered.

Often the timetable for the research programme is determined by external constraints such as the launch of the advertising campaign or a change management programme within the organization. If this is the case, then timing is not open to negotiation. Other projects may be less constrained and allow some flexibility in the timing.

Budget

The client may or may not include a research budget in the brief. This sometimes stems from the belief that stating a fixed budget will encourage proposals that 'use up' the budget, even if it is not required. Alternatively, the client may believe that, without the 'limitation' of a budget, the researcher will develop the ideal research structure. Occasionally a lack of budget indicates a lack of thought about the project and a lack of commitment to the work.

From the researcher's point of view, a lack of budget means no goal posts. There is no ideal structure. Research proposals are put together on the basis of getting the best research outcomes from the budget available, especially in a competitive tender. The researcher wants to win the project – why else would he or she spend a day writing a competitive proposal with no guarantee of work at the end of it? Given a budget, he or she will work hard to provide the best and most appropriate structure within this budget. Without any idea of budget, there is a risk of writing a hugely comprehensive and expensive research proposal that the client cannot afford. It is a wasted day. If at all possible, it is best never to agree to write a proposal without at least an approximate budget.

HORSES FOR COURSES

Of course, there is no such thing as an average client, and the relationship between client and agency will vary greatly. Where there is an established relationship with the client, or where the project is fairly straightforward, then the communication between researchers and client can be quite informal. In other situations, such as a new relationship, when many stakeholders are involved or a complex, lengthy project, communication is often more formal. However informal the arrangement between client and researcher, it is always important to confirm details of the research in a letter or e-mail. In particular, it is essential to spell out the research structure, the timing, the costing, and what is included and not included in the costing. Equally, any additions or changes as the research rolls out, especially if they have cost implications, must be notified to the client in writing. This will prevent any misunderstanding.

Having had a taster of the client perspective on qualitative research, we will return to the nuts and bolts of the research process and re-visit the issue of proposal writing, in response to the client brief, at a later stage.

5 Research issues that call for qualitative methods

There are certain research questions that naturally favour quantitative approaches. For instance, collecting retail audit data (what was bought, from where and when) lends itself to this approach. Equally, other research questions naturally favour qualitative approaches. The understanding and insight gained from a perceptive piece of qualitative advertising development would probably be impossible to replicate through a quantitative study. However, these examples represent the extremes. As Imms and Ereaut (2002: 37) point out, there are many questions that would lend themselves to either qualitative or quantitative methods or to a hybrid approach using both.

Nonetheless, there are certain types of project that cry out qualitative research. These include:

- exploratory studies;
- understanding a specific market, brand or social issue;
- developing consumer typologies;
- new product or service development;
- developing a communications campaign;
- advertising development;
- changing organizational culture;
- exploring global/cultural issues.

This list is not exhaustive and different industries and product categories may have different terminology for these types of studies.

Studies that fall into these categories are discussed below, with case histories as illustrations. Often a qualitative project will incorporate several of the areas outlined below.

EXPLORATORY STUDIES

Qualitative research is particularly well suited to the exploration of research areas in which the client has little previous experience, where the organization may not know what it does not know. For example:

- An organization may want to enter a market that is very different from the one it has traditionally operated in.
- Significant market changes may be taking place, such as new competitors or a shift in consumer spending, so the organization needs to gather up-to-date information and understanding of the changes.
- The organization is introducing its existing products into a new country and needs to understand the cultural context.
- It needs to understand the current marketplace in order to identify opportunities for new product or service developments. For instance, the 2008 recession dramatically changed people's attitudes towards consumption, and manufacturers needed to understand the implications for their businesses.
- New markets may be emerging, for example using new technologies. Organizations may need to develop consumer vocabulary and product descriptors, and to understand how the innovation may change the marketplace.

Qualitative research is flexible so, with broad research objectives, such as these, the researcher has the freedom to explore and discover what the key issues are from a consumer perspective.

Case study: Understanding the female big-spender segment

Courtesy of Stancombe Research & Planning, Australia, www.stancombe.com.au

Stancombe Research & Planning conducted a significant study for women's fashion magazine *marie claire* (Australia) into the valuable female big-spender segment. The approach used was a combination of primary research plus insights gained from current consumer themes identified by Stancombe's cultural forecasting 42 Insights-bank. This is our bank of insights regarding the key themes that shape the consumer context.

The challenge

The challenge for Pacific Magazines, Australian publishers of *marie claire*, was to demonstrate to their advertisers in an increasingly competitive marketplace that they understood, better than other magazines, the hearts and minds of their clients' most valuable market segment, big spenders – and how to communicate with them.

Although we already had a sense of the female big spender from a demographic and expenditure perspective, we needed to dig down and get to know her from the inside. We wanted to understand in what way, other than discretionary spend, she was different from other women of her age and generation. What really made her tick? What were her core drivers? And, lastly, we needed to discover the best way to engage with these big-spending women and activate their purchase.

The research solution

A bricolage study (ie one combining different methodologies) was conducted to get close to and build a rich and personal understanding of these women. This helped us dig deeper into the lives and motivations of the big spender and discover how best to tap into her world. There were four phases of the research:

■ *Phase 1*: Each participant was given a pre-task (to articulate her thoughts on style) before attending a two-hour in-home interview and a 'wardrobe audit' that involved the participants showing us the contents of their wardrobe and drawers while providing commentary; twelve of these 'immersions' were conducted in Australia's largest cities, Sydney and Melbourne.

■ *Phase 2*: A 20-minute online survey with 406 respondents.

■ *Phase 3*: A three-hour workshop with 12 big spenders facilitated by two moderators. Learning from Phases 1 and 2, coupled with themes from Stancombe's 42 Insights-bank, was used to develop stimulus boards that were fed into Phase 3.

■ *Phase 4*: A consumer collaboration workshop (see Chapter 10), involving some of our big spenders, representatives from Pacific magazines and Stancombe strategists consolidated the findings and helped shape future strategy.

Core drivers readily set her apart

Our research, along with previous research investigating her lesser-spending 'heartland' consumer counterparts, allowed us to identify the core drivers that set big spenders apart from other members of the female population.

As Figure 5.1 illustrates, the big spender's underlying confidence and desire to explore her world and its boundaries sits in stark contrast to her 'heartland' sisters who, in comparison, are driven more by a desire for security and structure, revealing an underlying fear that confident, optimistic big spenders simply do not share.

So, while heartland consumers were reacting to perceived threats in their environment with a bunker mentality, the comparatively wealthy, generally better-educated big spenders, riding high on 10 years of good economic times and full employment, saw few, if any, real threats. They confidently stepped beyond the known, taking risks and exploring tangents. Core drivers that particularly resonated for big spenders were

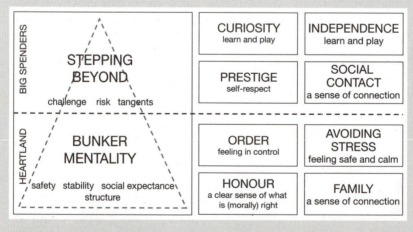

Figure 5.1 *Differences between big spenders and 'heartland' consumers*

curiosity, independence, prestige and social contact; for them, the journey is the destination.

Summary

The study demonstrated that *marie claire* has an instinctive grasp of the big spender mindset. It also provided some firm and conscious markers with which to ensure that the magazine continues to offer content that truly resonates with its market and also speaks to its readers in a language they understand.

UNDERSTANDING A SPECIFIC MARKET, BRAND OR SOCIAL ISSUE

A more focused approach is used when a client wants to explore a particular, clearly defined, market such as fragrances or a new internet service. The client may need to understand how consumers evaluate brands within this market and how brands – in particular their own – are evaluated in relation to other brands. It is important that clients understand the consumer criteria for this evaluation, because these may differ from the way in which the client differentiates between brands.

Clients may need this understanding because they want to launch a new brand into an existing market or because they want to change their existing brand in some way, for example by introducing new packaging, a different recipe, new advertising or brand extensions (new products under the same brand name). The understanding of brands and how they are perceived in the market place is a central part of much qualitative research.

The same basic questions arise, whether the product is a bar of soap, a sports car or an academic book.

Case study: Conducting research at an academic congress

Courtesy of Attfield Dykstra & Partners, Germany, www.a-d-p.net

Increasingly, qualitative researchers are being asked to conduct research ethnographically, that is, to observe and/or interview research participants in their own environments (their homes, schools, places of work, shopping arcades, etc), rather than – or in conjunction with – conducting the research in a dedicated viewing facility. There are two main reasons for this. First, there is now considerable evidence that people behave differently in different contexts. If we need to understand, for instance, how people select a bar of chocolate, then one element of the research might involve interviewing them at the point of sale, to try to understand what influenced their decision. We are more likely to get an accurate response at this time than a week later in a focus group when they may have difficulty recalling the purchase decision. The second reason for carrying out research in the research participants' home, work environment or elsewhere is practical. It may simply be easier or less costly to go to the participants rather than have them come to you.

It was practical necessity that led us, at Attfield Dykstra and Partners, to conduct research (quasi) ethnographically at an academic congress. Our client, Springer Science+Business Media, headquartered in Heidelberg and with offices in Europe, the United States and Asia, is one of the world's leading publishers of scientific and professional content, publishing over 1,700 journals and more than 5,500 new books a year as well as offering the largest scientific and technical e-book collection worldwide. Springer wished to take advantage of an international congress in Dublin in summer 2008 to research a planned new academic title. The idea was to 'capture' senior academics from around the world whilst they were in one location, and conduct focus groups with them.

As Springer's qualitative research partner we were faced with a number of challenges. First there was the issue of where to stage the groups. A room at the Dublin congress venue was one option, but it lacked specialist focus group facilities such as technical support, one-way viewing mirrors, professional recording equipment and high-quality catering. However, the nearest viewing studio was 20-minutes' drive away, which would certainly deter participants. Improvisation was called for. It was decided to use a seminar room at the university, but a video camera and tripod, along with a digital voice recorder as back up, was brought over from Germany. Basic refreshments were bought in and the researchers, slightly nervously, launched into the research. In the event, the informality added to the occasion by making participants feel more at ease and willing to 'help the researchers out'.

The second challenge was recruitment. Normally, professionals are recruited from telephone lists, but neither Springer nor the congress organizers were able to provide these. Attfield Dykstra could have recruited on the spot by approaching delegates during congress breaks, but this was rejected as too risky; what if no one could be recruited at short notice? It was decided that recruitment lists would be created by searching university websites, which generally contain good contact details for faculty staff, so that a representative selection could be made. There was also the list of congress speakers, which was a useful start. The phoning began. However, the next problem soon emerged. The summer vacation had already started; the target audience had scattered to the four winds and was no longer reachable by phone. Days went by and there were no firm recruits. Departmental secretaries suggested trying e-mail. Thankfully, this worked. Within 48 hours both groups were fully recruited, with 18 participants from a total of 11 countries in East and West Europe, America, Africa and Australasia.

This project illustrates the adaptability and ingenuity that is often required of researchers, and the benefits of going to respondents. The conditions for research are rarely perfect and researchers often have to improvise in order to talk to or observe the right people, in the right place, at the right time. However, when the logistical issues are sorted, there is a strong sense of satisfaction. Conducting the research in the academics' own conference environment encouraged involvement and was a very positive experience. Academics are fun to work with – refreshingly open and respectful with one another, articulate, honest and robust in expressing their opinions. While less familiar with market research than some business-to-business audiences, they are very accustomed to discussing in a small group format, and eager to contribute ideas. Sometimes the moderator's biggest challenge is to get them to stop talking!

The congress also gave us a rare opportunity to bring together participants from a range of cultures and to experience their widely differing takes on the proposed publication concept. An intriguing finding was the scepticism among academics from developing countries about using online data: 'Byte for byte of information, our internet access in Africa is 150 times more expensive than yours in Europe.' Altogether a project that was as enlightening as it was challenging.

DEVELOPING CONSUMER TYPOLOGIES

Alternatively, rather than starting with a particular market – and segmenting people by demographics (age, gender, social class etc) and in terms of their brand or product usership – a client organization may start with the individual consumer. Clients may want to gain an understanding of the differences between consumers in terms of their more general motivations, beliefs, attitudes and behaviour, and then segment them according to psychological profile. This is often referred to as psychographic segmentation. It has grown in popularity as societies are becoming more fragmented and traditional demographic segmentations seem less useful.

For instance if a client organization is interested in launching a new, technologically advanced phone, it may be more useful to segment people in terms of their curiosity, openness to new ideas, and awareness of and involvement with technology, rather than their demographic characteristics. Using these criteria, a 70-year-old may have more in common with a 17-year-old – when it comes to phones – than with a neighbour of the same age.

Once typologies have been defined (which usually requires some initial exploratory qualitative research), they can act as useful templates for the development of new products or services targeted by psychographic typology. Alternatively, they can help shape appropriately targeted advertising for existing products.

It is important to note that typologies are not the same as types. 'Types' implies a fixed, immutable set of personality characteristics, so that an individual will behave according to his or her 'type' regardless of circumstances. This is not what happens in 'real life'; we all adapt our behaviour and attitudes according to our context. 'Typology' is a tendency rather than a fixed set of behaviours. For instance, we might predominantly fit a 'saver' typology, but occasionally, we will push the boat out and exhibit 'spendthrift' tendencies.

Case study: Developing a customer-focused strategy within a financial market

Courtesy of Campbell Keegan Ltd, www.campbellkeegan.com

A major financial group in the UK wanted to re-think the way in which it categorized its customer base. Traditionally, financial companies have segmented their markets by product – mortgage borrowing, car loans and so on – and developed departments to handle each product. However, people see themselves 'holistically', as individuals with a variety of financial needs. The company wanted to move toward this customer-centric way of structuring its departments. It needed to understand people's basic needs and motivations – their drives, fears, hopes and expectations within the context of their particular life stage and within the current social and cultural climate – and link all this to financial requirements.

The project lasted a year and involved three stages of research interspersed with client workshops in order to steer the process. The research objectives were clearly defined, but the process was iterative. With each research stage it became increasingly clear where the next stage needed to focus.

Stage 1

The starting point was two day-long breakthrough events (Langmaid and Andrews, 2003), held in hotels in different parts of the country. It was important that there was enough space for whole group sessions and also for convening smaller breakaway groups. Thirty-two people attended each event, including a client as a research participant. The objective of this first stage was to pull out key personal and cultural themes: to identify what mattered to people. Given this broad objective, we ensured that the mix of participants was sufficiently diverse. We had an age range from 17 to 70, men and women, and included a broad spectrum of jobs, education and social class.

The day was introduced as a 'Workshop on people's expectations of life'; we wanted people to arrive in a state of anticipation. The invites were enticing, promising a day of challenge and discovery. People were asked to bring an object that was particularly meaningful and a photo that said something about them. The hotels were comfortable and spacious. There was good food, goodie bags and endless coffee and biscuits. People arrived early, expectantly.

The day involved a variety of sessions, with changes in pace and activity to ensure that people stayed engaged. There were large group sessions involving everyone, and many break-out sessions, followed by sharing with the whole group. The conversations were largely initiated by the participants themselves;

they chose discussion topics and invited others to join them. A spectrum of projective techniques (see Chapter 9) was introduced, many of them physical, to ensure that everyone's brain and body were in good shape.

The two days produced a wealth of rich data: ideas, threads and hypotheses embedded in drawings, photos and collages, as well as tapes and written material. As a micro-community, the large group highlighted social patterns outside the group. A 17-year-old 'hoodie' and 70-year-old granny struck up an unlikely friendship. As the 17-year-old explained, 'I don't have any grandparents and I've never talked with anyone of that age before. No offence [to his new friend]. I'm amazed at how much we agree on things.'

Participants created collages of 'My hopes for the future', initially on their own, using photos torn from magazines, scrawling on them to clarify their meaning. Later, they explained to the group what their collage represented. The richness of data came less from the drawing or collage itself than from the process of making it and the subsequent exploration and explanation of the meaning.

The events flagged up many themes that could be explored, verified, developed and particularized in the subsequent research stages: the financial hot spots, times of change, hopes and aspirations.

Stage 2

Subsequent research involved a mix of extended group discussions, family interviews conducted at home, and paired husband and wife 'at-home' depths (see Chapter 6). The aim was to focus in on different lifestyle and financial needs.

From these two stages, we developed seven psychographic typologies that encapsulated different attitudes and behaviour in relation to money. These were tendencies rather than fixed character traits, and they needed to be treated as crude but useful models rather than depictions of real people in all their complexity.

One of the typologies we named Cool Dude. Cool Dude was sharp, streetwise and opportunistic. S/he was often self-made, status conscious and had made money from property. S/he was dismissive of equity investments because s/he didn't understand them, and was suspicious of, and alienated from, traditional financial institutions. S/he liked to get one over on the establishment.

Figure 5.2 shows how a Cool Dude drew himself, with his wife and family safe inside the walls of his 'castle'.

'Life Balancers' viewed money as a means to an end. They sought safety, predictability and continuity in a mad world. They wanted the best for their children and enough money to mean they did not to have to worry. They knew their limitations and set comfortable boundaries. They regarded themselves as lucky in life. Talking about money was considered rather unsavoury. Occasionally, a Life Balancer might be Whimsical – splashing out on expensive shoes or an exotic holiday. The importance of balance is illustrated in the drawing in Figure 5.3.

Stage 3

The typologies developed in the previous research stages were employed in the recruitment of participants for Stage 3, so we had groups of Cool Dudes, Life Balancers and so on. This stage filled out the typologies and we started exploring the notion of holistic financial services: what it would mean in terms of financial advisors, access, product packages and the like.

Figure 5.2 *Cool Dude*

Figure 5.3 *Life Balancer*

NEW PRODUCT OR SERVICE DEVELOPMENT

Qualitative research has proved invaluable over the years in helping organizations to develop and define new products and services at various stages in their development, the key stages being:

- understanding the market and how the brands that already exist within it are positioned, so that potential gaps can be identified;
- screening a large number of product concepts or ideas in order to determine which routes are best for further development;
- giving guidance on the ways in which the ideas should be developed, the potential strengths and weaknesses;
- development of each component of the package: product, packaging, positioning (how it fits into the particular market), promotion, advertising for the product or service, so that each element builds on and reinforces the branding.

Case study: Rejuvenating a brand

Courtesy of Patricia Sabena Qualitative Research Services, USA,
www.qual.com

This is the story of Herbal Essences shampoo and how qualitative research helped to shape and rejuvenate the brand. It maps the brand's journey from its initial launch by Clairol in 1971 through to its repositioning in the late 1990s and its subsequent brand leadership.

Herbal Essence (as it was originally called) was born into the 'flower-power' seventies. It was the first brand to talk about 'natural ingredients', and its bottle and advertising reflected the spirit of the times (Figure 5.4). It was a huge success.

Introduce your hair to
Clairol herbal essence shampoo
with natural protein. It will smell as fresh as the first day of spring.

Figure 5.4 *Herbal Essence in the 1970s*

However, during the 1980s, other brands jumped on the 'natural' bandwagon and Herbal Essence began to look and seem dated. Eventually advertising support was withdrawn and the brand languished on the shelf.

In the 1990s, Clairol decided to look again at the brand. Between 1992 and 1999 a series of focus group projects was commissioned to explore a variety of aspects of Herbal Essence, including perceptions of the brand itself and possible routes to re-launch the brand, new ingredient combinations, environmental packaging styles, alternative print and TV campaigns, and even other products as spin-offs from the shampoo.

The research was carried out using focus groups with female mass-market shampoo users in different areas of the United States. The target market for the new Herbal Essence was women aged 15–50 but, in order for the groups to work most effectively, the sample was clustered into groups of women in the same life-stage. In general, the younger the age group, the smaller the age span in the group. Therefore, teens were recruited in a tight age span (15–17), whereas it was possible to have a broader age span with older respondents.

The research explored the perceived strengths and weaknesses of the old Herbal Essence. Whilst the brand was viewed with nostalgia and affection – and the scent and herbal base were liked – it was seen as outdated. It seemed too strong, harsh, 'chemically', something respondents' grandmothers might use.

Following on from this initial research, Clairol developed a number of re-positioning concepts (alternative ways of presenting the brand) that incorporated the following themes:

■ ancient herbalist;
■ environmentalist;
■ aromatherapeutic;
■ science-and-nature;
■ nostalgia/born again.

More focus group research was carried out on these repositioning concepts and other aspects of the brand. In the groups, the moderator explored a number of issues such as the relative appeal of these themes, their appropriateness to Herbal Essence, how distinctive they seemed within the shampoo market, and how they could best be developed.

The findings from the research, which were fed back to the brand development team, helped Clairol to develop a new positioning for the brand (re-named 'Herbal Essences' to indicate newness and multiple ingredients/benefits) and it was re-launched into the marketplace. In addition to the new positioning, there were new ingredients and a striking new crystal-clear, see-though packaging to indicate gentleness, herbal ingredients and refreshing scents.

The ad agency, Wells Rich Greene BDDP, used key consumer insights gleaned from the research as the basis for advertising development for the new Herbal Essences. They created highly memorable TV advertising that touted the refreshing benefits of 'an organic experience' (Figure 5.5).

Figure 5.5 *Advertising for Herbal Essences*

Qualitative research carried out on the re-positioned Herbal Essences indicated a very different feel or 'personality' for the brand than it had possessed before: younger, more contemporary, nature oriented, carefree, caring, sensitive and so on. This was illustrated in consumers' drawings of Herbal Essences as a 'person' (Figures 5.6 and 5.7).

The Herbal Essences brand was also expanded into other product categories: hair styling aids, body wash, facial care and hair colour. The brand changed the shampoo market by becoming the new standard of packaging excellence for all other shampoo brands and spawned a multitude of copycat brands. In 1998, revenues for all Herbal Essences products were more than $300 million.

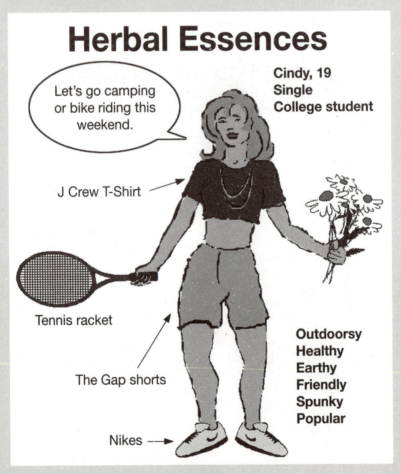

Figure 5.6 *Herbal Essences personified*

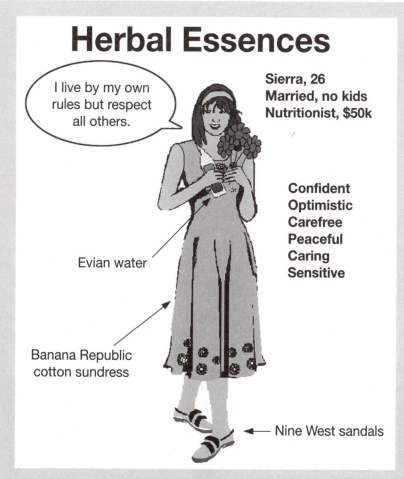

Figure 5.7 *Herbal Essences personified*

As with all consumer brands, Herbal Essences cannot rest on its laurels. It must constantly be in step with – if not ahead of – its customer base. Scrap-art team collages (see Chapter 9) from more recent qualitative research with consumers highlights consumers' desire for the brand to stay cutting edge, maximizing its serenity, 'natural' attributes and performance, whilst softening the sexuality.

Overall, qualitative research helped to provide a deep-rooted understanding of what women wanted in this market, as well as a wide range of consumer insights that fed into strategic outcomes. It highlighted the residual affection consumers felt for the brand, the ways in which 'natural' could be recast in a contemporary way, and the way that breakthrough packaging could help contemporize the image of the brand. It pointed to provocative advertising as a way of breaking through the clutter of shampoo brands and highlighted the opportunities for brand extensions.

DEVELOPING A COMMUNICATIONS CAMPAIGN

Every communications campaign involves understanding what needs to be said, how to say it and what media to use. The nature of the communications – and the best way to deliver them – may also change over time. This is particularly the case with public sector campaigns, which are often complex and multi-faceted, and involve a variety of different target audiences.

For instance, the issues to be explored might involve people's attitudes to a particular health risk, such as childhood measles or HIV. The purpose of the research in these cases is to help develop health messages that the target audience will listen to, understand and act on. People are selected to be part of the research on the basis of their existing behaviours or attitudes, such as their sexual history or whether or not they have chosen to have their child immunized. These are not simple research issues to address and they often include elements of deliberative research and consultancy (see Chapter 6).

Case study: Developing a communications campaign to promote the Australian government's Drought Assistance Package

Courtesy of Open Mind Research, Australia, www.openmind.com.au

In 2005, Open Mind Research was asked by the Australian Department of Human Services (DHS) to develop a communication campaign aimed at farming communities across Australia. The purpose of the campaign was to promote the Australian government's Drought Assistance Package.

Initial research was conducted in June 2005. Sixteen community workshops were carried out, complemented by depth interviews with representatives from the general community, health and allied-health professionals, social service professionals and the sensory impaired. Following on from this, research was conducted specifically with the 'farmer' audience.

The research identified a key theme: that farming communities were already aware of the major changes and expansion to the Drought Assistance Package. Whilst they were not familiar with all the details, they acknowledged that it had been broadened to include more farmers in more areas. Word had spread through community services' rural accountants, media releases and news programs. The problem wasn't awareness, but uptake of the Drought Assistance Package. Open Mind and DHS agreed that further research would be required to develop and shape a campaign that would work beyond merely 'providing information'; it needed to identify and break down the barriers to farmers asking for help.

The research had identified an important shift: the growing expectation amongst audiences of government communications that they be treated as capable, actively engaged partners rather than passive information recipients. It also highlighted the potential role of a 'spokesperson' to deliver government-to-community (G2C) information. The 'spokesperson model' could shift perceptions, positioning the government as providing ongoing and engaged conversation at a personal level.

The campaign also needed to be shaped in a way that would address key barriers:

- *A predisposition of farmers to 'self-assess'*: Farmers often assumed that they were not eligible for the package.
- *Pride*: They were reluctant to 'ask for assistance'.
- *Stereotypes*: Farmers were hypersensitive to any message that appeared to them to be patronizing or to parody 'rural life'.
- *Emotional distress*: Many farmers felt defeated by their circumstances. The campaign needed to inject a sense of hope and empathy.

On the basis of the research, a spokesperson who connected with audiences but who did not 'take over' was recommended: a subdued figure who could diffuse the highly emotive context, allow messages to seep through and act as a 'neutral conduit'. Ian Leslie (a respected journalist) was chosen.

> He [Ian Leslie] doesn't treat you like you're asking for something you don't deserve. (Farmer)

The research also identified the strength of using an appropriate image to communicate key messages. A 'swinging farm gate', coupled with the campaign's original tag-line, 'Drought Assistance: Now Open to More Farmers', was used, as it was very familiar to the audience and the message itself communicated an 'enhanced' drought assistance package.

> I like the gate… it's simple, to the point. We all open and close 20 of those a day… so it feels right, you know. (Farmer)

Research continued throughout 2006 and 2007. This provided an essential 'ear to the context' without which the subtle trends and shifts amongst the audience could not have been detected. It was a priority of DHS to 'stay in touch' with its audience, illustrated by their personal attendance at research workshops. Ongoing research consisted of community workshops with farmers, their partners and rural business representatives across various states. Research was conducted in areas declared by the Australian government to be experiencing 'exceptional circumstances' due to the drought.

Following each stage of research, additional tweaks to the campaign were made in order to refine not only the content but also the tone and implied messaging. For example, research identified the need to incorporate more of a 'community feel'. As awareness of the campaign grew, the need to subtly change its 'look and feel' grew also.

Research identified a clear need to maintain key campaign components such as the use of Ian Leslie, the use of the 'gate' image, and a clear call to action ('Don't Self Assess, Call the Infoline'); while other elements could be tweaked as required. Research established the most suitable layout and need for subheadings to increase message uptake.

Research also identified the need to shift the tone to reflect the impact the extended drought conditions were having on families and rural communities in general (by changing the message on the gate image to indicate that drought assistance is 'supporting drought-affected communities' as opposed to only 'farmers'). The concept of 'family involvement' was also subtly introduced.

> Drought assistance has always been about helping farms and farmers... this is about the whole community. When we suffer, so do they. This goes into that fact. (Farmer)

Despite these changes to content, tone and layout, the research identified a clear need to maintain the 'don't self-assess' message as this remained a primary barrier. Utilizing the message on the farm gate to continually state 'don't self-assess' was complemented by Ian Leslie's emphasis on this point in the communications. Message take-out was clear.

> It says 'don't self-assess', and we're all guilty of that... It's an important message. (Farmer)

Ongoing quantitative tracking of the campaign (by Open Mind) further demonstrates that awareness (across all key audiences) of the Ian Leslie campaign continued to grow over time (Figure 5.8).

Although both ongoing qualitative and quantitative research reported increased awareness, the success of the campaign was (and continues to be) evaluated by the effectiveness of its call to action: hits to the Drought Assistance Infoline. The campaign has delivered a tangible outcome in terms of calls made as illustrated in Figure 5.9.

Overall, the development and ongoing refinement of the Ian Leslie campaign resulted in increased effectiveness and a clear call-to-action response. Its success lies in its ability to convey essential messages (to combat key barriers) by

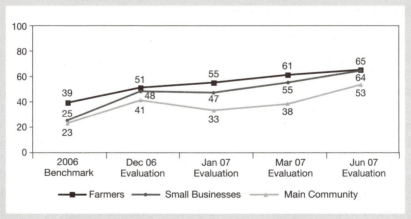

Figure 5.8 *Response to the campaign*

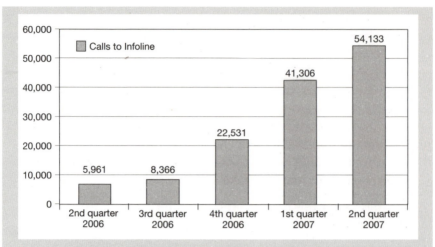

Figure 5.9 *Calls to the Infoline over time*

defusing the emotional response and allowing messages to quietly seep through. The Ian Leslie campaign continued into 2007.

ADVERTISING DEVELOPMENT

Advertising development research may be carried out at one of three stages in the development of the advertising campaign, as outlined below.

Strategy development

This stage of research involves exploring the attitudes, beliefs, needs and aspirations of the target audience. Its purpose is to help the creative team at the ad agency (and others involved in the process) to understand – or get inside the heads of – the particular group of consumers that the client is interested in. This may include their language, humour, tastes, music, dress and so on. It is very difficult to create advertising aimed at people whom you do not know or understand. This input will help the creatives develop an advertising strategy (the key communication and style of the advertising) that closely fits – and is relevant to – the target audience, rather than strategy that fits their stereotype of that audience. From the researcher's point of view this is often the most relaxed stage of advertising development, because the advertising ideas have yet to be developed.

Executional guidance

At this stage one or more advertising routes (usually in the form of story-boards or other rough formats) have been developed. The researcher's job is to nurture the creative ideas that appear to have the potential to be distinctive, memorable and relevant, and that fit the advertising strategy. Equally he or she will be expected to reject those that do not match up, or highlight elements that could be changed in order to develop the idea further.

Pre-testing

The advertising is in a finished or near-finished state, and the purpose of the research at this stage is to check its communication and appeal, and the extent to which the target audience engage with it. Because the commercial is in a near-finished form, it is useful to try to replicate 'real life' viewing, as far as possible, for example by showing the ad without any preamble, or asking people to write down their individual responses.

Pre-testing may be carried out in a hall in a town centre. People from the target audience are recruited from the streets to be interviewed briefly and shown the ad. Sometimes quantitative pre-testing is carried out simultaneously, so that both breadth and depth of understanding can be gauged.

Advertising pre-testing may also be carried out online. Research participants watch the commercial or view press ads and respond to the researcher, either individually and/or as a group, through online forums (see Chapter 6). With press advertising, they can use virtual crayons to make comments directly on to the ads (Sabena, 2009, personal communication)

Case study: Developing advertising for Weight Watchers

Courtesy of Campbell Keegan Ltd, UK, www.campbellkeegan.com

The company

Weight Watchers was founded in the United States by Jean Nidetch in the early 1960s. Its aim is to help people to lose weight. The company now operates in dozens of countries worldwide from Brazil to New Zealand, with the core of the business centring around weekly meetings in which Weight Watchers' members are supported, encouraged and educated in weight loss by Weight Watchers' leaders – themselves successful former members. The company also franchises a wide range of foods, drinks and related products and also has an online weight loss programme.

Recent history

In the last decade Weight Watchers and its competitors in the UK have achieved considerable success. However, the accessible and down-to-earth nature of weight loss meetings in general (and Weight Watchers in particular) has encouraged parody (eg in the high-profile comedy show, *Little Britain*). Paradoxically, this has existed alongside the popularity and commercial success of slimming clubs. The task for Weight Watchers has been: How can it reinvent, re-describe, and interest new generations in a brand that has the conflicting values of proven success and heritage versus elements of anachronism and farce?

Understanding the psychological landscape

Over the last four years, Campbell Keegan has conducted more than 20 qualitative research studies for Weight Watchers. Most of these have focused on helping to develop the meetings business, although studies on the licensed food and drink product ranges, the online offering and the holistic brand imagery have also been undertaken.

Qualitative research has played a central role in helping Weight Watchers to understand the perceptions of issues and cultural influences on women who consider themselves overweight. Research identified different psychological groupings (or 'mind states') amongst people trying to lose weight; this enabled Weight Watchers to build a clear picture of the best way to talk to those with different 'mind sets' and to ensure that the messages and tone of voice were appropriate for these different groupings.

Women have complex relationships with weight; it is never a 'single issue' and it is often differently constructed in different contexts: weight in terms of self-image, weight as a 'societal problem', weight as a feminist issue, weight as a day-to-day issue related to mothering and family food provision, weight as a psychological 'mask' and so on. In the weight loss arena, behaviour, thought and response to advertising can seem contrary and often paradoxical; women often express the opposing pressures they feel in relation to weight (Figure 5.10).

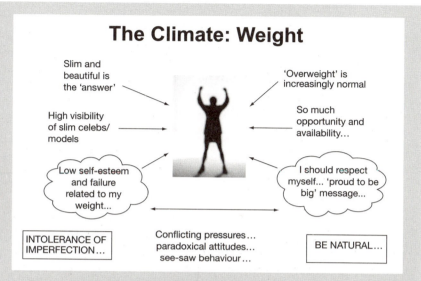

Figure 5.10 *Conflicting attitudes towards weight*

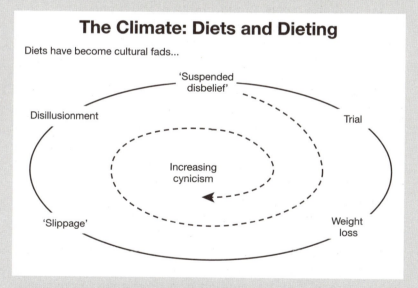

Figure 5.11 *The weight loss spiral*

Over time, there is often a spiralling towards cynicism, as repeated attempts to lose weight are unsuccessful (Figure 5.11).

Because of the inherent contradictions in attitudes and behaviour, the research methodologies adopted to explore the psychology of weight needed to be very varied, in order to obtain as many different perspectives as possible. This allowed Weight Watchers to obtain an evolving and very holistic understanding of the market, as well as providing direction for the brand to communicate effectively.

For instance, group discussions were commonly used; they provided a comfortable forum where women could talk with others who shared similar weight problems. Depth interviews were useful in order to probe individuals' history of weight gain and attempts to lose weight, over a long period of time. Ethnographic 'interview and observe' sessions, in supermarkets or at home for instance, allowed the researcher to see what participants actually did rather than what they said they did.

A particularly valuable qualitative approach was a series of 'triad' interviews (see Chapter 6). These involved a moderated 'debate' between a Weight Watcher enthusiast, a professed 'rejector' of any weight loss meetings and a neutral/undecided participant. This process was very useful in creating a template for the real arguments, brand strengths and brand detractions, as voiced in the language of peers. It replicated the process that often takes place when women 'argue with themselves' about whether or not they will sign up to Weight Watchers' meetings.

Why Weight Watchers?

The Weight Watchers' brand needs to constantly keep its offering, its programme and its image up to date and relevant to younger women – but without alienating or evoking cynicism amongst the very many older women and ex-members who feel comfortable with the familiar routines of Weight Watchers. This is a tough challenge for the brand.

Weight Watchers has used qualitative research to help understand its 'attribute bank' (the brand characteristics or values that make up the brand). These values, which relate to the brand's motivating, historical reputation for honesty, efficacy and 'success', can then be isolated and developed. Conversely, those values that tend to drag it down towards dowdiness and anachronism can be downplayed.

It is particularly important in complex research areas to present research outcomes simply and clearly. Figure 5.12 is an overview of negative attributes, as perceived by slimmers who were not Weight Watchers' members. The detail has been omitted, in order to highlight the four key 'attitude clusters' that need to be addressed, by the client and ad agency, in order to 'convert' these groups of slimmers into Weight Watchers' members.

Inevitably, developing communications for Weight Watchers that are powerful enough to motivate interest is fraught with a particular problem. Weight Watchers might simply be creating interest in the idea of losing weight through attending meetings – a 'generic effect' – rather than motivating specific, 'branded' interest in Weight Watchers. This has been especially problematic given a relatively promiscuous target group. In practice, even a quite pronounced preference for one style of approach over another (in the UK, Slimming World, Rosemary Conley and Scottish Slimmers are all significant competitors) is outweighed by highly pragmatic or social influences; having the meeting at walking distance from one's home, or having a friend who has successfully lost weight, can be a stronger lure for most women than any 'brand'. So Weight Watchers, as the biggest, 'premium' player is always in danger of 'selling the competition' in broadcast advertising.

Skilful and cumulative qualitative inquiry has ensured that advertising messages that maximize the 'brandedness' of Weight Watchers' communications are developed. In practice, it has been the layered and subtle qualitative exploration of Weight Watchers' and its competitors' brand imagery, strengths and weaknesses that has tightened up the creative brief.

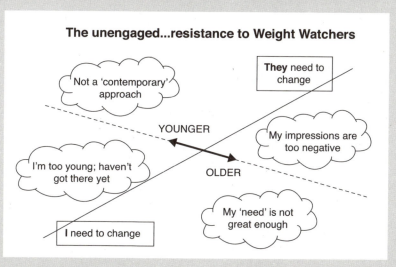

Figure 5.12 *Attitude clusters that Weight Watchers needs to target*

In spring 2006 Weight Watchers launched a campaign, 'Start Your Story', through advertising agency Euro RSCG that generated high levels of meetings registrations. One of the key insights that led to the development of this campaign and subsequent advertising was recognition of the 'personal' offering from Weight Watchers. There is genuine flexibility in Weight Watchers' weight loss plans and no single or formulaic image of 'success' is imposed. This reflects the positive experiences of Weight Watchers' members as well as a differentiated brand position for a 'potential' audience of 'undecideds'. Press advertisements from the campaign are shown in Figures 5.13 and 5.14.

Figure 5.13 *Press ad for Weight Watchers (courtesy of Euro RSCG London www.eworscglondon.co.uk)*

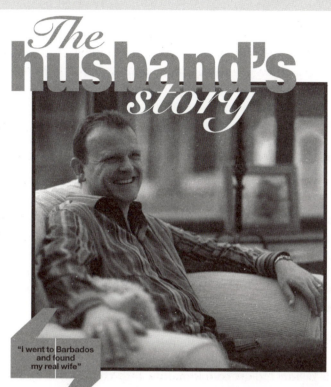

Figure 5.14 *Press ad for Weight Watchers (courtesy of Euro RSCG London www.eworscglondon.co.uk)*

CHANGING ORGANIZATIONAL CULTURE

Understanding cultural trends and communication within an organization is just as important as understanding them in the consumer environment. Arguably it is more important, because corporate culture inevitably 'bleeds' into the consumer world through the customer interface. For better or worse, product quality, level of customer service and speed of answering the phone all tell the customer something about the corporate culture. Growing awareness of this has boosted organizational research in terms of examining the customer interface, developing change management programmes and highlighting training and communication needs.

Case study: Attracting top talent from India's leading business schools into the Tata Group

Courtesy of Piyul Mukherjee, Proact Research & Consultancy Private Ltd, India, www.proact.co.in

This case study illustrates the way in which qualitative research can help change perceptions of a major company amongst a key group of potential employees. It also illustrates how the choice of research methodology can, in itself, give a message to future employees about the nature of the company and what it would be like to work there.

Background

The Tata Group is India's largest private sector organization. It is a US $15-billion Indian conglomerate that contributes nearly 3 per cent of India's GDP. Historically, Tata attracted a steady stream of high-potential managers, the best from leading Indian business schools. However, in the 1990s international recruiters began to cream off Indian talent and, simultaneously, Tata's image began to seem conservative and 'fuddy duddy'. This deterred dynamic, thrusting MBA students with a mission to reach the top in the corporate world. There was an urgent need for the Tata Group to update and differentiate the Tata brand in the high-calibre youth campuses of India, amidst global competition.

Proact was commissioned to carry out a two-year study, in order to understand the perceptions of various stakeholders, including students, faculty and business leaders. The study would help Tata to devise a 'brand reinvention programme' that would change perceptions of the company and, in doing so, encourage the best students to join the Group.

How research helped

A comprehensive qualitative programme of research was carried out over the two-year period, including:

- four or five focus groups from each of the 10 top business schools in India;
- observation of life at each campus, by researchers living there;
- twenty-six in-depth interviews with core faculty who shape perceptions amongst students, respected recruiters from competitor companies and a spectrum of Tata Group heads and human resources directors.

The research provided a wealth of understanding, and inputs from the research were regularly fed into the comprehensive brand reinvention programme.

Just touching on a few of the areas of opportunity that were highlighted and how Tata tackled them:

- In India, student-life and work are discrete life stages; Indians rarely go back to academic study once they have begun work. Consequently, the few senior students who had spent three months of 'summer training' in various organizations were an important source of knowledge for their peers. Summer trainees had the potential to be brand ambassadors, and Tata chose to focus specifically on this area.
- Pre-placement talks (PPTs) to showcase companies and potential careers within them are routinely carried out on campus each year by large corporations hoping to recruit graduates. Students recognized the importance of these talks but, with 50–60 PPTs taking place over a few days, differentiating between organizations was exhausting and difficult. Tata worked hard at presenting a distinctive face, for example by using unexpected posters and humour, and introducing innovative spokespeople to introduce the Group. Young and dynamic Tata managers in their early 30s came on campus and interacted with the students.
- The United States is seen as the Mecca of MBA education, so marketing professors of Indian origin from US business schools were invited to judge the Tata case study that students were undertaking on campus.
- The Tata Business Leadership Awards (TBLA) was introduced to ensure that students could compete and pitch their skills against one another. Soon, business schools started writing in, asking to be allowed to participate. The Tata Business Leadership Awards went on to become the largest business school event in India in the second year of its launch.

- Exciting case studies, especially those that were also used by the Harvard Business School, were provided by Tata to the institutes for use in class.

During the second year of the study, Proact adopted a more fluid research approach in order to fit more easily with student availability and lifestyles. Rather than replicate the previous year's structure, they customized the research to fit with each institute. They wanted to keep the element of surprise, using more observation, informal mini-groups, staying on campus and intermingling. This allowed the research to extend beyond the boundaries of the usual focus group discussion. The interaction was orientated to 'campus life' and some groups were conducted in dorms at midnight, as this was often the best time to get the students to unwind.

Outcomes

The research fed into the Tata brand reinvention plan, which successfully changed perceptions of the Tata Group. Amongst the target audience, as of 2003–04:

- Brand rating of Tata as a preferred recruiter improved from 31st position in 2001 to 19th in 2002 and then sixth position in 2003 (independent CampusTrack survey by ORG-MARG).
- The percentage of offers accepted improved from 65 per cent in 2001 to 96 per cent in 2004.

Proact highlights the key factors that helped the successful completion of the project as the high level of trust, an intuitive mindset, a spirit of fun and teamwork between Proact and the Tata team.

EXPLORING GLOBAL/CULTURAL ISSUES

In organizations that operate globally, there is a constant tension between the need for uniformity across countries and awareness that subsidiaries in different countries need to operate in different ways in order to be successful in their specific markets. Qualitative research may be carried out within specific countries to compare approaches, so that areas of commonality and of difference can be defined more closely.

Case study: Business-to-business research

Courtesy of Amber, China, www.amberinsights.com

This case study looks at business-to-business qualitative research in China for SGS, a Swiss company that provides product inspection, verification, testing and certification on a diverse product range from furniture to petrochemicals to agricultural goods.

Challenge

With 10 independent business units operating in China and globally under the SGS name, it was difficult for the regional head office of SGS to control external communications. The marketing team was concerned about fragmentation: that the marketing message was being diluted. Managers at head office needed to understand how their main customers perceived SGS in relation to its competitors and how the company could strengthen its communications to customers.

Research objectives

The aim of the research project was to better understand SGS's reputation amongst key customers, within each of the main business units. In particular, there was a need to identify inconsistencies between the business units that could be addressed in order to facilitate a strong top-down marketing approach. SGS wanted to gain a thorough understanding from each customer of SGS's customer service, communications and brand reputation.

Design

Twenty face-to-face, in-depth interviews were conducted with business customers across four of the key business units. This project was part of a wider study that also included interviews with senior managers within SGS.

Approach

There are particular protocols that have to be observed in China. Senior executives are often suspicious of talking with a stranger by phone, so face-to-face interviewing is essential. In addition, the most informative interviews – those that provide greatest insight – are always conducted face to face in China. In this instance, the client made the initial approach to its customers. This paved the way for the research agency and made it relatively easy to fix up interviews. Nonetheless, each interview had to be pre-arranged and a gift was presented to every respondent. Normally, cash incentives are acceptable for middle management, but at more senior levels an introduction through a contact is more important for securing an interview. All interviews were conducted on site, behind closed doors, at the respondent's place of work.

The discussion guide was devised in collaboration with the client and all the interviews took place over a period of one month. After the preliminary stage of interviews had been completed, minor changes were made to the discussion guide. Questions about brand perceptions were changed in order to make them clearer for respondents. Typically, Chinese company managers do not have a strong understanding of the value of a company's brand and are reluctant to offer thoughts on the brand imagery of a company. To address this, questions on brand were tweaked a little and visual images were introduced. The visuals comprised a range of images, and respondents were asked to select the images that they felt most closely represented the SGS brand. This enabled the researchers and the client to understand the respondents' perceptions more clearly than would have been possible through simply asking them to describe the brand.

The client was presented with transcripts of each interview as well as a detailed presentation of findings, analysis and recommendations.

Result

The research enabled the client to comprehensively re-assess the SGS brand within China and to develop a forward plan for improving key customer retention in the four focus business units.

I have tried through these international case studies to give a flavour of the variety of research issues that are addressed through qualitative research. Having looked at the research issues holistically, we will now specifically examine the role of qualitative methodologies in these processes.

6 Qualitative research methodologies

THE CHANGING FACE OF QUALITATIVE RESEARCH

During the late 1970s and throughout the 1980s, qualitative research experienced huge growth in developed countries. Most qualitative research was carried out using face-to-face interviews, and the industry was largely wedded to group discussions and individual/paired depth interviews. The view was that group discussions are fairly straightforward to set up and groups are easy and convenient for clients to view. This methodology came to dominate the thinking, and the automatic choice became group discussions or depth interviews. This reliance on a single methodology, driven as it was by the high volume of work and time pressures, encouraged a degree of commoditization of qualitative research (Gordon, 1999: 60–64).

However, in the last 10–15 years there has been something of a sea change, leading away from interviewing as almost the sole methodology. Although group discussions and depth interviews still account for 85 per cent of qualitative research worldwide (Esomar, 2008: 6, 15), other methodologies are growing in strength. Observation and ethnographic approaches, deliberative inquiry, web-based methodologies, semiotics and cultural analysis – all of which will be discussed in this chapter – are being used either as an alternative or as a complement to interviewing (Desai, 2002: 117–27).

It is tempting to view these methodologies as competing with one another. Those who favour ethnography sometimes criticize group studies, and vice versa. In practice, methodologies overlap, providing different perspectives rather than different outcomes. They are discussed separately in this chapter for the sake of clarity, but in the field researchers use whatever method is appropriate in order to help them understand the particular research issues.

Terminology

It is important to talk about terminology – which is something of a minefield – before launching into a discussion of qualitative method-ologies. The language used in qualitative research was largely borrowed from quantitative research and a classical science mind-set. However, it now seems inappropriate to researchers who work from an interpretivist perspective (see Chapter 3). For instance, 'findings' imply things waiting to be found whereas interpretivist researchers would say that we construct research outcomes. The former is passive, the latter active, and they reflect quite different philosophical positions (Valentine, 2002; Keegan, 2005: 11–17). There is a move towards the use of more active terminology that emphasizes a jointly constructed, interactional style of research – but this is work in progress. Here are some examples of alternative ways of describing research activities:

passive	active
research	inquiry
reporting	feedback/discussion
respondents	participants
findings	outcomes, constructs
interview	conversation
briefing	discussion
consumer	partner (possibly)

Rather than constantly qualifying the terms used in the following chap-ters I will use the terms that I personally am comfortable with.

THE RANGE OF QUALITATIVE METHODOLOGIES

There is a variety of methods by which commercial qualitative research can be carried out and numerous permutations within each of these methods. The main methods used are:

- Interviewing people individually, in pairs, or in groups. Interviews can be conducted face to face, by phone, internet, letter, blog or other methods. Some researchers refer to interviews as conversations, to reflect the shared, informal nature of the exchange.
- Observing people, either without actively interacting with them – for instance using fixed cameras in a supermarket aisle – or observing them overtly though without actively participating.
- Engaging in an activity with people as a co-researcher. The emphasis here is on the interaction: developing relationships and gaining understanding through participating in their lives.
- Setting people tasks to do by themselves or with others, which they then report back on: for example, taking photos, visiting a particular store, keeping a diary, writing a blog. This may be linked with other methodologies, particularly group discussions.
- Deliberative research. Where research issues are complex and participants require knowledge before they can express an informed opinion, they are gradually given information – in an impartial manner – and allowed time to consider the research issues, before commenting on them.
- Semiotics and cultural analysis. Semiotics starts by exploring the cultural context rather than starting with consumer understanding. Consumers are viewed as products of culture.
- Researching accessible data sources, such as newspapers, magazines, social networking or other internet sites, or reading existing qualitative reports.
- Creative forums in which participants, chosen for their creative abilities, work together on problem definition, idea generation and evaluation (see Chapter 10).

INTERVIEWING AS A RESEARCH METHODOLOGY

Interviewing has obvious advantages as a methodology. The researcher feels in control, in the sense of having the research participants in front of him or her, at the end of the phone or, virtually, online. He or she can set the agenda, ask questions, observe and/or listen to or read responses. It is a relatively efficient, effective and versatile methodology.

Group discussions

The most common form of interview worldwide is the group discussion. This is often referred to by the US descriptor 'focus group', but many qualitative researchers in the UK dislike this term because it implies homing in on people's responses to specific questions or stimuli. In practice however, most group discussions are open, discursive processes, concerned with understanding the way in which people make sense of their worlds and how products, advertising and so on fit within it. Nowadays the terms focus group and group discussion – or simply 'group' – are used interchangeably.

The standard group discussion comprises 6–10 individuals. In the UK it usually involves seven or eight people and in the United States, between 10 and 12, although smaller numbers are increasingly being used in the United States (Sabena, 2009, personal communication). A typical group lasts 1½–2 hours, although it can be longer (eg with elderly participants or if it incorporates creative tasks) or shorter (eg with children). The participants are recruited according to a recruitment specification ('spec'), which includes demographic variables such as gender, age, social class and life-stage as well as other criteria specifically related to the project, such as purchasing behaviour or product, service or brand usage. Each group discussion has a research moderator who facilitates the group.

When to choose group discussions

To create a relaxed and open environment
Research participants readily feel at ease and are willing to open up with other participants with whom they share similar experiences. In general, group discussions are fun as well as productive.

To foster a creative forum
Participants can expand and build on the views and experiences of others without self-consciousness. Often the communal expression of shared experience leads to fresh insights. A group discussion is a cultural forum that reflects behaviour and attitudes in the wider world – or a particular sector of the wider world.

They can hothouse diversity
Groups highlight the way in which different participants make sense of events or experiences. It is possible to capture and explore these differences with group members in a relatively short space of time.

Group discussions offer a versatile environment
A large range of stimuli can be explored: advertising ideas, concept boards, packaging and product; or creative exercises such as drawings or role-play, can be introduced into the group context.

They enable clients to view the research process
Last, but not least, group discussions are popular because clients can view the group through a one-way mirror in viewing facilities or by video relay, or it can be web streamed around the world in real time.

When not to choose group discussions

When detailed histories are required
The researcher may need to understand the detail of a participant's ongoing medical condition, or to explore the extended process of house purchase. A group context would not allow for gathering individual history in this way.

Practical difficulties and confidentiality
If participants are geographically scattered, it might not be possible or cost effective to convene them in groups. Alternatively, if they work for competitor companies, there might be issues of commercial confidentiality that would preclude groups.

When observation in situ is needed
It may be important to understand how a research participant behaves in a particular context, for instance when engaging in automatic behaviour such as driving or loading the washing machine. These situations may call for observation or ethnographic approaches – sometimes in conjunction with interviewing.

Taboo subjects

There are some topics that are widely regarded to be 'taboo' for group discussions, for example:

■ intimate subjects: sex, personal hygiene, drug usage;
■ where people have very different levels of knowledge or understanding of an issue;
■ where there are strong social norms, for instance in relation to parenting or healthy food;
■ complex political and social issues;
■ matters of fashion and taste, where personal preferences are likely to be very varied.

There are two issues here. First, there are different cultural norms in different countries (see Chapter 15). In Europe, the United States or Australia, for example, it is acceptable for many intimate subjects to be discussed in a group, whereas in other parts of the world this would be unacceptable. It is essential that researchers understand the cultural context in which they propose to carry out research and, if they do not have prior research experience in that country, they must seek guidance from local researchers. Even in multi-country projects where the aim is to create a uniform methodology, consideration of the norms and beliefs in each country take priority. If these are flaunted, then the research itself will be compromised.

Second, even in the same country, researchers may have different opinions on what issues can be discussed in groups. For instance, some researchers would recommend conducting depth interviews on the taboo subjects above. My personal view is that, with careful planning and good moderation, these subjects can often be constructively handled in groups, and the benefits of group interviewing generally outweigh the disadvantages. In fact, sensitive subjects are sometimes better dealt with in groups. Participants feel relief that they can share their experiences with people who have had similar experiences or share similar views.

Different levels of knowledge present separate issues, which can usually be dealt with by careful recruitment and sensitive moderating. It is good to incorporate participants with different views and levels of knowledge in a group, but if the differences are extreme then moderation becomes difficult and the group may be less productive.

Variations on group discussions

There is no magic number for participants in a group. Although a group of 6–10 participants usually ensures sufficient diversity of views whilst still being manageable for the moderator, groups can easily be adapted to fit the needs of the project. The sections below outline some common variations.

Mini-groups

Mini-groups may either be ones that meet for a shorter time, perhaps an hour or less, or have fewer participants, or both. Having fewer people works well when potential participants are thinly spread so that it is difficult to gather six or eight individuals in the same location. Alternatively, mini-groups may be chosen for professional participants, such as doctors or business managers, who are very knowledgeable on their subject and have a lot to say.

Pre-teen children are often convened in shorter sessions because of their limited attention span. Children can usefully be interviewed in groups (with their parents' permission) from about the age of six. The groups are usually an informal mixture of chat and play, using lots of stimuli (toys, games, drawing) to encourage response.

Friendship groups
Children aged 6–15 are usually recruited as either three pairs of friends or, on occasion, as a group of five or six friends, in order to reduce feelings of embarrassment or shyness in the unfamiliar group situation.

Reconvened groups
Participants attend an initial group on the research topic. At the end, they are asked to carry out an activity over the following week: for example, to use – or not use – a specific product such as a toilet cleaner, to visit a particular store or to visit a specified website. Typically they are asked to keep an actual or virtual diary of their activities and impressions and/or to take photos. The purpose of these tasks is to sensitize participants to the research issues and for them to become more knowledgeable. The group is reconvened a week later, by which time they are 'experts' with on-the-ground experiences to share and discuss.

Reconvened groups are an excellent way of combining interviewing and ethnography. They have fallen from favour because they are costly. This is a shame, because they can provide much invaluable consumer understanding.

Incorporating quasi-ethnographic approaches into groups
Group discussions are a very malleable methodology, and there are ways of combining interviewing and *in situ* experiences that to some extent replicate real life situations. Products, packaging, advertising and so on are regularly incorporated within groups, so that participants can experience them 'live'. This is common in car clinics, for instance, where group discussions are combined with a detailed exploration of a new model of car.

A chocolate manufacturer wanted to know if it should sell its Easter eggs as whole eggs that could be broken to reveal the chocolates inside, or as two halves that fell apart when the wrapping was removed. It was six months before Easter, so there was no possibility of observing Easter egg consumption in its natural environment. Instead, we asked the manufacturer to make both types of egg and participants tested them to destruction, with relish, in group discussions. To my shame, I cannot remember which option they preferred.

Individual depth interviews

Depth interviews (known as IDIs in the United States) are one-to-one sessions with a research participant, recruited according to specific criteria, and moderated by a trained qualitative researcher. Typically a depth interview lasts an hour, but this will vary according to the research needs. Often depth interviews are conducted in the participant's home or place of work.

In the early days of motivational research, the individual interview was the primary deep-digging tool (Gordon, 1999: 83). Depths have become somewhat neglected in recent years, in part because they are time consuming and this has cost implications. However, perhaps more importantly, they have been overshadowed by the extensive use of viewing facilities, which favour groups. Depths are expensive to conduct in facilities and are less engaging for clients.

There is an erroneous belief that depths are easier to moderate than groups, so they are often given to junior researchers to conduct. In reality, a one-to-one interview is highly intensive. The moderator needs considerable experience and sensitivity in order to quickly establish rapport with the participant, to delve beneath cultural norms and surface attitudes and explore the rich, personal seams beneath. This can only be effectively achieved as a shared exploration between researcher and participant, and this in turn requires a degree of trust and parity between the two individuals.

One of the fundamental problems with depths is that they are still regarded as an alternative to group discussions, which ignores the fundamental differences between the two methods (Gordon, 1999: 84–85). Ideally, groups and depths should be used to enrich and complement one another.

When to use depth interviews

For sensitive or socially taboo areas
As discussed earlier, some researchers choose depths for sensitive topics, such as sanitary protection, financial issues, redundancy and incontinence.

Where a detailed history is required
The sole focus is on the research participant and this allows him or her to recall and explore detail, without feeling that he or she is dominating the conversation or worrying about what other research participants might think.

Where finished advertising or other communication needs to be explored

In a depth interview it is easier to gauge the participant's immediate reaction, uncontaminated by the opinions of others. Misunderstandings in the communication, or unusual interpretations, can therefore be easily picked up.

In topic areas where under or over-claiming is common

Personal hygiene, household cleaning and alcohol consumption are typical topics. An experienced moderator can easily detect and help the participant to express more private emotions and behaviours.

Where practical issues dictate

Depth interviews are necessary if there is geographic dispersal of potential participants, or a need to interview them at their place of work. For this reason, most business-to-business interviews (B2B) are individual interviews.

Understanding context

Interviewing individuals in their home or place of work can provide invaluable insight into the research issues. Participants are often more comfortable in their own environment, which can provide a wealth of contextual information to help the researcher make sense of the data.

Variations on depth interviews

In paired depths, participants may either know each other or be strangers. Husband-and-wife pairs are common, with the partners offering their own perspectives on a joint venture. Equally, paired depths can provide a degree of interaction when it is not possible to convene a full or mini-group.

Triads are also very useful as, for instance, when each of the three participants represent a different stance on an issue. Triads were successfully used for Weight Watchers. Three overweight women – a Weight Watchers' member, a rejecter of slimming clubs and a non-slimmer – each tried to convert the others to their way of thinking. In the process, they all clearly articulated their different positions on weight loss (Rosie Campbell, personal communication).

Short depths can even be conducted 'in-hall'. Participants are recruited from the street and brought into a nearby venue, where a qualitative researcher interviews them for 10 or 15 minutes. These short, rolling mini-depths are useful for exploring focused issues, such as evaluating near-finished advertising executions. This short exposure injects some realism into the viewing situation.

Case study: Understanding and communicating to pregnant women and new mums

Courtesy of Bounty and Discovery Research, UK

Background

Bounty is the UK's largest parenting club and online community (www.bounty.com), offering information, advice, solutions and support to pregnant women and young families. Bounty is also an established media owner, working with leading brands in the young families market that advertise via Bounty's on and offline channels.

Bounty needed to demonstrate to potential business partners:

■ how the internet is integral to the lives of parents with young families;
■ that Bounty itself is a credible and influential media channel.

Equally, Bounty had recently recruited a new online client services team – many of whom were not parents – who needed a rapid immersion into the joys and challenges of parenthood so they could understand the Bounty audience and offer the most creative and compelling solutions to clients.

To achieve these aims, Bounty wanted to build a visual and emotionally engaging picture of today's 'digital native' mum, through her journey of pregnancy into motherhood, demonstrating how this journey impacts on the media she chooses and how she consumes it.

Research approach

The study, which included pregnant women and new mothers, incorporated a range of research approaches. The research team needed to understand the everyday experiences of pregnant women and new mums, as they happened. They also needed to understand participants' interpretations of their experiences. To achieve this, a combination of ethnographic and interviewing methodologies was employed, as described below.

In-home immersion depth interviews

These enabled researchers to spend extended periods of time with participants and their families in their own homes, capturing behaviour as it happened and observing internet usage.

Ongoing contact

Phone, e-mail and face-to-face contact was maintained over a 10-day period.

Video diary

Each participant was left with a digital video camera and encouraged to record a short video every day, particularly in relation to internet usage.

Triad discussions

Mini-groups of all participants were convened to share views and impressions of how pregnancy and motherhood influence media consumption.

Research outcomes

- The presentation and voxpops developed from the research were delivered to 40+ clients and digital media agencies, offering a new and engaging story that established and reinforced business relationships.
- The online client services team, through their immersion in the world of pregnancy and parenthood, were empowered and felt better equipped to manage effective client relationships.
- The new depths of understanding of the audience could be applied across Bounty media, not just online.
- Last but not least, the research re-affirmed the positioning of Bounty's in-house research function within the business.

Phone interviews

Depth interviews can be conducted by phone, for instance to reach geographically dispersed research participants or to save on costs. The same principles apply as with face-to-face interviewing, but there is a greater pressure to establish rapport and engage the participant quickly. Participants can easily lose focus in a phone interview. There is less tolerance of silence and woolly questioning, particularly if the participant is in an office and/or other demands beckon. This generally means that the interview needs to be shorter – no longer than half an hour, unless the participant is extremely interested in the subject – and more structured than in the equivalent face-to-face interview. The interview structure should flow well and questions need to be direct. It is more difficult to explore emotional issues by phone.

The protocols of phone interviews are very important. The interview needs to be pre-booked and time keeping is essential. Phoning late will aggravate participants and risk losing the interview. Ideally, interviews should be confirmed in writing, once the appointment has been made.

Specific ideas, concepts or ads can be posted or e-mailed to participants before the interview, provided they have the facility to download the particular stimuli. With the participant's permission, interviews can be recorded, leaving the researcher able to focus on the conversation without having to make notes.

Doubts about the validity of interview data

In recent years there has been a groundswell of criticism about interviewing as a qualitative research methodology. Current thinking within psychology and other disciplines has led to concerns in two areas. First, there is the issue that what people say they do, think or feel may not be true. Second, there is the supposed artificiality of the interview situation, which may skew responses. There is some truth in both these criticisms.

People do not always say what they mean and mean what they say

When they are being interviewed, people may not necessarily tell the truth or the whole truth (Seale, 1998: 204). There are a number of possible reasons for this. People may be lying; they may not want to admit to embarrassing, antisocial or illegal behaviour. They may over-claim when describing how often they brush their teeth or clean the toilet. More likely they may not remember, because it was an insignificant event, or it was a long time ago, or they muddle it with another occasion. How can someone remember why they chose a particular chocolate bar two weeks after the event?

Perhaps the issue that we should be most concerned about, however, is that much of our behaviour takes place below conscious awareness. Participants may simply not know why they did something or even whether they did it. Tim Wilson (2002: 6), a Professor of Psychology at the

University of Virginia in the United States, discusses the importance of the adaptive unconscious in everyday behaviour.

> The mind operates most efficiently by relegating a good deal of high-level, sophisticated thinking to the unconscious, just as a modern jumbo jetliner is able to fly on automatic pilot with little or no input from the human 'conscious' pilot.

It is difficult to be certain how much of our behaviour is relegated to the unconscious. It includes breathing, walking, but can also include driving or making a cup of tea – in fact, most habitual behaviour. How often do we do something absentmindedly and then 'come to', wondering why we did it? When we don't know, we may make up a plausible explanation to sound rational – and this explanation too can come from the unconscious.

Implicit within the interview format is the assumption that people are, or can become, aware of their actions and motivations – but this is shaky ground (Desai, 2002: 4).

By its nature, in an interview situation participants are invited to tell their story, to create a narrative. This narrative is constructed retrospectively, by selectively choosing, omitting and reinterpreting aspects of the past. It is not, and can never be, a transparent account of events. It is created to fit the needs of the situation. This does not make the story untrue, but it gives it a particular perspective that may need to be balanced by other perspectives, such as observing actual behaviour.

The importance of context in understanding people's attitudes and behaviour

Critics have long argued that data, gathered in group discussions that are convened in rather sterile viewing facilities, or other contexts far removed from research participants' normal environments, are suspect. This alien context, they claim, distorts people's responses, which means that the data gathered is inaccurate or not to be trusted.

We have all had experience of how context can affect us; our behaviour during Sunday lunch with our new partner's parents is different from our behaviour when out clubbing with our mates. The environment in which the interviewing takes place of necessity influences the responses to some extent.

Are these criticisms of interviewing approaches valid?

To an extent, yes. Both criticisms have some validity. There is much evidence to support the view that context is important in influencing people's attitudes and behaviour. Equally, in group discussions participants are often discussing their buying behaviour, beliefs and aspirations out of context, and this is likely to colour the views they express. We cannot be sure that what people say in a group is what they actually do.

However, the argument is not quite as black and white as it appears. The assumption behind most of these criticisms is that we are asking research participants to remember past behaviour, to simply lift a memory from their brain and bring it into the present as a complete unit. This is impossible. Our brains do not work like that.

It also assumes that there is one unitary truth waiting to be found and, if only the researcher can dig deep enough or ask the 'right' question or see the event as it 'really' happened, then he or she will truly understand what is going on.

However, neuroscience (Damasio, 2000: 148) indicates that, when we remember, we do not simply retrieve past events and replay them, as if they were CDs. We re-live and re-interpret the experience we are describing. Our memories, therefore, come to life in the present as we are describing and feeling them, as well as being rooted in the past. People are constructing what they think and feel as they speak.

All research is 'artificial'

It is worth reminding ourselves that almost all research is contrived and in this sense artificial. Whether we convene eight people in a discussion group or watch their behaviour in a pub or shop, the researcher's presence has an effect. The researcher, in turn, biases the research outcomes in his or her interpretation and analysis. Bias is always there. It is inevitable. As researchers we need to ensure that our bias (or, phrased positively, our interpretation) is grounded in strong theory, rigorous analysis and constant reflection on the way in which we are shaping and being shaped by the data (Keegan, 2008, 31–32; Shaw, 2002: 129).

If we accept that all truth is partial and constructed, then we can welcome different perspectives. For instance, we can combine understanding from both group discussions and observational research in order to develop a fuller picture composed of different but interlocking truths. What is learnt when mingling with drinkers in the pub may be different from the learning obtained from the same drinkers in a group discussion, but neither is right or wrong. Using these methodologies in conjunction provides a well-rounded picture.

In all, interviewing, in spite of its limitations, has proved to be a robust and productive qualitative methodology. It has survived and thrived precisely because it provides such useful input to client decision making.

QUALITATIVE RESEARCH USING DIGITAL MEDIA

The current state of play

There is much debate about the current and future role of digital media within the qualitative research community. The impact of the internet on quantitative methods has been considerable and is likely to grow. Online accounts for 25 per cent of quantitative research spend worldwide (Esomar, 2008). However, qualitative research by its nature has relied upon direct contact between researcher and participant and the use of group dynamics, body language and tone of voice. These form part of the data analysis (Desai, 2002: 100). So what do digital media mean for qualitative research?

Enthusiasts point to the benefits of using digital media with audiences for whom this is their natural environment, eg arguing that people under 25 are likely to be more authentic, that is to behave and speak more honestly, in an online community – their natural environment – than they might in face-to-face interviews. Enthusiasts also emphasize the convenience of recruiting difficult-to-find people on line and argue that people reveal more in this environment than when physically in the same room as the researcher. Participants may also have more flexibility, for example commenting on a bulletin board when it is convenient for them rather than at a set time.

Meanwhile, critics point to the difficulty of verifying participant identities, the limitations of not being able to see participants or, perhaps more importantly, of them not being able to see each other. They question the authenticity of participant responses and point out that interaction is not as full or lively as in face-to-face sessions. There is little of the important 'body language'.

Sarah Davies (2009, personal communication), who ran some of the first online focus groups in the late 1990s, believes that there has been limited development of digital media in qualitative research in the intervening time. She attributes this to misguided attempts to replicate traditional qualitative research online, rather than using digital methodologies where they are the best choice for the research needs. She favours digital media for tasks they are particularly well suited for, such as using blogs as follow-ups to discussion groups – especially for international projects, where they can be instantly received – or mobile texting from teenagers 'on the move'.

The practicalities of using digital media

Web-based interactions have three distinctive aspects compared with face-to-face ones:

- The medium is text rather than speech.
- The researcher and participant are not in the same physical place.
- The interaction can be more flexible and does not need to take place in real time.

These characteristics could be seen as potential benefits rather than problems to be overcome. In fact, there is evidence that online research is different in a variety of ways that we can capitalize on (Pincott and Branthwaite, 2000; Desai, 2002: 102).

- In some situations, eg where there are strong shared interests, intimacy can be established very quickly.
- Participants are probably alone, may be more focused and therefore might spend more time responding.
- A text-based medium might be more considered, formal, thought out, or casual, informal, playful, with responses lending themselves to games and fantasy – depending on the context.
- People tend to express more extreme views online. Opinions may be clearer, more polarized.
- It is a democratic, sharing forum, where social hierarchies can be suspended.

There are a number of digital forums that can be employed for qualitative research, including online groups, bulletin boards, blogs, e-mail forums and online communities.

Online groups

Online groups attempt to replicate face-to-face discussion groups, using web-based chat room technology. Six to eight participants are recruited and asked to log on to a password-protected chat room, where the discussion takes place. Often, because of the range of tasks that need to be carried out, two moderators conduct the group. The client and researcher are able to communicate without the participants' knowledge, new browsers can be launched on the respondents' computers, and the researcher can communicate by e-mail with individual participants if necessary. If, for instance, a new website is being tested, participants might be asked to visit the site during the group session and then discuss their reactions. In this situation, online groups can provide spontaneous, immediate responses that mirror real life fairly closely.

Often participants are recruited by phone from lists so as to maximize response rates. Some researchers who use online groups emphasize that participants can express themselves easily and that groups provide valid and reliable data (Walkowski, 2001). This does, of course, depend on the topic under discussion and the nature of the research sample. More sceptical researchers point to the importance of fast typing skills and the lack of interaction (Sarah Davies, 2009, personal communication).

Bulletin boards

Bulletin boards use a web-based technology in which participants are invited to log on to the board once a day. The researcher posts questions and the participants can post replies at their convenience. Everyone can see the comments and can follow the threads of discussion. A new question is posted every morning, and the researcher reviews the answers at the end of the day.

Bulletin boards are particularly useful where participants are required to absorb detailed information or read stimulus materials and make a considered response. They may also be used to encourage communication and cross-fertilization between two different communities. Busy professionals – indeed most of us today – could fit their participation around other commitments.

E-mail forums

E-mail forums take place over a week or two. The researcher e-mails questions to participants, who then e-mail back their responses. After each set of questions and answers, the moderator produces a summary of responses that is sent to the group for their comments, along with further questions. This gives the researcher considerable control over the discussion, summarizing and feeding back what he or she wants the participants to see. E-mail forums allow time and space for consultation with clients and for re-shaping the topics of interest, so that the research becomes an iterative process. However, they offer limited opportunities for probing, clarification and interaction.

Blogs

Blogs are particularly useful for ongoing follow-ups on group work, where participants can provide daily or weekly input, including pictures, text, drawings, virtual collages and so on. They are especially relevant with younger audiences, because of their familiarity with the medium; in this sense it is a consumer-driven qualitative methodology. The speed and accessibility of blogs means they are often chosen for international projects. Clients can access them directly and the researcher can choose to share content with other participants, if appropriate.

Online research communities

An online research community is a group of people who have been provided with an online environment in which to interact with each other (and the client and researcher) about topics related to a research interest. Typically they are constructed in content management systems (eg Community Server) that provide functionality, such as forums, blogging, polls, personal spaces, videos and e-mail contact mechanisms (Comley, 2008). The reasons for setting them up include:

- to monitor key issues within a market on an ongoing basis;
- to tap into leading-edge consumers/innovators;
- to build a panel of consumers who will be available throughout a development process;
- to collaborate, two-way, with consumers;
- to monitor markets around the globe;
- as a cost-effective and versatile research tool.

Online communities have developed as a result of three influences. Firstly, the open source movement has enabled easy access to software and encouraged a wider atmosphere of participation and sharing. Online communities are often explained as the natural expression of customers' desire to be treated as equals by the companies they deal with. Secondly, online has become normalized and we now have a whole new generation of consumers for whom online is becoming the lead medium. There is a belief that techno-savvy young people will simply not participate in traditional research methodologies. Thirdly, the emergence of Web 2.0 has provided an array of collaborative tools with which to develop new research approaches, such as wiki (software that allows users to freely create and edit Web page content) and 3D images (Cooke and Buckley, 2008).

Challenges to be overcome

Online communities present challenges to traditional methods of conducting research, although there are many logistical issues to be resolved. For instance, it has proved to be difficult to build and sustain online communities, and take-up rates are often lower than expected (Comley, 2008: 679–94). Then there are issues about recruitment and retention. What is the longevity of the community and how regularly will it need to be refreshed? Once such communities are built, there are questions around whether they can be steered towards the client's agenda. If this is attempted too overtly, then the community may reject the interference, but if the community goes too much off track then it is of questionable value to the client. Some researchers believe that online communities cannot be presented as 'research' at all (Phillips, 2008: 41–42). When there is a community of equals, is the client prepared to participate as much as everyone else? Is it feasible for clients to be always available? Are clients happy to accept criticism and not correct negative comments that appear online? Who actually owns the community?

In spite of these difficulties, online research communities have attracted a good deal of interest and appear to be flourishing, with over a thousand being set up worldwide (Comley, 2008). It is early days, but Comley predicts that they will become the preferred method for proprietary customer panels and that the adoption of short-term communities for conducting online qualitative research is likely to increase rapidly.

The future of digital media

The jury is still out in terms of the long-term effect of digital media on qualitative research but, for certain types of project and for certain audiences, they may be particularly appropriate, especially if combined with other methodologies. Digital media can less easily be categorized as 'qualitative' or 'quantitative' and this may encourage greater blurring of the boundaries between the two paradigms.

OBSERVATION AND ETHNOGRAPHIC RESEARCH

Ethnography is about understanding a social and cultural context from the insider's perspective: that is, understanding how the individual's group that is being researched interpret the world. Academic ethnographers may take years to complete a thorough ethnographic study. Commercial researchers adopt a rather pared-down version, in line with commercial budgets and time-scales, but they aspire to the same principles. Research participants are observed, interviewed and/or act as co-researchers with the agency researcher, within a context that is relevant to the research issues.

This interest in ethnography partly reflects a backlash to the 'over-use' of groups, but it is also rooted in the current near obsession with observed 'reality' exemplified by *Big Brother* and its spin offs.

There is a spectrum of approaches that can be termed observational or ethnographic (the terms are often used interchangeably), including:

■ The researcher acts as 'detached observer' and the participant does not know he or she is being observed.

- In participant observation, the researcher observes and interacts with participants; they may work as co-researchers.
- The researcher covertly gains access to a group in order to study them. This latter approach is rarely used because it would create ethical issues for commercial research.

Within most commercial projects, a middle path is struck. Researchers act as participant-observers, in order to explore how participants give meaning to their behaviour and attitudes within their everyday environment.

Desai (2002: 15) describes commercial ethnographic research as characterized by:

- a focus on the social and cultural context of people's actions and beliefs; looking at people as whole individuals, rather than compartmentalized consumers;
- seeing the world from the point of view of the participants, and avoiding imposing the researchers' cultural frameworks;
- allowing people to use their own language to describe their world;
- looking at behaviour in the place and time at which it actually occurs – in the home, the office, the car, the supermarket;
- a long-term involvement with individuals or groups;
- the use of a range of data collection methods, including interviews, group discussions, informal conversations and observations of behaviour, and also the inclusion of cultural artefacts as part of the data – eg photographs, films, drawings.

Ethnography in practice

Ethnography is not new to commercial research and was particularly prevalent in the 1930s. In recent decades, the 'accompanied shop' has been a standard feature of the qualitative researcher's repertoire. As the name suggests, the researcher accompanies shoppers whilst they go about their normal business, shopping for groceries, electronic equipment, a car or whatever. The researcher observes, asks questions, tries to understand the shoppers' behaviour, attitudes and buying decisions, and tries to make sense of their experience *in situ*. Accompanied shops have been adapted to a variety of situations: hospital visits, navigating airports, online purchasing, store layouts and so on.

Ethnography used in commercial research has become more complex and sophisticated in recent years. Siamack Salari has spent large chunks of his working life living with families and videoing them. Often, his starting point is making a film of the specific consumer group that the client is interested in. The film involves hanging out with subjects to capture the detail of how the client's products and brands fit into their lives. He also captures the broader context, including the group's environments, influences and decision making, in a naturalistic, unprompted way. By analysing the film, showing it to both clients and the consumer group, he starts a dialogue that is intended to trigger questions no one has previously considered. These questions are fed back to the target consumers and their responses are recycled as the client's understanding of its target consumers grows (Salari, 2009).

India is one of the fastest growing markets in Asia. TVS Motor Company, a motorcycle manufacturer, is increasingly doing research at the product development stage, and with people who have never owned a car or motorbike before. Spending time with people in their homes – coupled with diary research – unearthed a valuable insight. Many female customers had never learnt to ride a bike, felt that they did not know how to balance and thought that they would not be able to ride a scooter. They wanted a scooter but did not want to be taught to ride it by a male relative. TVS's response was to target an easy-to-ride scooter at the female market with a balancing wheel at the back for stability, supported by a learn-to-ride school taught by women.

Esomar Industry Report (2008)

Ethnography can be useful as a complement to standard interviewing, providing a different perspective, or it can be relevant on its own when interviewing is difficult or where it is felt that interviewing would not provide an accurate picture. There is, inevitably, a degree of overlap between interviewing and ethnographic approaches.

Hard-to-reach target audiences

Some individuals or groups are more amenable to being interviewed than others, and talk of 'focus groups' or 'market research' will send some target audiences running for cover. In particular, they may feel intimidated in a plush viewing studio, being watched by unseen observers behind a one-way mirror. Ethnographic research can be a user-friendly alternative. Recruitment can be carried out through informal networks such as groups of friends, and the exercise can be presented as 'getting ideas' rather than market research.

Ironically, the desire to minimize the research effect created by an alien environment was one of the reasons that group discussions in the UK were traditionally carried out in the home of the recruiter, who lived in the same neighbourhood as the research participants and offered a familiar environment. The reduction of in-home groups in the UK and the move to viewing facilities has arguably led to greater artificiality in the group discussion context.

Research areas where ethnographic approaches or observation are useful

Ethnographic approaches are particularly useful when there is a need to understand the social context of particular behaviour and/or to look at details of behaviour: the routines and habitual actions that we take for granted. For example:

■ Exploring cleaning behaviour, either personal or in the home: watching how participants clean their work surfaces or observing their skincare routine.

■ Understanding how technology is used: the behaviour patterns of people using their computers, watching television, listening to their iPods or, indeed, doing all three at the same time.

■ Examining the layout of shops, banks, airports and other public spaces. How do people use the space? Is the siting of the tills or changing rooms or check-in desks appropriate? This approach can be used to observe the interactions between staff and customers. Are staff helpful? What specific behaviour conveys this? Are customers satisfied? How does their behaviour show it? Exit interviews with customers can be used to check that the researcher's perceptions match the customer's experience.

■ Nights out, with the researcher as participant observer, examining drinking/eating behaviour – often with a follow up group discussion.

■ A day in the life: shadowing someone to observe particular behaviours, such as how they use transport systems.

■ Ethnographic immersion: long periods of time, perhaps a week, spent with consumers, watching and possibly videoing them.

There are endless permutations that can be crafted to fit the needs of the research programme.

Mixing methodologies

Pike and Gordon (1997) describe an experiment to compare qualitative understanding derived from three methodologies: group discussions, accompanied shopping and participant observation. The subject was toilet cleaning attitudes and behaviour. Not surprisingly, each methodology had its strengths and weaknesses. Participant observation, based on videoing the toilet cleaning, was particularly good at bringing the consumer alive for the client. Group discussions were strong on highlighting emotional issues and placing these in a social and cultural context, and accompanied shopping provided insight into the brand–consumer interface. Pike and Gordon discovered that the approaches complemented one another and provided a richer and broader picture.

Using a mixture of complementary methodologies, either as separate elements that are combined in analysis or by incorporating two methodologies within the same research event (eg group discussions in-store combined with observing store layout), allows the researcher to create multiple perspectives in which the whole is more than the sum of the parts. Each method provides a slightly different view of the research issues, which leads to well-rounded analysis, interpretation and client recommendations.

THE PARTICIPANT-RESEARCHER

There are many useful ways in which research projects can be enhanced by research participants, briefed by the researcher but carrying out research tasks on their own. This cannot really be considered as a stand-alone methodology because it is coordinated by the researcher and typically supplements other elements of the research. Generally the researcher sets the participants one or more tasks to be carried out around the research session, such as:

■ To encourage participants to focus on specific behaviours, especially habitual behaviour that is low-awareness. If you are a manufacturer of low-wattage light bulbs you might want to understand the detail of why and when people turn lights on and off. A detailed log of consumer activity can, as it were, illuminate the issue.

■ To gather contextual data on participants' lives outside the research situation, eg photos, diaries. This helps the researcher to make sense of the research data gleaned from other sources.

■ To provide material that will help to explain participants' lives to the client.

■ To increase participants' knowledge of the subject under discussion.

These activities are often – but not invariably – linked to group discussions or depth interviews. The interview context provides an opportunity for the researcher to explore the materials produced. Tasks can be set before attending a research session (pre-task), between a first and recon-vened session, or after the session (post-task). The participant forwards the task material to the research agency after it is completed. Equally the interview can precede, follow or be integral to ethnographic studies.

Research participants as photographers

Photographs offer a great way of broadening our understanding of research participants' lives outside the research context. Two purposes can be served by giving participants disposable cameras (often better than digital because this ensures a level playing field) and asking them to take photos relevant to the study, get them developed and bring them along to the research session. This sensitizes participants to the research topic and produces research data to explore, with others, in the research session. Instructions can be as broad as 'Please take photographs of anything important in your life' or as specific as 'Please take photographs of all the pairs of shoes that you own, photographing each pair separately.'

In the discussion phase, the participant photographer explains the meaning and importance of the photo. In a dynamic group situation, when participants are engaged in creating shared meaning out of their individual photographic contributions, they are very much in the present. The story is being created as they speak.

There is a danger that photographs can be seen as self-explanatory, especially when they are visually powerful. However, photographs need to be viewed as a primary source of data. They offer the potential for insights that are not accessible through interview methods alone, but they need analysis and interpretation. This needs to be instigated by the photographers themselves, as only they can say what the visual means to them. The wider meaning may subsequently be developed by the group.

Photographs serve the secondary role of bringing the consumer to life in a subsequent client presentation. Conveying the full breadth of consumer experience, particularly if the medium is a PowerPoint presen-tation, is notoriously difficult. However, photographs or other materials that participants have created, help to bridge the – often considerable – gap between the consumer and the client. Participant photos can often say much more than words.

Keeping a diary

Whether handwritten, an e-mail or a blog, a consumer diary can be extremely helpful for monitoring the detail of ongoing situations. For instance, the process of changing an energy supplier can go on for weeks and it is difficult to recall the detail of specific telephone conversations. Equally, during the first few weeks after childbirth, there is a sea change in the mother's life. It is difficult to remember the stages if they are not recorded.

Mementos

These can be potent symbols in people's lives. It is a simple task for people to bring an object of importance with them to a research session. Mementos can trigger off all sorts of relevant memories.

> Campbell Keegan carried out a project for a holiday company to identify factors that make a holiday memorable. The company's aim was to enhance their customers' holiday experiences and encourage customer loyalty. We undertook a series of workshops and asked people to bring a memento of a really good holiday. They arrived with postcards, shells, a stick of rock, an umbrella! Holding their memento, they each described their holiday experiences. Many were vivid and emotional. The memento had become an embodiment of the holiday, allowing participants to access and re-live their memories. The stories and language fed into development of a customer loyalty programme and future advertising campaign.

The researcher as photographer

The researcher can also take photos as supplementary data. This may involve taking photographs of participants (with their permission and after explaining exactly how the photos will be used), photographing their homes or work environments, their possessions, their family and so on. These photos may later be discussed with the research participants and the meaning of the content explored, and / or they may be used by the researcher to examine differences between participants so that generalized themes may be drawn out. Again, these can be very useful in helping clients understand the lives and priorities of their target audiences.

Increasingly videos are used in these situations instead of still photographs, although physically holding a photograph, which represents a frozen moment in time, can be very effective in allowing participants or the researcher to reflect on the meaning of the action or setting without the pressure to move on to the next scene.

DELIBERATIVE RESEARCH

Deliberative research is a process of hot-housing people's views and experience over time. The purpose of this process is to attempt to replicate – as far as possible – what the general public would think if they were informed and engaged citizens. This is achieved by:

■ providing research participants with relevant information, new ideas and/or access to professionals in the topic under discussion;
■ allowing them time to consider the issues (an extended group session, day-long events or reconvened sessions);
■ encouraging personal and shared reflection;
■ fostering a comparison of different – sometimes conflicting – viewpoints.

Deliberative research has something in common with reconvened groups, in that both can involve an initial, moderated group exploration of a topic, followed by activities that sensitize and inform participants. Both approaches often culminate in a further moderated group session, in which learning is shared and integrated, and participants evaluate the topic under discussion from a position of greater knowledge.

Deliberative research is used for exploring complex, multi-layered issues. Key audiences are taken through a complex series of arguments in workshops in which all sides of the debate can be presented, competing arguments tested, witnesses examined and facts scrutinized. Sometimes a combination of video, audio and real-life situations will be used to provide deeper understanding of how people make up their minds and are likely to react to complicated arguments.

This area of research is growing in importance, particularly in the public sector, in which there is a requirement to involve and engage the general public in decision-making processes. The key idea underlying deliberative research is that when ordinary people are presented with clear, unbiased information about complex issues, they can understand the topics and make sensible recommendations. The general public normally do not have the time or access to such information themselves, so they are assisted and accelerated through the deliberative process (Desai, 2002: 74).

Deliberative research in action

Examples of deliberative research projects are:

■ providing policy makers with an understanding of the public's perspective on new and developing scientific research and technology;

- exploring public attitudes towards the BBC and facilitating active engagement of members of the public with the issues that face the BBC and the media-consuming public in the 21st century;
- engaging members of the public and arts professionals, in order to help develop a 'value framework' that would steer the Arts Council's future policies, guiding how it allocates resources and evaluates its work.

This was a fairly straightforward deliberative research project, carried out by Campbell Keegan and sponsored by government. Eight groups of eight participants, representing a cross section of local populations, were recruited. The aim was to seek the opinion of the general public on the proposed restructuring of a professional regulatory body. To give a flavour of the many proposed changes, one involved changing the balance of experts and the general public on the Regulatory Council and the second meant stricter sanctions on members who were found to have broken the code of conduct. This was a specialist area, one that research participants were not – and were not expected to be – familiar with.

Initial discussions established their level of knowledge about the area. Participants were then shown a series of informational boards. The first set of boards explained the basic structure of the regulatory body. The second set provided key information on each of the proposed changes. Some of these proposals were complex and needed to be broken down into several stages. The language used on the boards is obviously key. Not only does it have to be as accurate and factual as possible, but it also needs to be expressed extremely clearly and succinctly.

There was considerable discussion around each of the boards, some need for clarification and some disagreement amongst participants. At the end of each three-hour session, we reviewed all the material and noted the spectrum of views. This enabled us to develop overall recommendations on the proposed restructuring of the statutory body and specific responses to each of the proposed changes.

Although deliberative research is used predominantly in the public sector, the growing interest in collaborative and co-creation research approaches means that it is likely to grow in popularity within the private sector.

SEMIOTICS

Semiotics, unlike many qualitative approaches, does not focus on the individual or even the group. It is concerned with understanding signs (including language as a sign system), about how things stand in relationship to other things, and how those mediated relationships help us to understand things better (Shank, 2008: 806–10). Put another way, consumers are viewed as products of culture, constructed and largely determined by the popular culture within which they live (Desai, 2002: 84). So, to understand the consumer, the researcher must first understand the cultural context. Semiotics assumes that, as meanings are constructed within popular culture, its key role is in cultural analysis.

Semiotics challenges traditional qualitative research, in that it does not require direct interaction with the consumer. Instead, the focus is on the mechanisms by which advertising, brands and products acquire their meaning and place consumer responses within a wider cultural framework.

Semiotics and cultural analysis have been used by commercial qualitative researchers to explore:

■ the meaning of advertising and marketing communications;
■ consumer cultures and how they are structured;
■ how brands speak to their consumers: the stories and myths surrounding them.

Greg Roland (2003) describes how Pot Noodles, an instant snack in a pot (just add hot water), was re-invented as an iconic youth brand through the use of semiotics. By deconstructing the characteristics and cultural associations of the brand – and highlighting its contrast with 'real food' – he concluded that Pot Noodles 'occupied a unique cultural space'. Building on this, he looked for other 'cultural constructs' that filled a similar cultural space. The answer was pornography. Consequently, a campaign was constructed based on 'Pot Noodles: the slag of snacks'; a spoof of sexualised popular culture. This campaign produced a record number of complaints to the UK Advertising Standards Authority and a 26 per cent spike in sales of Pot Noodles.

Harvey and Evans (2001) describe how semiotics was used to decode the unwritten rules that existed within the beer market and to map out an international language of beer. This map provided broader vision and deeper consumer insight, and was developed into a decoding kit that is used throughout the Guinness world to add new rigour to brand proposition development. Harvey and Evans claim that semiotics 'develops a visionary perspective on where culture and communications may be taking us, helping client brands to lead rather than follow the market'.

Although semiotics has been around in research for decades, and there are a few dedicated semioticians, it is still regarded as a rather peripheral area within commercial research (Valentine, 2007). Possibly this is because qualitative researchers tend to crave human interaction and semiotics is rather lacking on this front.

RESEARCHING ACCESSIBLE DATA SOURCES

This area used to be called desk research, but internet trawling is now probably more apt. Given the huge online resources available, it is perhaps surprising that internet trawling is not more common. It is easy for researchers to get caught up in an ongoing project, re-inventing the wheel, when useful background and contextual data, gathered online, could accelerate learning. For instance, in the UK the government has placed large numbers of its qualitative research reports on line, which can be easily accessed.

Equally, clients often seem unaware of the wealth of understanding they have stored in past projects. Research outcomes, it seems, are only valid from current research projects. Reviewing past research is an excellent start, before instigating a new study.

Social networking sites

There is growing awareness that social networking websites have a wealth of data about consumer interests, lifestyles, brand choices and so on that can help build up a picture of different target audiences.

> Whiting and Sagne (2005), from Hennessy Cognac, noticed an
> increasing number of hyperlinks between the brand's website
> and an American website called BlackPlanet.com, a community
> web portal with over 5 million members. BlackPlanet's visitors
> had a close fit with Hennessy's core consumer base in the
> United States. Using internet-based ethnography, Whiting and
> Sagne describe how they managed to gain an intimate perspec-
> tive of their consumers' lives 'first hand'.

These emerging techniques do raise some ethical issues about what consti-
tutes 'personal'. The UK Market Research Society has specified that the
processing of personal data obtained from normal networking sites may
only occur with the informed consent of the individuals concerned (MRS
News, November–December 2008).

THE FUTURE OF QUALITATIVE RESEARCH METHODOLOGIES

The changing consumer

The general public is becoming more marketing literate; business studies
and marketing are now taught in schools and 'focus groups' are part of
the culture.

This has encouraged a shift away from marketers and market
researchers 'using' consumers, in the sense of keeping them in the dark
about the objectives of the study and taking what they need. Consumers
are wise to what is going on and communication is becoming a two-way
street. In fact, the term consumer has itself been criticized as patronizing
and uni-dimensional.

There is growing interest in 'co-creation', in which consumers, advertisers and marketing people work together on a problem and share their
different perspectives on the same situation, product or experience. It is
too early to tell whether this will become the dominant mind-set for the
future. It may simply prove easier for time-pressed clients to watch
consumers from behind one-way mirrors.

Changing client needs

In spite of criticisms about the artificiality of group discussions, they
remain popular because they provide useful outcomes and because clients

like to watch groups. Viewing group discussions through a one-way mirror was common in the United States long before it became established in the UK. Nowadays it is the 'norm' in most countries in the world and many clients want to observe consumers at first hand, so that they can more fully understand their target audiences. There is no substitute for a client experiencing a participant's unmediated reaction to an ad or a new idea.

With the advent of web streaming, it is not uncommon for clients in different continents to be simultaneously viewing the group in 'real time' and feeding back comments by e-mail to those who are behind the one-way mirror. This technological capacity offers obvious benefits to clients in terms of time saving and sharing the experience, and this is likely to encourage greater use of viewed groups. However, participants' reactions are only part of the story and there is a danger that 'the experience of watching' becomes the research. Inexperienced clients may jump to conclusions based on first impressions, partial knowledge and the group they happen to have attended. It is important that the researcher's experienced attention to the group and the subsequent analysis, interpretation and structuring of the research outcomes is not diminished by the spectator aspect of groups.

The technological revolution

Technology has thrown open possibilities for qualitative research that are still emerging. Traditionally, qualitative research has been a people-focused, skill-based activity. The development of web-based methodologies has provoked widespread debate within the qualitative research community. Can we carry out effective qualitative research projects when we cannot see or even hear research participants – or when we cannot verify their online identities? What are the ethics of using social network material as research data? Is it valid to carry out research with virtual people? Jack Tatar, a US researcher, conducted a project on Second Life in which avatars sat in a 'focus group' discussing restaurant design. This enabled him to simultaneously involve experts from around the world (Tatar, 2008).

Online focus groups, blogs, bulletin boards and social networking communities have opened up new opportunities, both in terms of methodology and because they allow researchers to access certain research participants in environments in which they feel at home.

The area where collaboration and co-creation really seems to be taking off is online. Social networking sites, blogs and bulletin boards have fostered a spirit of collaborative self-governance, which has encouraged the direct involvement of consumers in new product development and other research areas (Leadbeater, 2008: 98–108).

7 Improving interviewing (and other) skills

COMMUNICATION: THE ROOT OF ALL QUALITATIVE RESEARCH

The two essential qualitative skills are good communication and thorough, insightful analysis, although in practice these skills cannot easily be separated. Good communication is needed at all stages of the research project, but particularly in relation to research participants and clients. This chapter deals mainly with participant communication and Chapter 12 deals with client communication.

There is sometimes a belief that the skills needed for qualitative research are very different from those used in everyday communication. This is not strictly true. Qualitative communication skills are a development of the skills that we have all built up over our lifetimes. With training, guidance and experience, we can all become more aware of, and broaden, our repertoire of skills. This, in turn, enables us to become more effective in research situations: to see, hear, feel, experience and to make sense of research data in a more productive way.

For simplicity, this chapter focuses mainly on group interviewing skills, because all qualitative researchers need to be proficient at moderation ('moderation' implies interviewing in groups, whereas 'interviewing' can refer to all types of talking research). However, interviewing is not just a verbal skill. All interviews involve ethnography: watching people's behaviour, how they express themselves, how they respond in the particular situation, how they interact with the moderator and other participants. Therefore, all of the issues covered in relation to interviewing are equally applicable to ethnographic, deliberative and other interactive research approaches.

The role of the moderator

The moderator has a complex role: covering the client's agenda and making sense of participants' perspectives at the same time, with the aim of bringing the two perspectives together to create a useful way forward. Essentially he or she needs:

- To create an atmosphere that is conducive for participants to share their attitudes, behaviour, feelings and thoughts with the rest of the group.
- To be aware, at all times, of the objectives of the study and to ensure that the conversation covers the areas that are relevant and of interest – and that have been agreed with the client. This needs to be done in such a way that the free-flowing conversation within the group is not inhibited. The aim is to foster an environment in which research participants are relaxed, comfortable and feel as if they are having normal, everyday conversation. There is an obvious contradiction here. The moderator must act like a duck: smooth and unruffled on the surface, but paddling madly under the water as he or she steers the conversation subtly in order to cover all the research objectives (Chrzanowska, 2002: 16–19).
- To recognize important areas when these emerge and encourage the group to discuss these in detail, using a variety of verbal and non-verbal moderating skills (see Chapter 9).
- To deal with the group dynamics constructively and encourage participants to speak and feel comfortable doing so.
- To use research stimuli as appropriate, to explore key areas and to encourage research participants to identify and articulate thoughts and feelings that may not be readily accessible to them (see Chapter 8).
- To manage client expectations, especially where there are high levels of anxiety around the project.

This is quite a tall order. How does he or she do this?

Leading and following as an interviewing style

A research interaction is like an improvisational dance between participants, both researcher and researched. The researcher's job is to explore, as far as possible, the research topic he or she has been commissioned to investigate, and to generate understanding that will help the client's decision making.

This cannot be achieved by simply asking a string of direct questions. Firstly, that is likely to alienate research participants, so they will not open up and engage with the researcher. Secondly, the researcher may not know the nuances of the market or subject area – which is why the research is being carried out. There will be areas that emerge from the research that neither the client nor the researcher had any previous knowledge of. A series of predetermined questions would simply bypass these areas. Thirdly, research participants may themselves discover aspects of their own behaviour or attitudes of which they were not previously aware.

During a depth interview that involved exploration of a particular brand of after-dinner mints, a participant suddenly realized that she bought the brand because it reminded her of her late mother. She had not previously made the connection and became quite emotional when it became clear.

The role of the researcher is to both lead and follow: to lead in order to ensure that the client's objectives are being fully met, and to follow in the sense that he or she must recognize and encourage interesting conversational paths that are also relevant to the research objectives. This style of interaction with research participants reflects informal everyday conversation, and so is more natural for participants. The real skill, of course, is to recognize when to lead and when to follow, and this takes considerable experience.

When I talk about leading, I am not referring to the actual questions asked but to the process of steering the research participants through the relevant topic areas. This is different from asking 'leading questions' that may influence the research participants and colour their responses. These are best avoided unless the researcher is absolutely clear why they are being used.

Developing moderating skills

There is a paradox in qualitative interviewing, and particularly in moderating a group discussion. A 'good' moderator will make the process look easy, and it is common for a client observing the group to comment, 'That was a really good group.' In fact, it was a really good moderator, but really good moderation is invisible.

Becoming really good at moderating takes time, practice and the guidance of an experienced and sympathetic mentor. Gordon and Langmaid (1988: 51) estimate that it takes 'an absolute minimum' of two years to train a novice researcher to the point where he or she feels relatively comfortable, competent and collected in the interviewing situation and will have attained a thorough grounding in both group and individual interviewing skills. I would add that it takes perhaps another two or more years before the researcher is able to fully understand, analyse and present the relevant learning from the research data in a way that is most useful and practical for the client.

Experienced researcher Joanna Chrzanowska describes how interviewing in qualitative research is a delicate balancing act, involving the integration of the client, moderator and research participant agendas, managing the power relations between interviewer and participants, choosing how to frame questions and when to make interventions and being sensitive to the group dynamics as well as the feelings and issues of the individual participants – all at the same time. In particular, Chrzanowska highlights a critical aspect of qualitative research interviewing, namely that the integration of all of the above:

> happens as a set of moment-by-moment interviewer choices. Colloquially speaking, these happen in the interviewer's head; since the interviewer or moderator is working simultaneously on several different levels it might be more accurate to say they happen in the 'bodymind' (using inputs from the physical, emotional and intuitive levels) (Chrzanowska, 2002: 1).

This may seem quite an esoteric claim and difficult to grasp initially. Certainly, in the early stages, it is normal for a new researcher to interview 'from the head'; in other words, the interview is largely a cerebral process as the researcher struggles to stay in control, get through the client's agenda and keep the group on track. However, over time and with experience, more of the senses come into play. Experienced researchers may choose to loosen their intellectual control and allow their senses to inform their understanding of what is going on. Rosie Campbell (2009, personal communication) describes this type of awareness as:

> a bit like butterflies in my stomach... hard to describe. It's like I know emotionally, before I get the intellectual understanding. I'm on to something important and I have to just wait and be alert. Sometimes it's when things are confused or when, for no apparent reason, I get really interested in what is going on.

There are a number of ways in which these skills can be developed but it is worth pointing out – if the above comments have triggered off minor terrors – that the most important research skill is establishing rapport. Research participants will be extraordinarily forgiving of glitches or hesitation in a new moderator, provided they feel a sense of rapport with him or her.

Self-awareness

Self-awareness is important. As researchers, we need to be aware of how we are presenting ourselves and how others are responding to us, and develop the ability to monitor the ongoing interaction between us and others, whilst at the same time being 'in the flow' of the conversation.

When we are aware of how we are acting and being perceived, we can make choices about how to behave, speak and interact with the individual or group in such a way as to create the appropriate environment to explore the particular research issues. I do not mean being 'false'. Research participants will immediately pick up on insincerity. An essential characteristic of a good qualitative researcher is being someone who is genuinely interested in understanding other people and what makes them tick – research participants will recognize this quality and respond to it. 'Being aware' is to do with choosing a facet of ourselves that is appropriate with this group, within this context, when talking about this subject.

As researchers we are, even if nominally, in charge of the research situation. Often this generates some power play between researcher and research participants or amongst participants themselves. The group situation may provoke long-buried memories. Does the moderator – or the situation – remind a participant of a disliked teacher? Does this foster over-compliance or, alternatively, passive resistance or hostility? Does a participant feel the need to dominate in a group, or to become invisible?

We can never truly know how participants experience the situation but, if we stay sensitive to what is happening in the group interactions, we can often gauge the mood and adjust our behaviour in order to keep the group on track. This means being aware, moment by moment, of the interaction. We can plan what we want to achieve in a research situation, but the plan is just a guide. We also need improvisational skills.

COMMUNICATION BEFORE THE RESEARCH SESSION

Recruitment as a 'taster'

We think of moderation as starting with 'the interview' but, from a research participant's perspective, this is not so. The way in which he or she is recruited, the language used to describe the session and so on, inevitably colour expectations and responses. We need to consider the message we want to convey. Is it a creative session? Then the invitation needs to stir excitement and anticipation. Will participants be helping to shape future government policy? Participants will take this seriously and it should be reflected in the tone of recruitment. Equally we need to be honest with participants about the time commitment and what is expected of them.

Controlling the research environment

The context in which the research takes place will colour the way participants respond. This is fairly obvious in ethnographic projects, but it also needs thinking about for groups. The layout of the room – for example in a boardroom style or with chairs arranged as a circle – conveys messages about what is expected of participants. Care needs to be taken to ensure that the environment supports the particular group of participants and the topic to be discussed.

Looking the part

It is a truism that we make judgements within seconds of meeting new people. When participants walk into the room, they immediately evaluate the moderator; will he/she make this fun, boring, interesting? Clearly there are certain factors that we cannot change – our gender, age, accent – and different participants will interpret these in different ways. A young, 'cool' researcher will provoke a different response from a group of teenagers than, say, a middle-aged woman who reminds them of their mum. The moderator's behaviour can overcome stereotypes to a large extent, but not eliminate them.

We need to think about the elements we can change, such as dressing in a way that will not seem intimidating or odd to the particular audience. On most occasions it's appropriate to look neutral, unless there is a reason not to, for instance if it is important for the study that we are seen as one of the participants.

THE FIRST FIVE MINUTES: ESTABLISHING RAPPORT

This is the most important stage of the research session and rapport needs to be established quickly during the initial introductions. Until we can achieve a sufficient level of rapport, empathy and trust with our research participants, we will be unable to get beneath the superficial platitudes of their lives. Rapport is a prerequisite of good qualitative research.

Essentially, it involves meeting individuals in their model of the world. We all have different upbringings, experiences, capabilities and identities: different ways of being. We see the world differently. To establish rapport with others we need to acknowledge them and their view of the world. As Carl Rogers, the founder of humanistic psychology, puts it, we do not have to agree with people, just recognize and respect them (Rogers, 1961: 243–79).

Greeting people in a friendly but professional manner and mirroring their style in the introduction helps people to relax. For instance, a degree of formality might be appropriate with a group of business people. They may need some reassurance about who the other participants are (competitors? potential clients?), what exactly the topic will be, who the commissioning client is.

Conversely, with a group of mums, greater informality might be appropriate, for example allowing a few minutes for them to relax if they have rushed to the session after the 'school run'.

Emphasizing that people have been invited to give their views – which will probably differ – gives permission for diversity. Equally, stressing that everyone's view counts sows the seeds for discouraging the over-talkative.

It is a good idea for the moderator to write participants' names down at the beginning of the session when people introduce themselves. Focusing on individuals and using their names ensures their attention and makes the interaction more personal.

Neuro-linguistic programming (NLP), although it sounds daunting, offers very practical, 'hands on' techniques which can be used to establish rapport quickly (O'Connor and McDermott, 1996: 10–16):

■ Matching voice tone and speed of speaking, not in the sense of mimicry but more like two instruments harmonizing, helps create rapport.

■ Using the same technical vocabulary, where appropriate, is a way of establishing professional credibility.

■ People will often mark out words and phrases that are important to them. Using the same words or phrases in your reply show that you hear and respect their meaning.

■ Body and voice matching with the research participant creates rapport at the behaviour level.

■ The strongest rapport comes from acknowledging people's identity, that is, their values and way of life.

USING NON-VERBAL COMMUNICATION

Human beings have an extraordinary ability to communicate with one another in a myriad of ways. In Western culture, we tend to over-play language because we prize rational communication over other forms of communication. However, non-verbal communication is also important; eye movements, frowning, grimacing, the way we walk, can all complement (or undermine) the words we use. Equally, the words we choose and the way we use them – our intonation, silences, tone of voice – are just as important as the words themselves. Some communication is overt and intentional, whereas much communication is outside our conscious awareness (see Chapter 6). As qualitative researchers we need to develop our awareness of this huge range of communication tools, because they open the door to a greater understanding of consumer groups and their needs, attitudes, behaviours and so on. The range of non-verbal communications discussed below is relevant across all qualitative methodologies.

The role of body language

Non-verbal communication (NVC) or body language is communication without words. It includes any bodily expression, such as eye or facial movements, posture and actions to which an observer attributes meaning. It also includes vocal cues or signals – crying, shouting or silences – although these cues are, strictly speaking, verbal.

Body language often acts at an unconscious level; we may leak signals. Equally, body signals can be learnt and consciously used by the sender, for example maintaining eye contact or smiling to encourage rapport. Body language is often described as more primitive and powerful than verbal communication and acts in different ways. For instance, communication containing strong emotional content (comfort, love, and apology) may be better communicated non-verbally as these messages can be more ambiguous and subtle.

Verbal messages can be replaced or reinforced by body language. Topics that are rarely discussed tend to have underdeveloped vocabularies and body language can 'fill the gaps'; for example it might be easier for a participant to demonstrate rather than explain how she brushes her teeth. Most importantly, non-verbal clues enable conversation to flow, by offering a common code that all of those involved in a dialogue will understand, for instance when taking turns to speak, adopting another's mood state (empathizing, consoling etc).

Body language also differs from country to country and there are recognized and reliable cultural differences in non-verbal communication. Consider differences in greetings: in parts of Europe it is appropriate to bow with a slight click of the heels; in Japan, the deep respectful bow is required; the gallant hand kiss is used in France, the bear-hug in Russia. The fact that body communication is in part culture specific means that inter-cultural communication can be fraught (Furnham, 1999: 67–68). This has obvious implications for multi-country studies.

We are all expert at using body language; we do it all the time. However, becoming more aware of what we do and how we do it enables us to choose the most appropriate body language for the situation.

Using body language in research contexts

Body language is especially critical when establishing initial rapport with research participants, but it also acts as an important tool for managing the research session. This may involve giving positive cues such as leaning forward, silent expectation, smiling encouragingly at the quiet ones, or negative cues like avoiding eye contact and shifting one's body away from participants who are dominating the conversation.

The energy level in a group can also provide important signals about its response to the material being researched. Researchers are not just reading non-verbal behaviour in a simple 'body language' sense; they are also looking for consonance or dissonance between verbal and non-verbal clues and attempting to understand why this is happening. When body language contradicts speech, so that we receive a 'mixed message', this is a clear sign that something interesting is going on and it is important to dig deeper. For example:

Participant: Yes, I like that ad [for a new facial moisturiser]. It's good, yes. I'd go for that one [shaking head, leaning back, arms crossed].

Moderator: What do you like about it?

Participant: Well, it just tells you what it does [slightly irritated tone, looking away].

Moderator: What is it telling you?

Participant: That if I use that I'll look like Kate Moss [definite irritation].

Moderator: And?

Participant: It's a complete load of tosh, isn't it? It's a product to get rid of wrinkles. Kate Moss hasn't got wrinkles. Of course I want to look young and sexy, but I'm a middle aged woman. It's about time they got real about skin care…

Expressing ourselves through our senses

Non-verbal techniques such as drawing or role-play are used to access and interpret different types of data. These techniques help move the researcher–participant interaction away from the purely verbal and offer a different perspective on the issues. These techniques can enable access to emotional content and are also useful with participants who are less verbal (see Chapter 9).

We all have preferences in the way in which we use our senses. Some people think in words. Others are visually oriented and think in pictures. Some trust their feelings or instincts. In NLP, these different sensory preferences are called representational systems, which can be expressed as:

Sense	Representational system
Sight	Visual
Hearing	Auditory
Feeling	Kinaesthetic
Tasting	Gustatory
Smell	Olfactory

The ways in which people express themselves provide clues to their preferred representational system. Someone who repeatedly starts a sentence with 'I feel' is likely to be strongly kinaesthetic, whereas a person who starts 'Sounds like' may be more auditory. Mirroring a participant's language can encourage them to open up and expand on a subject.

Equally, those with a visual preference may be interested in drawing, visual arts, film or interior design. With an auditory preference they might be interested in language, writing or drama. Kinaesthetic people are typically interested in sport or working 'with their hands'. These are, of course, stereotypes and people can use all sorts of combinations of these representational systems at different times.

The important thing, from a qualitative research perspective, is to be aware that people think differently. Knowing this, we can use different ways of accessing how participants make sense of the world. It is important to employ different sensory routes in order to achieve this. Therefore, qualitative research may well include a range of activities such as drawing, making collages, role-play, story writing and the like in order to tap into the different sensory preferences of research participants.

THE POWER OF WORDS

Active listening

Much of the time we only half-listen to the person we are speaking with; we are worrying about catching our train or preparing a response to what the other is saying. We are not fully there. By paying attention to in-the-moment interactions in conversation, by being present, we can absorb much more.

The goal of active listening is to attend entirely to the speaker, not to oneself or one's own inner dialogue. It is to hear and interpret the speaker's verbal and non-verbal communication. This may include focusing on the face and orienting the body towards the speaker. It also involves a neutral, open attitude toward the speaker so that even remarks that are shocking or distressing are understood – not judged – by the listener. The goal is to receive information not to give it – and to be a witness, not a critic (Ayers, 2008: 8).

In qualitative interviewing, there is a number of strategies that can be useful in developing active listening.

Paraphrasing

The interviewer may re-state the content of the communication in slightly different words, for example:

> So, can I check I've got this right: You think this ad is less effective that this one?

Simply repeating the participant's comments back to him or her creates a sense of being understood and this, in turn, can give the participant confidence to disclose more, or to reveal more private feelings.

Reflecting

This is more likely to involve non-verbal content: for example, 'It sounds as if you are pretty angry at the way you were treated in the surgery.'

This gives participants the opportunity to confirm, deny or clarify what they have said. In doing so, they may delve deeper into their own experiences and be able to give a fuller or more emotional description of their feelings. It is important in these situations that the researcher is acutely focused on the emotional state of the participant. Research is not therapy and it is unethical for researchers to delve into areas that might unleash emotional trauma in the research participant. However, it is not always possible to predict what might trigger trauma in an individual. This means that the researcher must be constantly vigilant to any sign of distress in research participants and, if they are concerned, back off from the areas of concern.

Summarizing

This may help a smooth transition to the next topic or be used to confirm understanding. It is also an opportunity to clarify. A participant's meaning when he or she uses certain words may seem self-evident, but sometimes just asking, 'What does it mean when you call him xxxx?' reveals quite surprising answers.

Silence

When appropriately used, silence can be a very powerful way of communicating respect, empathy and interest in something a participant has just said. It also allows participants to work through their own thoughts, which is especially important when exploring areas in which they cannot easily articulate.

These strategies demonstrate to the research participants that the researcher is both concentrating on and actively processing what they are saying – the hallmarks of active listening.

Open and closed questions

Questions can be either open or closed. Open or non-directive questions often start with 'what', 'why', 'where' or 'who' and provide space for the participant to answer in his or her own words and to decide how to develop the conversation. For example, 'Describe a typical day at work' gives participants considerable leeway to steer the conversation in whatever way they choose and to focus on areas that they consider to be important. This type of question is good when exploring broad topic areas, because it helps the researcher to highlight key areas that are important to participants and that can be explored in more detail.

Neither open nor closed questions are better. Each has its place and the skill is in understanding which type of question is appropriate at a particular moment in time, in order to elicit the type of response that is needed. It is common for novice researchers to ask more closed questions, because they feel that they have greater control over the answers. However, this makes for a staccato conversation, which may neglect the key issues, for example:

Researcher: Do you take your child to school?

Participant: Yes, I do.

Researcher: And does she take a packed lunch?

Participant: Yes, usually.

Researcher: When would she not take one?

Participant: On Fridays, because it is a half-day.

Researcher: What do you put in her packed lunch?

Participant: A sandwich and some fruit.

Researcher: Anything else?

Participant: A drink.

Researcher: What sort of drink?

Participant: Squash, water.

This is hard work for both researcher and participant. The participant does not grasp what the researcher is getting at and so mirrors his or her staccato style and answers the questions literally. It is difficult for the researcher to get beneath the surface detail, to the meaning of the participant's behaviour: what she is concerned about, what she wants for her child, what she feels about packed lunches.

An alternative scenario, with more open questions, could go something like this.

Researcher: I want to chat with you about how you deal with packed lunches. Some women I talk to find it quite a chore, but others quite enjoy it. I don't know how you feel about it. But first, tell me a little bit about your little girl. What is her name?

Participant: Marie.

Researcher: OK, and does she enjoy school? Is she a good eater?' Is she picky?

Participant: Well, she's seven next month, the youngest, the baby of the family.

Researcher: Ah, so you have older children as well? Are they all having packed lunches or is it different for the others? How do you sort it all out?

Participant: Well Hanna is 11 and Sophie 9. They all have packed lunches so it's quite a hassle trying to get it all organized in the morning. And they all like different things. I take them with me to the supermarket and they are allowed to choose what drinks they have in their packed lunch.

Researcher: Ah, so they only get to choose their drinks? (Laugh)

Participant: That's the only thing they're allowed to choose, otherwise it gets manic. They have a good breakfast before they go to school and I always give them a cooked meal when they come home, so I'm not over-concerned about lunch. But I do insist that they have a drink at lunchtime, otherwise they can go the whole day without drinking – that's why I give them something they like that I know they'll drink. And they have a sandwich – Marie always wants cheese! And they have a piece of fruit. I try to get them to eat three pieces of fruit a day. I put a little treat in, maybe twice a week, a chocolate biscuit or a bag of crisps.

With this style of open questioning, the researcher concentrates on establishing rapport with the participant. The relaxed, conversational style of the researcher is mirrored by the participant. She describes the packed lunch scenario in her own words, from her own perspective, giving priority to those aspects that she considers to be most important. Rather than asking questions from a script, irrespective of the participant's answers, the researcher 'follows on' from the participant's comments – as you would in 'normal' conversation – whilst at the same time ensuring that the content remains relevant to the objectives of the research. This interviewing style provides a richer, fuller, contextual understanding of the issues because there is both factual information and greater understanding of how the participant feels about the issue of packed lunches. She reveals her anxieties about her children drinking enough liquids and her attempts to get them to eat enough fruit. But she stresses her balanced approach. She can monitor what they eat at breakfast and supper, so she is not over-concerned about their midday meal.

If the hypothetical client who commissioned this hypothetical project manufactured cheese niblets, it would be crucial to understand the attitudes and behaviour of mothers who prepare packed lunches. For this particular mother, cheese niblets would fall into the category of the twice-weekly 'little treat'.

Often, the researcher will start an interview with open questions, in order to provide context for the study. Gradually he or she will home in to specific areas that that the client wants to address. For instance, towards the end of the interview, when more evaluation is required, the following type of questions might be appropriate:

Is this the type of product you might put in your daughter's lunchbox?

Would it be an everyday thing or a treat?

The meaning of language

Language lies at the heart of qualitative inquiry. Even when we employ imaginative, innovative research techniques, we describe them and convey the outcomes of the research largely through language. An aesthetic interest in language is an essential for any qualitative practitioner (Campbell, 2008).

What people say and what is created in conversation (or written in discourse) creates reality, not least because we hear it as we speak it. Listen to a participant explaining her laundry routine:

> I'm afraid I'm the one who has the obsessively tidy house. I plump up my cushions at night. I have to put clean clothes away. I don't feel comfortable with myself until I do.

This woman is not just describing what she does. She is relaying a well-rehearsed story. 'Obsessively tidy' is a personal theme that is used to explain and contextualize who she is.

The way in which people use language is hugely revealing. Listening to people's stories – the way they describe events, the words they use, what they choose to focus on – tells us a great deal about who they are as people. Indeed, the way we use words contains the code for our beliefs and motivations (Campbell, 2008).

In the hurly burly of fast-turn-around research – and the belief that what you see and hear in a research session is all you get – it is hard to make time to reflect seriously on language. But if we do, we can unearth an Aladdin's cave of cultural, social and personal meaning. At best, this requires listening to recordings of interviews, because it is only through hearing the language, with its intonation, hesitation, pace and all the rest, that we can absorb the full flavour of the communication – bearing in mind that we inevitably fill in the gaps to create our own unique meaning.

Language can be analysed at different levels. Below are a few examples of the ways in which it can reveal meaning on a cultural, social and personal level.

Cultural discourse

We often use language in ways that are so rooted in our culture that we do not notice how odd they are until we question them. The bizarreness of the language becomes what Professor John Shotter, a communications specialist, calls 'rationally invisible' (Shotter, 1993: 60).

'What's he worth?' is generally understood as 'How much money has he got?' In a society where one's wealth is the definition of worth, this is normal, but in societies in which wealth is measured by other criteria, such as status in the community or supporting others, it would seem very odd.

'…the security of bricks and mortar…'

'You can't go wrong with property!'

'Safe as houses'

These quotes reflect cultural assumptions, which were regarded as truths until the 2009 world recession proved otherwise.

Social meaning

We often adopt family or group truths that become shared reality, so that denying the truth is particularly upsetting.

In my family, debt is always frowned upon.

For this participant, 'getting into debt' would bring more than simply anxiety about money. It would bring shame, and challenge her family allegiances.

Personal meaning and storytelling

Money just slipped through my fingers.

'Slipped through' and 'my fingers' are very close up, 'worried' descriptions, in which the teller feels things 'happen to him'. This is a common use of language, in which the narrator distances him or herself from the activity and denies agency. It was 'not my fault'. An area where this is particularly pronounced is in weight loss:

It was the car that put the weight on me…

I look and think, 'What are these rolls? Why have they decided to settle on me?'

Language as storytelling

Equally, language is the food of stories that both describe the past and define the future:

When I had a thin summer in my mid-twenties, I wasn't actually all that happy… I felt like I was waiting all the time, feeling anxious that the weight would come back… and of course, it did… sometimes I wonder why I'm obsessed by losing weight…'

BRINGING IT ALL TOGETHER

As the project progresses, these individual elements of spoken and body language and making meaning come together and we begin to see the patterns that are forming. We start to understand the bigger picture of research participants' attitudes, beliefs, behaviour, expectations and so on in relation to the research issues. In NLP terms, we move from 'small chunk' to 'large chunk' thinking.

Making sense of participants' experience

In real life, the way we experience something is dependent on a complex mix of intellect, bodily reactions and emotions, in a soup of personal history. A truism of NLP is 'The meaning of the communication is the response you get.' This may seem odd, initially. We tend to think that we are the source of the communication and, therefore, if it is misunderstood, then it is the fault of the recipient. However, turning this around gives quite a different perspective. We may get curious, ask how the misunderstanding is possible. What is the participant's 'world view' that encourages him or her to interpret the communication in this way? By paying attention, staying curious and asking questions around a topic, we can gain an understanding of where the participant is coming from. This is particularly important when making sense of responses to research stimulus materials.

I was exploring some potential press advertisements for a cosmetics manufacturer with a group of '30-something' women. They liked the bold, confident, colourful ads that I had shown them and felt that they worked well as part of a campaign to launch a new lipstick. I showed them the final ad and, as a body, they rejected it. They reacted viscerally; there was a physical drawing back in some of the participants.

> That's horrible.
> Oh no, you can't use that.
> Use the others, not that.

It is always interesting when you get such a strong physical reaction because you know it is not tempered by reason. Something quite basic, almost primeval, is being triggered and often the participants themselves do not immediately know why they have reacted in this way.

The participants did not want to discuss the ad further, but I needed to know what was causing this reaction. I had a suspicion, but I had to validate my hypothesis with the research participants. I needed to be able to explain to the client why this ad should not be included in the campaign, if this was what I was proposing, so I pushed them a little.

> You liked the other bold, colourful ads. You liked the challenging style, the tongue in cheek humour. Why not this?
> It's different. Too in your face.
> It's too close in.
> Vulgar. It's vulgar.

We were getting closer.

> The lips. It's too close to the lips – they take up the whole page [giggle].
> What is wrong with that?
> Oh look, its just like, well, it's just, you know, like it's not lips, well, not those lips...they're like, well, sexual.

The group tittered, glad that we had finally got this out in the open.

> 'So it just embarrasses you that the lips look too much like they could be sexual organs?' I asked.

> There was a chorus of 'Yes's'.

The client, I presume, had not intended to convey this association at all, but this is what the research participants took out of it. The visual triggered feelings of shame, of feminine privacy being violated. Gaining an understanding of how participants interpreted the communication from within their world view made it possible to explain to the client why this image would not work and to steer the company in a more appropriate direction.

OVERCOMING COMMUNICATION PROBLEMS

There are certain 'classic' problems that, sooner or later, moderators will experience in a discussion group or other research environment.

The 'quiet' group

Groups are not necessarily what they seem. A novice qualitative researcher is often fearful of 'the silent group'. There is anxiety that people will not say 'anything'; that long silences will lead to… well who knows what… ? Embarrassment? The collapse of the group? Client anger? With the current predominance of viewing facilities, there is the added pressure of ensuring a good performance for the clients, who want articulate, lively, entertaining research participants.

The reality is that the entertainment value of the group – participants who are articulate, energetic and put on a good show versus those who are taciturn and 'difficult' – bears little relationship to the usefulness of the session. Some of the most stilted, 'difficult' groups I have conducted have produced the most useful insights. Not all participants are articulate and comfortable in a research setting with a group of strangers, being viewed through a one-way mirror. (This is often an argument for using more ethnographic-style research.) In a 'difficult' group, non-verbal cues become particularly important and the researcher watches how people interact, their bodily movements, sensing any discomfort.

If a group is particularly stilted, a change of pace or style may be needed. It can help to break the group up into syndicate groups, working on particular issues and then reconvening in the main group. Projective techniques (see Chapter 9) can also come into their own. Some participants may feel more comfortable drawing or writing. Each group is unique and therefore unpredictable. The role of the moderator is to work with the group in whatever way is necessary at the time. The moderator has to be versatile, a chameleon, willing to change tack if the first approach is not productive.

One of the best ways to judge the 'usefulness' of a group is to transcribe it. When moderating a lively group, there is often a feeling of 'Yes, this is going OK', whereas a silent group often provokes anxiety, so we come away feeling less satisfied. However, if we ignore the anxiety and listen to the recording with an attentive ear, we may get a very different perspective. Words and phrases leap out; we hear things in a different way than we did when interviewing. This is the reason that I mourn the shift from researchers transcribing their own groups (now considered too time consuming) to getting interviews 'professionally' transcribed. Listening to our interviews with a critical ear is one of the best training grounds. We can pinpoint what we did well or what we might do differently. It also acts as an immersion in the data, which makes it much easier to carry out the subsequent research analysis.

The silent individual

What about the individual who sits silently in an otherwise lively group? This requires a degree of tact to encourage such participants without putting them on the spot and embarrassing them – and the rest of the group – to such a degree that they refuse to participate for the rest of the discussion. People can be silent for a number of reasons. They may feel nervous with a group of strangers. They may be preoccupied with personal issues that have nothing to do with the group, or they may simply be cynically attending the group to get the incentive reward.

The simple technique of getting all participants to introduce themselves at the start of the session and say a little about their background or interests breaks the back of nervousness about talking in the group, and also allows the moderator to learn everyone's names and so be able to address them individually. Alternatively, participants can be paired up and asked to talk to one another for a few minutes and then introduce their partner. This is good as an ice breaker and can be less intimidating than participants introducing themselves. If several attempts to involve the silent participant have failed, it is usually better to simply accept his or her silence, rather than risk creating 'an atmosphere' that disrupts the rest of the group.

There is a common misconception that all group participants contribute equally. This is no more the case in a discussion group than in other areas of life. Some people in the group are more talkative – though not necessarily more productive. Some simply have a greater grasp of the research area and so can contribute more. A 'good' group is one that works together on the research issues and this often means that there are those who lead, those who support and those who challenge or summarize.

Having said this, it is important, first, that each member of the group is encouraged to contribute to the best of his or her ability and second, that they are encouraged to help the group be as productive as possible. Experience is a great teacher and, over time, a moderator learns the most effective strategies that help to keep balance in the group and optimize productivity.

Dealing with 'difficult' participants

Very occasionally participants are rude, disruptive or intimidating to other participants. Participants are 'difficult' for a reason and it is important to try to understand this reason, otherwise there is a risk that the group will be compromised. Giving these participants space to air their views, reassuring them, non-verbally, that their voice is being heard or even asking them outright what the issue is, are all possible remedies. If these efforts fail, they must be asked, politely, to leave the group. The other participants will probably be so grateful that they will work extra hard during the session!

More commonly, the participant just 'niggles'; this is often not sufficiently disruptive to address head on, but it makes other participants uneasy. It may take some time before the 'problem' can be identified.

We had been commissioned by a government department to carry out research on literature to be sent to all parents of children about to undertake GCSEs in the UK. We were exploring how best the information should be presented. The research involved a combination of:

■ pre-placement of 'mock up' leaflets, so that parents could read them in a more natural setting and report back;
■ individual interviews, so we could go through the detail of the leaflets;
■ group discussions to examine the context in which the leaflets would be received and the overall content.

The leaflets needed to be accessible to all parents, including those with limited literacy. In one group, a particular participant was being belligerent and disruptive. He repeatedly challenged the purpose of the leaflet and dismissed its worth. It created 'an atmosphere' in the group and I did not know what to do. I needed to understand why he was being 'difficult', so I decided to talk with him specifically, asking him about the content of the page he was examining. It suddenly dawned on me that he could not easily read the page; the language was too complicated. He did not want to admit this. Obviously I did not want to embarrass him by exposing his lack of literacy, but understanding the root of his 'problem' behaviour allowed me to explore the style of language used in the leaflet, how paragraphs were structured, the layout and so on from the perspective of (the rather euphemistic) 'ease of use'. When approached in this way, the participant was extremely useful in pointing out specific areas of text and presentation that needed to be 'clearer'. There were many people with reading difficulties who would receive the leaflet. This participant, once he was 'on side', provided really useful input to the leaflet development.

Dealing with the participant who 'dominates'

It is not uncommon for one participant to hog the floor. He or she may be a 'natural soapbox speaker' who is oblivious to normal cues on social interaction. Such people may have particularly strong views on the topic or they may consider themselves expert and wish to share their knowledge with others. Many novice moderators feel that it would be impolite to intervene and so let the talker dominate. It is important to remember that other participants probably feel just as irritated by the domination, and consider it to be the moderator's job to stop the talker.

In general a clear, polite and firm request to let others talk is the most successful route to silencing 'over-talkers'. It can also be useful to understand why they want to dominate and address the underlying issues. A 'know-it-all' may be silenced by acknowledging their expertise, but politely asking them to keep quiet:

> I know this is your area and you're quite an expert [smile], but we also need to get the views of others who have less experience in this area [the moderator decisively moves her body to face the non-speakers].

Those who have strong views need acknowledgement that the moderator has taken their views on board, that they are being taken seriously and that their views will be included in the feedback to the client, even if the discussion moves on to other areas.

> I know this is an important area for you and I'm not minimizing its importance, but I also need to get the views of people who are less involved in the issue [said seriously, looking directly at participant].

A 'talk the hind legs off a donkey' type might need to be dealt with more directly:

> Right, Fred, you've had your say for now. I'm just going to park you for a minute and let someone else get a word in edgeways [said lightly, with humour and a smile].

If these issues are not dealt with promptly, they will escalate as the session progresses and other participants will feel irritated and, eventually, 'punish' the moderator for not doing his/her job, through silence, irritation or withdrawal.

Talking over one another

Participants sometimes find a topic so interesting that they start their own mini-conversation within the group. It is important that this is

stopped immediately or the group will go out of control and other participants become irritated. Deal with this firmly and directly.

> Please can we just have one group. It will be impossible to understand
> what's going on when I listen to the recording.

Usually participants will feel chastised and promptly shut up. There will
be a feeling of mild discomfort in the group whilst everyone waits to see
what will happen next. Be pragmatic but light hearted.

> Oh, whenever I do that, everyone shuts up altogether [grin]. Now where
> were we? Oh yes, so did I get it right, that some of you think…

And on you go.

GENERALIZING TO OTHER RESEARCH METHODOLOGIES

I have addressed these interaction issues between participants and
researchers within the context of face-to-face interviewing and, in particular, in a group context. This is partly because groups are still the
predominant methodology within commercial qualitative research and
partly because it is easier to illustrate the dynamics of the exchange
through conversation. However, the same basic human exchanges take
place whatever the research context, and many of the issues covered can
be applied to other types of face-to-face interviewing, such as depth interviews, and to other research approaches, such as ethnographic and observational research, as well as to creative problem solving, deliberative and
consultative research and to research using digital media.

8 Research stimuli

This chapter deals with two areas. First, it covers stimulus materials that are used in the development of new ideas, for new products, packaging, new services or store layouts for example. Secondly, it covers stimulus materials used in the development of advertising. Although the same basic principles apply in both areas, the way in which stimuli are used in advertising development is different and, to avoid confusion, they are dealt with separately. In advertising development, the stimuli are inextricably bound up with the research analysis and interpretation, so these issues have been covered together.

WHAT ARE RESEARCH STIMULI?

Research stimuli are any materials or prompts (visual, auditory, written, tactile) used in a research situation to augment – or sometimes take the place of – interviewing. The aim is to focus participants on the key research issues in a non-directive and often non-verbal way and to stimulate a response. Some form of stimuli will be used in almost all research situations. Stimulus materials are a way of making the research situation less abstract. Participants can react to concrete objects in front of them, rather than just to an idea. If this sounds rather vague, it is because the scope of stimulus materials and the way they are used is very broad.

Research stimuli and projective techniques

Another issue to be addressed up front is how research stimuli relate to projective techniques, which are discussed in the next chapter. In reality, the two overlap and sometimes serve a similar function. This can be confusing. Clients (and their ad agencies, designers etc) create 'direct' materials to help people visualise ideas that have not yet been fully developed, such as mock-up packs and rough advertising executions. However, they may also produce 'indirect' stimuli (Gordon and Langmaid, 1988: 209–12) such as mood boards (magazine pictures that depict a mood, eg indulgence, freedom), which are used to help research participants talk around a theme that might, for example, be used in developing brand imagery (Figure 8.1).

Meanwhile qualitative researchers use a wide range of materials and techniques that help them to understand people's feelings, aspirations, associations and so on, within particular markets (see Chapter 9). These are called projective techniques and they may include mood boards and other stimuli that are similar to those produced by the ad agency, design company and such organizations.

One crude distinction between stimuli and projective techniques is that stimuli are usually provided by the client and projective techniques are introduced by the research agency. This chapter will concentrate on stimuli produced by the client and worked on by research participants.

Figure 8.1 *Mood board (courtesy of isobel advertising, www.isobel.com)*

Cautionary note

It is important to be familiar with the research stimuli, to be clear about how they will be used and in what order, before the research session starts. The midst of the session, while perhaps being observed by clients, is not the best time to be searching for the right concept board. Strategically placing stimuli for easy and sequential access is strongly recommended.

Equally, research participants can get unexpectedly excited about the most unlikely stimuli, especially if they can handle them and pass them around. Carbon monoxide alarms, for instance, can provoke paroxysms of delight (Lydia Fellows, 2009, personal communication). It is important to retrieve one set of stimuli before the next is introduced, especially if they are delicate 'mocks-ups'. Otherwise chaos may ensue.

THE ROLE OF RESEARCH STIMULI

There are three broad roles for research stimuli in developing new product or service concepts:

■ to explore current market dynamics;
■ to communicate and explore a specific idea or concept for consumers, such as a product, packaging, or even an environment such as a store or a restaurant;
■ to engage consumers and encourage them to explore and express themselves within a general area of enquiry.

The type of stimuli and the way in which they are used differs between these three areas, which are discussed separately below.

Stimuli to explore current market dynamics

Before developing potential new concepts, it is important for clients to understand how the current market 'works'. How do brands relate to one another? Are there currently 'gaps' – or could they create gaps – for new products or services?

Brand mapping, understanding the existing market, is often the first stage of developing new products. Using products currently on the market enables the researcher to understand the ways in which participants evaluate products and brands within the market and the criteria they use to do this.

A drinks company wants to launch a new brand of instant hot chocolate drink. It needs to understand the market: how customers (current or potential) evaluate existing brands of hot chocolate and how each brand is viewed in relation to others. On what basis do customers select brands? Cost? Taste? Packaging? Imagery – and what specifically? Advertising? Availability? Habit? Other? And how do these factors interact?

A collection of competitor brand packs are introduced into a discussion group and participants are asked to physically group the brands in whatever way seems 'right' to them. There may be an agreed clustering of brands, so the researcher can determine the characteristics of that cluster – what they have in common – and then probe the characteristics that make each brand unique. Another cluster may represent a different set of characteristics. When participants disagree, the researcher must delve into the reasons behind the disagreement. Maybe one participant sees the brand as poor quality because of its taste, whereas another views it as high quality because he or she trusts the brand.

In the process of physically comparing and contrasting brands in this way, research participants are creating a vocabulary and 'map' of the market, which provides a context for further discussion. The criteria for evaluation in this market are spelt out along with an understanding of packaging cues and possible market gaps. This is a simple use of existing products as stimuli that engages participants, through providing a physical (kinaesthetic) and visual activity.

Exploration of advertising

Existing brand advertising within a particular market can be mapped in a similar way. TV or press advertisements can be grouped in terms of their similarities and differences and the reasons for this clustering explored to create a brand map.

Stimuli to communicate specific ideas and concepts

It is expensive to develop prototype products or packaging for use in exploratory research. Therefore stimuli are created to give participants an idea of what the finished product might look like. The role of these stimuli is to enable people to indicate how they might respond to the idea when it becomes a reality in the future (Gordon, 1999: 241). Stimuli can vary from almost finished products to very rough approximations. They provide guidance on whether ideas are 'on track' and also elicit consumer input on how the idea can be developed further. There are many different forms of stimuli, for example:

- *'Mock ups'* are prototype packages used for research. Three-dimensional packs, which look quite similar to the (hypothetical) finished product, are produced. These can be handled by participants, enabling more realistic evaluation.
- *Packaging designs* are two-dimensional drawings mounted on boards. These may include acetate overlays, which can be turned over to explore the effect of adding a brand name or design feature.
- *Photographs* can be used as visual prompts, for example of a range of shampoo brands, of a store layout or a hospital reception area. These help to focus participants on the topic area and aid recall of the detail, such as how the brands looked in store or people's experiences as patients.

  For example, when trying to evaluate a proposed layout for an out of town shopping centre, photographs of similar shopping centres might be shown to enable discussion of what 'works / does not work'.
- *Concept boards*: A set of alternative propositions is presented on individual boards. These outline the nature of the idea. These may be simple statements and/or visuals, the aim being to convey the nub of the concept. Product ideas may be presented as a written concept, outlining the nature of the product or service, and may have accompanying visuals to try to get the idea over more clearly to research participants.
- *'Experience'*: Stimuli can also include experiences such as trying out a restaurant, store or bar, or using a new gym. Stimuli, in these instances, are complex and we move into the area of ethnography or mystery shopping (in which an individual is recruited and briefed to act as a shopper and give feedback on the experience).

  For instance, in car clinics participants may be interviewed in a car showroom especially set up as a research forum, where they can observe, sit in or drive different models of car, explore alternative car designs and give their feedback.

  Equally, kitchens may be set up in which food can be prepared during the course of the interviewing and participants can observe, join in and try out different cookers or food ingredients for themselves.

These scenarios allow people to have a 'hands on' experience of the topic under discussion as well as discussing it. They are attempts to replicate the experience that participants would have in a natural setting. By physically examining the materials, handling them, through the senses of touch, smell, taste, participants can give a very full response to the stimuli. This enables the client to make a more realistic assessment of the idea's potential.

Where it is possible for the researcher to have input to the format of the stimuli – ideally this would always be the case, but often it is not – it is important to ensure that the central ideas are clearly presented. Research participants are not marketers. If they are forced to wade through a lot of extraneous detail, they will quickly become confused and bored and start to respond randomly.

Research stimuli to explore a general area

'Mood boards' are used to display a range of visual images, with each board attempting to capture a different theme or mood such as happiness, success or energy. The boards are pre-prepared and can be used in a variety of ways to explore participants' thoughts and feelings about brands, companies and service experiences, and the participants' relationships with them. Often people will respond intuitively to the visuals and then work through their understanding of what they are feeling, so that they can express themselves clearly in words. The boards help people to respond to the topic under discussion in less conventional ways, using their senses and emotions as well as their thinking.

For instance, a company developed a new fragrance aimed at the 20–35-year-old market. It needed to establish how to position its new fragrance within the overall market and, specifically, what personality it should have. Six large mood boards were prepared. On each board there was a collection of photographs that represented one of the following themes: glamour, independence, escape, indulgence, romance, solitude. The boards provided a focus for participants to talk around the relevance of these themes for the fragrance and to suggest ways in which they might be expressed. They could also relate the themes to current products, in order to help establish how unique the particular positioning might be within the market.

Photographs: 'A picture speaks a thousand words.' Photographs and other pictorial stimuli can operate at a visceral level, which is appropriate when dealing with emotional content and brand identity. Photographs 'work' as stimuli because they are in some ways closer than words to the language of the emotions.

Vocabulary sort cards (a set of cards each containing a specific descriptor or mood) provide a simple but effective way of building up an image or attribute bank (collection of relevant words) that fits with a particular market or brand. This can be particularly useful when looking at directions in which the brand might develop. For example, a specific brand of chocolate might be associated with attributes such as luxurious, rich, indulgent, occasional, pure. The research question might be: To what extent, could these brand attributes carry over to a teenage chocolate milk drink?

Music, video collages, visual collages and scrap art, as well as particular environments, can all be used as research stimuli to provoke new reactions or challenge existing perceptions… and at this stage, we are firmly in overlap territory with projective techniques!

THE LIMITATIONS OF RESEARCH STIMULI

The concept is not the reality

By definition, research stimuli are not the 'real thing' and should not be assessed as if they are. This may seem obvious but participants – and sometimes researchers – can easily slip into acting as if the stimuli designed to illustrate an idea is the idea itself. This is a common mistake made by novice researchers who confuse the concept (the underlying idea) with the execution (its form as stimulus).

It is difficult for research participants to evaluate rough ideas. Stimulus boards may be developed in order to explore positionings for a new product. These are just ideas, and in practice elements from each of the stimulus boards might be combined. However, to research participants unused to thinking about ideas in this way, they appear to be finished products and so the participants evaluate them as if they are finished. The danger is that good ideas may be lost because research participants reject the stimulus, mistaking it for the idea.

In the absence of finished materials to present to research participants, it is the researcher's job to ensure, as best he or she can, that the idea does not get lost because of the rough nature of the stimulus material. This is not an easy task. It is a question of judgement, helped by experience. The researcher needs to explain, repeatedly, to participants that this is an idea, still in rough form. This will not totally solve the problem, but it will help.

The involvement of the researcher in the development of the stimuli can help, because he or she will know through experience what is more likely to 'work' or not 'work'. For example, keeping stimuli simple, breaking up complex concepts into a series of boards, keeping visuals and copy separate so that they can be 'mixed and matched' enable the researcher to explore individual elements more easily.

Stimulus materials are not necessarily cross-cultural

It is easy to assume that because stimulus materials 'work' in one culture they can easily be transferred to another. For instance, in multi-country studies it is tempting to use the same stimuli, 'to enable comparison'. However, the same stimuli may mean quite different things in another culture. The appropriateness of the research stimuli needs to be assessed within its cultural context and different stimuli developed if necessary. It is particularly important to keep stimuli simple and clear for multi-country studies, in order to allow for variations in moderator expertise. There may be core stimuli that local moderators can add to, using their own experience and knowledge.

THE ROLE OF STIMULI IN ADVERTISING DEVELOPMENT

Stimuli used in this context are, in a sense, peculiar in that we are using stimuli to research advertising – which itself can be regarded as a stimulus: the advertising is the first step, the product or service the second. This creates a particular dynamic that needs to be carefully managed.

In addition, there are now many advertising mediums. Alongside TV, print and poster advertising, web-based advertising has grown exponentially. Different advertising mediums require different approaches.

The dilemma of researching 'unfinished' advertising

There are many different opinions about when, how and what type of stimulus materials are suitable for use in advertising development research. The client-ad agency-research team is attempting to develop and/or evaluate ideas and concepts that have not yet been made concrete. However, much of people's response to advertising is in the detail: the tone of voice, the smile, the humour, the posture. Take these away and the essence of the ad is often lost. This creates a dilemma.

Clients cannot afford to create very expensive advertising campaigns without at least attempting to check that the target audience will be receptive to it. Do they risk researching an idea in a rough format, which may be very different from the final execution, or risk not researching it at all? For this reason, advertising development research is one of the most challenging areas within qualitative research.

Over the years there has been considerable controversy around the choice, use and interpretation of advertising research stimuli. Research participants are familiar with evaluating finished advertising; they do it all the time in real life. However, evaluating a press ad as a rough drawing, or interpreting a series of drawings that supposedly represent a TV commercial, is quite a different experience from evaluating glossy press ads in a woman's magazine or watching a well-produced 30-second ad on television. Translating responses to rough advertising ideas into directions for development of the finished ad requires considerable skill and experience on the part of the researcher.

How stimuli are used in advertising development research

Many different formats of research stimuli have been developed in an attempt to reduce the gap between the stimuli and the finished advertising, and to try to reduce the commercial risk of making a mistake.

Simple scripts

At one end of the spectrum are simple scripts that the researcher reads out. Obviously these provide very limited information for research participants and it is difficult for them to envisage what the finished commercial might look like. However, there is no concern that participants will view the scripts as finished commercials and criticize them for lack of production values! The script acts as a prompt to enable participants to discuss the storyline, the role of the brand and the characters in a very fluid and creative way. In the course of this conversation, the researcher can often obtain a good steer on how the storyline and characters might be developed in order to be relevant and appealing and communicate effectively to this particular target audience.

Narrative tapes

These use a professional actor to tell the story, with the aim of getting closer to a more professional effect. A narrative tape also ensures a standardized delivery of the stimuli between one research session and the next. However, without visuals to quickly convey cues about mood, lifestyle, characters and so on, narrative tapes can easily seem long and tortuous to participants, so that they lose interest half-way through.

Storyboards, animatics, stealomatics, photomatics

Various techniques have been developed to try to convey the movement and emotion of a TV commercial. Storyboards, which are a series of drawn visuals, are often used, sometimes accompanied by a narrative tape. A more sophisticated version is an animatic, in which drawings, voice-over and music are filmed and presented as a rough ad. A photomatic involves a series of photographed scenes that depict the storyline. This is often used if the finished commercial has high emotional content. Yet more sophisticated is the stealomatic, in which snippets from existing ads, along with a voice over and music try to convey mood and visual cues as well as content.

Cautions and caveats

All of these stimulus materials are attempts to obtain as realistic a response as possible to a commercial that is still in concept stage and may change before final production. This makes the presentation and interpretation of responses to these stimuli particularly problematic. The two cardinal rules in advertising development research – as with concept development – which need to be borne in mind are:

We are researching the idea (the proposition), not the stimuli

The stimuli are there to provide a steer. If participants do not like the stimuli, it is essential to try to understand why. If it is because they don't like the way the pictures are drawn in the rough stimuli, this is irrelevant. If it is because they feel the content of the rough commercial is insulting or boring, then this needs to be explored further. This may be relevant and we need to identify and understand the elements that trigger this reaction and establish whether these are artefacts of the rough stimuli or important elements to be taken into account in developing the advertising.

The level of 'finish' of the stimuli influences the nature of the research

Rough or abstract stimuli are useful in the early stages of developing advertising. Participants and researcher can play with and develop ideas, and there is little risk that the stimuli will be confused with finished ads. However, the corresponding drawback is that there is a huge gulf between the stimuli and the finished ad, so it is difficult to predict with any confidence whether the ad will 'succeed'.

Figure 8.2a *Concept board used in advertising development (courtesy of isobel advertising, www.isobel.com)*

Figure 8.2b *Concept board used in advertising development (courtesy of isobel advertising, www.isobel.com)*

Figure 8.3a *Concept board used in advertising development (courtesy of isobel advertising, www.isobel.com)*

Take home a more refreshing taste.

Figure 8.3b *Concept board used in advertising development (courtesy of isobel advertising, www.isobel.com)*

It might be possible to get a reasonable steer on the effectiveness of an ad, researched as an animatic, where the theme is: 'It does what it says on the tin.' However, if the ad involves a subtle flirtation between a man and a woman, say, this is more difficult, because so much depends on the way in which the ad is executed, the couple, their behaviour and so on. Similarly, ads that have a strong emotional/visual content generally need high production values to be effective.

With more finished stimuli, such as a rough-cut ad or stealomatic, it is easier to get close to the effect that the advertiser is trying to achieve in finished advertising. This will arguably enable the researcher to more accurately gauge the potential appeal, comprehension and effectiveness of the advertising. On the other hand, with stimuli that are closer to the finished ad, there is a greater risk that people will interpret and evaluate it as 'finished', and so judge it more harshly than they would rough stimuli. Research participants are not used to viewing unfinished advertising materials and there is a natural tendency to compare the stimuli they are shown with what they know, which is finished ads. It is important to regularly remind people that these are not finished. Such reminders will go some way towards reducing misunderstandings and evaluations provoked by the nature of the research materials, but the researcher must also be constantly aware of these issues.

The three stages of advertising development

It is important to bear in mind the stage of advertising development, because this will determine the way in which the research is approached, the stimuli that are most appropriate and the nature of the recommendations that are based on the research. In essence, there are three stages; developing strategy, creative development and advertising pre-testing, although sometimes the first two are conflated. This conflation can cause difficulties. Combining an exploratory stage with the development of creative ideas can lead to confusion unless both researcher and client are very clear about the potential tensions and limitations that result.

Developing strategy

At this stage, the researcher is trying to understand the nature and psychology of the market and, in particular, the relationship between consumers/potential consumers and the market and/or specific brands. Any stimuli that are used at this stage need to be subservient to this main aim. For example, although concept boards might be used, they do not represent advertising routes. Their function is to stimulate response: verbal, emotional, tactile, visual and the like.

There is often a tendency for the client or advertising agency to load up the researcher with stimuli under the mistaken impression that the more there are, the better the understanding that results. The opposite is often true. This is the time to listen. The role of stimuli, if used, is to spark off ideas, thoughts, associations, non-verbal cues. It is not about evaluation.

Ambiguous, open-ended stimuli that allow participants to project their own meaning on to the material, or enable the researcher to understand the complex interrelationship of signs and symbols that carry meaning in a particular product field or for a particular brand, can be used. Visual and video collages (scrap art, photos), vocabulary boards (eg containing a range of possible mood, activity or tone words), packaging shapes and so on can all be employed, depending on the needs of the research project. It is important that these are used, if appropriate, to elicit responses, rather than by rote.

Certain – very simple – stimuli can be useful in order to provide 'headings' for discussion, or to help fine tune the areas of interest. For instance, a list of adjectives on a board can help research participants to develop a 'character' for a potential product. Similarly a small selection of well-thought-out concept boards that outline the product to be advertised can help focus participants' attention. They might, for example, contrast:

■ Fruitolite – fewer calories, more satisfying!
■ Fruitolite – the drink you can have between meals!

It is easier and more satisfying for participants to build on core ideas rather than trying to find a core idea in a sea of irrelevance. These statements can be the trigger for a discussion that allows the researcher to understand the research participants' relationships with their own consumption patterns, individual brands and the market as a whole. Encouraging participants to write on concepts, or tear up those that they find inappropriate, reinforces the idea that this process is about playing with ideas, not evaluating them.

Creative development

On the basis of earlier exploratory research, the client and ad agency will have developed an advertising strategy and a number of potential creative routes. Sometimes ad agencies are reluctant to put in 'weak' ideas, because they think these will reflect badly on the agency. However, from a researcher's perspective, it is useful to have options, good and bad. Research participants are used to comparison in real life:

I like this ad more than that.

I prefer brand X to brand Y.

Having more than one route in the early stages of advertising development – even if the client would not want to develop the second route – will help participants to talk about and develop the ideas. Learning what doesn't work is extremely useful, and it is often easier for participants to explain what is 'wrong' than what is 'right'. Clients may need reassurance that this is a learning stage; it is not evaluation. It is important that this mind-set is carried through to the presentation. The issue is not, 'What didn't work?' (which is likely to trigger defensiveness in the client and/or ad agency), but 'What have we learnt from this that will help in the next stage of development?'

It is useful to ask participants to jot down their immediate thoughts on seeing an execution. This ensures that initial, diverse, impressions (which arguably is all there will be in 'real life') will be captured before the first participant voices his or her opinion.

Advertising pre-testing

This usually takes place with finished or near-finished advertising. The aim is to make the viewing situation as realistic as possible, given cost and logistic constraints. Sometimes ads can be researched 'in hall'. This means that research participants are screened and recruited in the high street and then invited into a nearby venue. The participant is usually shown the ad with little preamble and then a short interview is conducted. Whilst the situation is still artificial, there is little or no discussion of the topic area, so the participant is viewing the ad in much the same way as he or she would view it at home.

This style of interviewing is sometimes carried out in conjunction with quantitative evaluation. Some participants will be siphoned off for qualitative interviewing, others for quantitative interviews. Quantitative and qualitative 'findings' can then be integrated.

THE SKILL OF ADVERTISING DEVELOPMENT RESEARCH

Advertising development research requires considerable experience and judgement. The researcher needs to be able to make ongoing evaluations of the effect that the nature of the stimuli is having on people's responses to the idea. He or she needs to know when to discard the response because it is not relevant to the idea, and when to follow it up because it may be central to the success of the advertising route. The researcher also needs to make judgements about alternative ways in which the ad can be constructed or particular nuances that will add humour or credibility or

impact. These judgements come from having carried out scores of advertising development projects and, as a result, having developed finely
honed skills that help him or her to steer the project through the minefield of misinterpretations and confusion. But it is not an exact science.
Predicting the success of advertising (in terms of boosting sales) is notoriously difficult, because so much depends on factors outside the control of
the advertiser: the current economic climate, competitive activity, the
weather and so on.

Judith Wardle (2002: 102–04), an experienced advertising researcher,
describes 'the politics of stimulus material', and in particular highlights
the tension it generates between researcher, client and agency. In spite of
shared public agreement between these three groups about the purpose
of the research stimuli, the reality is somewhat different. The researcher
regards the stimuli as a means of developing the advertising, the client
essentially needs the research to evaluate the idea and the ad agency
wants to sell the idea to the research participants. In the ideal world, evaluating, developing and selling would require different stimulus materials. These different perspectives mean that often the researcher has to
negotiate a minefield of competing expectations. Wardle describes the
handing over of the stimulus material from the ad agency to the
researcher as 'like handing over the baby to the childminder'. The result-
ing anxiety is one of the reasons that the researcher is often laden down
with 'excess' stimulus material that actually obscures the idea to be
researched. Researchers need to be political animals, in that they must
effectively carry out the research project whilst simultaneously being
aware of and appeasing the sensibilities of all the parties involved.

9 Projective techniques

THE ROLE OF PROJECTIVE TECHNIQUES

In Chapter 1 we talked about how much of our decision making, habitual behaviour, attitudes and beliefs are below conscious awareness. How then do we, as qualitative researchers, attempt to access these areas? Qualitative research is not psychoanalysis and does not pretend to be. It can, however, help us to understand the triggers, motivations and aspirations that influence our behaviour but that may not be obvious either to ourselves or to others who may be watching us. Some of these behaviours, such as buying a particular brand of soap powder or coffee and rejecting another brand, or having a mug of tea every morning, may be so habitual that we never question them. They have become part of our identity; they define who we are:

> I'm a Foster's man.
>
> I have to have Schweppes tonic in my gin – with lime and ice – in my special glass.
>
> I'd never go to McDonald's.
>
> I like a tidy house.
>
> I always walk the same route to the station. It would seem odd if I walked a different way.

When asked to explain these behaviours, we are capable of giving a plausible response, but it may not be the 'real' or whole answer, sometimes because we do not know why we act as we do. Understanding developed from psychotherapy and the social sciences and, more recently, discoveries in neuroscience can help to explain how, perceptually and cognitively, we structure and make sense of the world. Over time, this understanding has enriched and shaped qualitative research practice and it can help us to better understand people's inner worlds and their interactions with the world outside. Projective techniques can help us to access attitudes and beliefs which are below our conscious awareness.

Terminology

Historically, projective techniques were differentiated from enabling techniques. Projective techniques required participants to create something (eg a collage or drawing), whereas with enabling techniques they were asked to do something that often had facilitating but not interpretive value (Gordon and Langmaid, 1988: 89). However, with the burgeoning of techniques, many of which involve creating and doing, the distinction became redundant. Nowadays, the term projective technique is used more loosely, to refer to a range of tasks.

CONTRIBUTIONS FROM THE SOCIAL SCIENCES

Before embarking on an exploration of the ways in which we can access people's inner worlds through the use of projective techniques, we will briefly visit some of the theories from the social sciences and neuroscience that underpin these techniques.

The influence of the social sciences, and in particular psychology and psychoanalysis, on qualitative research practice is usually taken as given. However, in truth, it is not easy to track the ways in which these disciplines have influenced practice because there was little generally available literature on commercial qualitative research history before the late 1980s.

Hy Mariampolski (2001: 14–21) provides a very useful summary of the way in which the intellectual heritage of qualitative research in the United States goes back to the middle of the 19th century and incorporates psychological and psychoanalytical thinking from Sigmund Freud, Carl Rogers and Edward T Hall as well as influences from sociology (Erving Goffman), social reality (Georg Simmel, Edmund Husserl and the symbolic interactionism of G H Mead). These influences have done much to shape the way in which qualitative research is conducted today. I have borrowed from Mariampolski, in order to highlight the influence of these thinkers on qualitative research in general, and in particular the way in which this thinking has shaped the use of projective techniques in qualitative practice.

Carl Rogers (1902–1987)

Carl Rogers founded client-centred psychotherapy. His impact upon qualitative research arose from his humanistic perspective on behaviour and his approach to patient interaction, which emphasized respect for the integrity and autonomy of the individual. In particular, he prioritized 'empathy', 'reflection' and 'self-actualization', and these Rogerian principles still act as the cornerstones of qualitative research, including the importance of establishing rapport and developing understanding from the participant's perspective. Equally, these principles are relevant to the way in which projective techniques are used with research participants and to the joint activity, between researcher and participants, of interpreting and making sense of the material produced.

Edmund Husserl (1859–1938) and phenomenology

Phenomenologists argue that the world can only become known through experience and intuition. Our perceptions are built up over time and we come to share our beliefs with other people through a process of 'intersubjectivity'. This, 'according to Husserl... is a coalition of common perceptions of the world' (Mariampolski, 2001: 16). Our everyday lives are, as a result, lived according to taken-for-granted rules that are largely below conscious awareness.

In qualitative research, we are attempting to look beneath the surface of our research participants' everyday lives in order to understand the rules and 'habits of mind' that shape perceptions – and, possibly, to change them. Projective techniques are a mechanism for helping us to do this.

George Herbert Mead (1863–1931)

Philosopher George Herbert Mead coined the term 'symbolic interactionism'. By this he meant the way in which 'the self' grows out of social interaction. Mead believed that we act on the basis of the meaning things have for us, rather than the things themselves. Meaning arises in interaction with others and we spend all our lives 'making meaning': interpreting, selecting, checking, challenging, revising meanings. This rather abstract explanation becomes real when we apply it to consumer goods. Commodities symbolize personal and cultural meanings; a Ferrari is not just a car; it represents success, confidence, the desire to stand out from the crowd, and so on.

Most qualitative research, in one way or another, is about exploring the meaning that things have – or potentially have – and how these meanings evolve. Projective techniques enable us to explore how people create 'meaning' from 'things', using their intellect, but also their sensory awareness: their visual, auditory and tactile understanding. They allow us to tap into this understanding and to move away from literal definition: moving from a car called a Ferrari, which is big and red and goes fast, to a FERRARI – with all the multi-layered meanings (personal, social and cultural) that this entails. Mead's theory suggests that the meaning we attach to things is inevitably cultural because we are essentially social beings. Working with brands is all about understanding cultural meaning, which is constantly evolving. Projective techniques allow us to tap into this changing, multi-sensory world.

Sigmund Freud (1865–1939)

If we focus on the influence of psychoanalysis in the development of projective techniques, then the undisputed champion is Sigmund Freud, whose thinking still has a profound effect on the way in which we view ourselves today. In particular, Freud introduced the notion of 'the unconscious'. He recognized that there is a gap between our controlled, conscious lives and the unconscious, which lurks beneath conscious, everyday behaviour. In his view, we could access the unconscious through the analysis of dreams, mistakes and slips of the tongue. Projective techniques, which try to circumvent rational thinking, were adopted by the Freudians as another way of tapping into the unconscious. It is this aspect of Freudian thinking that has been adapted and incorporated into qualitative research practice.

However, it is important to bear in mind that this use of projective techniques in qualitative research is not an attempt to 'analyse' or 'treat' research participants. The techniques are based on Freudian practice, but they are very far removed from therapeutic use. They are used light-heartedly with healthy research participants, and the participants are instrumental in understanding the material produced.

CONTRIBUTIONS FROM NEUROSCIENCE

Neuroscience is making huge contributions to our understanding of our minds and brains. According to some cognitive neuroscientists, we are conscious of only about 5 per cent of our cognitive activity, so most of our decisions, actions, emotions, learning and behaviour are dependant on the 95 per cent of brain activity that goes on beneath our conscious awareness (Zaltman, 2003: 50). Similarly, Mark Earls (2002: 89) suggests that more than 90 per cent of what is communicated by any speaker lies in the (largely unconscious) nuances of tone of voice and body language, and only 10 per cent of effective communication comes from the content of what is said.

Some experts, such as psychologist Professor Adrian Furnham (1999: 5–10) would dispute the scale of unconscious activity. Nonetheless, there is general agreement that, although we believe that we make considered and conscious decisions most of the time, neuroscience proves this is false. From the beating of our hearts to breathing, walking, shrinking from spiders, crossing the road without getting run over, we rely on our bodies to do the work for us, without our conscious awareness.

Gladwell's theory of 'thin slicing'

Malcolm Gladwell (2005), in his best selling book *Blink*, discusses the concept of the 'adaptive unconscious' (not be confused with the 'unconscious' described by Sigmund Freud, which is an altogether different concept). The 'adaptive unconscious' makes it possible for us to, say, turn a corner in our car without having to go through elaborate calculations to determine the precise angle of the turn, the speed of the car and its steering radius. We operate on 'automatic pilot', aware of what is happening, but not on a conscious level.

Gladwell (2005: 11) describes the 'adaptive unconscious' as the part of our brain that leaps to conclusions. We are all familiar with that sensation of 'knowing something' but not knowing how we know it. We use this ability all the time. We make judgements on people within seconds of meeting them and often we are proved right. Gladwell (2005: 12–13) reports on an experiment to explore this phenomenon. College students were shown three two-second videotapes of a teacher they had never met, with the sound turned off. They were then asked to rate the teacher's effectiveness – which apparently they could do without difficulty. He discovered that their ratings were essentially the same as evaluations of those same teachers made by their students after a full semester of classes. Watching a silent two-second video clip of an unknown teacher was sufficient for students to accurately assess that person.

In a different context, we are crossing the road and suddenly see a car heading straight towards us. What do we do? We do not rationally evaluate the risk. Instead, our 'adaptive unconscious' makes an instant evaluation of the risk and our body reacts immediately to avoid danger. Afterwards, we may wonder how we reacted so quickly. If we had depended on our rational brain, we would probably not be here today.

How does our brain do this? Gladwell describes his theory of 'thin slicing' or 'a little bit of knowledge goes a long way.' Our brain responds to myriad details in the situation that our conscious mind is simply not aware of. This detail may arise partly from our intellect, but it will also include input from our emotions, intuition and bodily reflexes. In fact it is a 'whole body', not just a rational, 'from-the-head' response. We leap to a decision or have a hunch. Our unconscious has summed up the situation in front of us, discarding everything it considers irrelevant whilst homing in on what really matters. Gladwell claims that our unconscious is so good at this that it often delivers a better answer than more deliberate and exhaustive ways of thinking.

In everyday life, we move back and forth between our conscious and unconscious modes of thinking, depending on the situation. Neither our rational thinking nor our understanding based on 'thin slicing' is infallible; we have all experienced situations when our 'snap decisions' have proved disastrously wrong. However, by using both modes and emphasizing one over the other according to the situation we can, hopefully, get the best of both worlds.

I have discussed the adaptive unconscious at length in order to illustrate the importance of attempting, in our research, to access those areas that are below conscious awareness. Our conscious mind takes up so much of our time that it is easy to forget the importance of what happens below conscious awareness. We can then delude ourselves into believing that what people say to us in a research interview is the total picture, all there is to be known.

The importance of emotion in thinking

Reinforcing Gladwell's views, Portuguese neuroscientist Antonio Damasio emphasizes, in his fascinating book *The Feeling of What Happens* (2000), how the brain knows more than the conscious mind reveals. Neuroscience is now confirming what many psychologists, psychotherapists and qualitative researchers have believed for decades; that consciousness is simply the 'tip of the iceberg' and that all sorts of activity that crucially affects our decision making goes on beneath conscious awareness.

What really does challenge our cultural preconceptions, however, is Damasio's assertion that emotion is a necessary component of reasoning. We tend to dismiss emotion as somehow 'lower order'. We talk about controlling emotion or having a rational conversation, and criticize those who are over-emotional or cannot control themselves. We distrust our emotions because we feel they are unmanageable and we cannot always understand where they come from. Uncontrolled emotion is seen as child-like and unpredictable and we have been taught to distrust what we cannot logically understand or control.

On the other hand, we think of rational, considered thought as being higher-order brain activity, the most effective way of communicating and an aid to effective decision making, especially within a work context. It is regarded as the evolutionary peak of our communication abilities.

However, this is simply not true. Damasio's research suggests that having either too much or too little emotion interferes with rational thought. Too much, we can accept, but too little? This seems counter-intuitive in our individualistic, rationally focused culture. It would not seem strange in many Eastern cultures, in which emotion and logic are not set apart as adversaries.

According to Damasio 'emotion probably assists reasoning, especially when it comes to personal and social matters involving risk and conflict' (Damasio, 2000: 41–42). He suggests that emotion helps with the judgement aspect of decision making. It provides the emotional intelligence that helps our reason to operate most effectively. It may seem rather paradoxical in our society that, in truth, we cannot make rational decisions without emotional input. However, Damasio is at pains to point out that emotion is not a substitute for reason, and those emotions should not be allowed to reign unchecked. He concludes, 'well-targeted and well-deployed emotion seems to be a support system without which the edifice of reason cannot operate properly' (Damasio, 2000: 42).

LINKING THEORY WITH PRACTICE

We have covered the territory in which projective techniques are rooted in some depth: the way in which culture shapes us, the role of the unconscious and taken-for-granted aspects of behaviour, how much of what goes on is below our conscious awareness and how emotion is essential in decision making. It is important, when using projective techniques, to understand that they are based on sound principles of social science and neuroscience. The next step is to examine how we link these theories with qualitative research practice.

We might question how we can ever reach an agreed truth, given that research participants cannot access their unconscious or adaptive unconscious and so cannot know the full extent of what they are thinking. Even if they were able to do this, how would they ever express this cocktail of verbal, emotional and intuitive knowing in a way that we, as researchers, could reasonably comprehend, gather, make sense of and transform into useful meaning for our clients?

This is the challenge for qualitative research. Of course we can never really get inside participants' heads; we cannot experience their ongoing feelings, hopes or worries. All we can ever do, with the help of the participants themselves, is access the shadows, the shades and nuances of meaning, both of individual participants and collectively as the cultural co-created beliefs and assumptions that are our shared understanding. To do this, we need to help participants to access their beneath-conscious selves and help them to share the meaning they are creating.

As Wendy Gordon (1999: 163) puts it:

> If we accept that qualitative research is fundamentally concerned with understanding the meaning that people bring to 'things' – events, objects, products, brands, places, people and relationships – we need to know how to open the doors to these perceptions. To do this, we must have the cooperation and goodwill of the 'meaning-maker'.

Projective techniques are an essential part of the armoury of qualitative research because they allow us to 'dig deeper and connect wider': to go beyond the rational, conscious, thinking part of our individual and collective brains into more complex, intuitive and emotional areas. Using a variety of techniques, we can gain some understanding of the meaning that lies within people's relationships to 'things'.

PROJECTIVE TECHNIQUES

What are projective techniques?

In essence, projective techniques are aids to reaching below the superficial, rationalized responses of research participants. They can be invaluable in certain research situations, when we need to get beneath the top-of-mind or rational data and achieve a deeper exploration of a participant's feelings about and relationship with a particular market, service or situation.

Projective techniques offer a structure for participants that makes it easier for them to access thoughts and emotions that are difficult to verbalize or to express publicly, and they help translate the intuitive, emotional and non-verbal into concepts that can be explored in the research situation.

These techniques also give permission for participants to express embarrassing or antisocial views through projection: that is, by attributing these views to other people and dissociating them from oneself, as in 'Everyone hates the government.' In this way, culturally unacceptable ideas can be expressed but personally disowned. 'The pot calling the kettle black' is a colloquial expression of projection.

Many projective techniques are borrowed directly from clinical psychology or psychoanalytic practice and are embedded in particular theoretical approaches. When using these techniques in qualitative research, it is not necessary to fully understand their theoretical roots, but it is important to be aware of the reasons for using the techniques and to consider how they can best be introduced to research participants.

Projective techniques in a commercial research context are used in a light-hearted way. I often introduce them as: 'Right, we are going to have a bit of fun now.' This helps people to relax and reduces 'performance anxiety'. Most techniques are relatively easy to administer and fun to do, so they help group bonding, as well providing important input to understanding.

A simple, but useful model for understanding the role of projective techniques is the 'Johari window' (Figure 9.1). Area 1 can be accessed through qualitative exploration, whereas areas 2 and 3 can be accessed, to some extent, through projective techniques. Area 4 is outside the scope of most qualitative research.

**The 'Johari Window' as a
Qualitative Metaphor...**

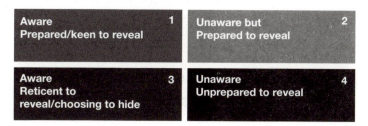

Aware 1 **Prepared/keen to reveal**	**Unaware but** 2 **Prepared to reveal**
Aware 3 **Reticent to** **reveal/choosing to hide**	**Unaware** 4 **Unprepared to reveal**

Figure 9.1 *Johari window*

Projective techniques in action

The best way to understand how projective techniques 'work' is to be a participant in a group discussion and experience the process; monitor how you feel when you are asked to draw 'My feelings about travel' in colour on a large sheet of paper... and are then asked to describe your drawing and say what it means. Or experience completing the sentence, 'The thing I wish I had done with my money is...'

The second-best way is to look at some of the material that has been generated by the use of different projective techniques. The techniques below are by no means exhaustive, but they represent a spectrum from the simplest to the more complex. Projectives can be crudely clustered into three groups reflecting the nature of the activity:

- exploring relationships;
- completion exercises;
- creative exercises.

In practice these techniques often overlap. Examples have been selected to illustrate each type of projective. There are numerous other techniques that could be used, or that can be created to suit the needs of the research.

Exploring relationships

These techniques enable participants to identify the patterns of relationship that they have created, such as those between different products or brands, between attitudes or beliefs, between different images and so on. They may not have previously noticed these relationships because they exist in Gladwell's adaptive unconscious. These techniques encourage participants to notice and articulate the patterns of relationship.

Association

Our minds work by association; if I say 'blue' you are likely to say 'sea' or 'sky'. If I say 'sports club' you may share some of the associations in Figure 9.2. Our brains are made up of millions of neural connections, and

Figure 9.2 *Word association*

understanding the connections that customers make with a particular brand or service gives us considerable factual and emotional information.

I ask: 'What is the first thing that comes into your mind when I say "Marmite"?' You are likely to respond in one of two ways. Either it will be 'nostalgia, distinctive taste, homely, childhood, addictive...' or 'horrible, strong, old fashioned, hate it...' We find it easy to cluster words in this way.

This is a very simple technique and a good warm-up exercise, but it can be very useful for unearthing brand imagery, product attributes and polarized views. Once these associations are articulated, we can ask participants to delve further, to find out why they have made these associations and what they mean in terms of their relationship with the brand.

Participants can be asked to write down their associations individually on Post-it notes and then stick them on one of two large boards, which might be headed 'Pro-Marmite' and 'Anti-Marmite'. Participants generally enjoy these exercises, especially if they are introduced in a playful way. Differences in perceptions are particularly useful because they point to conflicting brand or product imagery, which can be further explored.

Building personalities

This simple exercise can be spontaneously introduced to shift the focus or to enliven a flagging group. Participants need to feel relaxed and comfortable before being asked to participate. The aim is to build a personality for a brand, service or company. For instance:

> If this Mars bar came to life as a person, who would it be?
>
> A man... a big man... in his 40s...
>
> What would he do for a living?
>
> Definitely a long-distance lorry driver. He'd play football, Arsenal [laugh].
>
> Anything else?
>
> He'd eat it when he was driving – when he got bored. When he stopped for petrol...
>
> So what is it about a Mars bar that makes you think all this?
>
> Well, it's big and chunky. Lots of calories. Traditional, a good make... but not for girls. We're all too interested in weight watching for that [laugh].

A simple, playful conversation such as this, inviting the participants to join in the game, to be creative, can start to build up a picture of brand imagery and the strengths and weaknesses of the brand. It capitalizes on our inbuilt human processes of making meaning in the interaction (Mead, 1962: 80–81). This meaning can be developed and refined by other research participants who may have slightly different perceptions so that, gradually, brand imagery – including its contradictions and ambiguity – becomes clear.

Mapping a market

This exercise is described in Chapter 8 in relation to stimuli. Essentially, it explores the relationship between brands, companies, attitudes, imagery and so on in a particular market. Participants are asked to group a collection of products or brands together as those they find similar in feel, for example. If this is a group exercise, then there is much to be learnt through the discussion between participants about where particular brands fit and the criteria used to evaluate them. The researcher can encourage this discussion and it becomes a voyage of discovery for researcher and participants:

> Why are these brands grouped together? What characteristics do they share? Are there brands that stand alone? What is special/different about them? Which brands do you feel closest to?

Market mapping is particularly helpful for establishing where a new brand entrant might fit in the market. Having a physical product to hold and move around provides a greater sense of reality that just talking about brands would lack.

Picture sorts

A set of up to 50 cards is prepared, each showing a visual image. A line of brand names is placed on the table and participants are asked to sort the visual images into piles that fit most closely with their image of the brand. They are encouraged to do this quickly, without too much conscious thought. Once this task is competed, participants are asked to reflect on their choices. In a group interview, the choices act as a springboard for exploring perceptions and imagery of the range of brands or institutions, through questions such as: In what way does this visual reflect how you feel about 'X'? Could it also fit 'Y'? Why/why not? What does it say about 'X'? How could you change this? And so on.

Empathy maps

Understanding of brand imagery can also be developed through empathy maps. Participants write 'Me' in the middle of a blank sheet of paper. They then write the name of various brands either closer to 'Me' or further away, depending on how emotionally connected they feel to the brand. This does not necessarily mean they are users of that brand. For instance, a participant might position Virgin Airlines very close to 'Me' and Ryanair very far away, although he or she flies with Ryanair more frequently. This opens up an opportunity to explore the difference between empathy with a brand and brand usage.

These exercises, in different ways, are attempts to make the unconscious more conscious so that participants can examine and make meaning out of their habitual and unexamined behaviour, attitudes, beliefs and so on.

Completion exercises

These exercises involve giving participants partial materials that they must complete.

Thought bubbles

These are cartoons depicting individuals in various situations, such as in a supermarket or a football crowd, or filling their car with petrol, in which speech or thought bubbles are coming out the mouths of the characters. Participants fill in what the cartoon character is saying or thinking. They explain why they have written their particular comments and this can act as a springboard to more detailed and fuller conversation (Figure 9.3).

Figure 9.3 *Thought bubble*

Thought bubbles can be very useful when time is tight and there is a need to obtain feedback. For instance, they can be used to capture experiences at the beginning and end of a conference, when delegates are either arriving or before they rush off home at the end (Figures 9.4 and 9.5).

START OF CONFERENCE

Figure 9.4 *Thought bubble given to participants at the beginning of a conference*

END OF CONFERENCE

Figure 9.5 *Thought bubble given to participants at the end of a conference*

Sentence completion

This is another simple exercise that can produce useful input. Participants are asked to complete a number of sentences, such as:

> I would describe my attitude to money as…
> The thing I most worry about in terms of my children is…
> I think people who buy ready meals are…

This type of exercise is useful as a warm-up at the beginning of the interview process. It encourages participants to focus on the research area, compose their thoughts without influence from other people, and read out what they have written; this is a less arduous task for nervous participants than ad-libbing on the subject. The diversity of their responses encourages a rich conversation.

Completion exercises produce a mix of conscious and subconscious material. They can be particularly effective in giving participants permission to express embarrassing or antisocial opinions by projecting them on to others.

> People who never clean their toilets… are lazy, dirty and slovenly.

Creative exercises

A wide range of exercises fall into this category, ranging from simple projective questioning (What would a Martian think of this? Who do you suppose would use this new fresh pimento drizzling oil?) to complex exercises requiring thought and pre-planning, such as role-play, psycho-drawing (see below), creating collages, creating ideas for new products, generating imagery for advertising development.

It is important to remember, both when asking participants to carry out these tasks and when interpreting the outcomes, that this is a search for ideas. It is not the job of research participants to create advertising. The tasks need to be kept light-hearted, so that people can play with ideas, rather than feel they have to do a job that will be evaluated and judged; if this is how they feel, then their creativity will be dampened.

Life graphs

Life graphs are a useful device for allowing participants to re-live the detail of a particular experience. Often, when we talk about an event in the past, the detail becomes blurred; we slide one element of the experience into another. Physically drawing the different parts or stages of the experience on paper makes it easier to pull out the different elements. For example a group of business managers were asked to:

> Draw a graph of a plane journey you have taken recently, starting from the time you left home for the airport and finishing when you touched down at your destination airport. Was it a business trip? A weekend break? A family holiday? Note the highs and lows of the trip. Then think about what happened to trigger these highs and lows. What were you experiencing at the time? What did you feel? What did you hear? What did you see? Was it comfortable? Uncomfortable? What precisely caused these feelings? How would you have liked it to have been? What would have improved that situation?

Introducing the task in this way encourages participants to re-live the experience and, in particular, to access what they were feeling, seeing, hearing and so on. The aim is to unearth below-conscious experiences and make them accessible, so the experience can be explored.

Encouraging people to engage with these activities requires a mixture of sensitivity, matter-of-factness and humour. Introduced in this way, participants very rarely refuse and most enjoy rising to the challenge. The life-graphs below were drawn by the business travellers (Figures 9.6 and 9.7). They arrived from work, in suits, carrying briefcases. In spite of initial reluctance, within half an hour, their jackets and ties were off and they were kneeling down on the ground drawing, totally engrossed in their task.

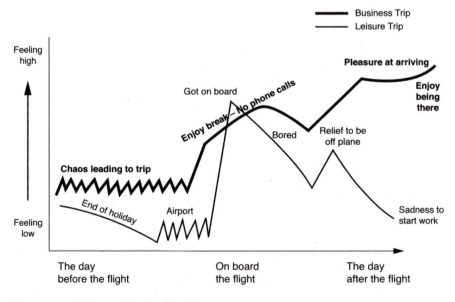

Figure 9.6 *Life graph of a plane journey*

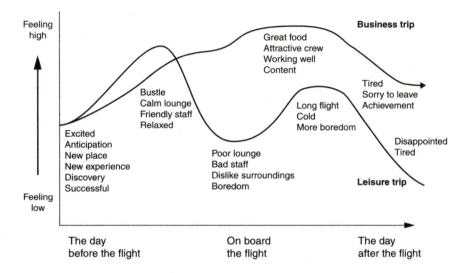

Figure 9.7 *Life graph of a plane journey*

The most important element of life graphs is asking each participant to hold up his or her graph and take the group through the journey. In the process of describing what is going on at each stage, and prompted by questions from the moderator and the rest of the group, the participants often discover additional insights that they had not realized before.

Collages

Research participants are given large sheets of paper, scissors, glue and a stack of magazines. They are also given a theme and asked to tear out pictures that represent the theme to them. The pictures, along with drawings and words, are used to build up the representation and arrange it on the board. The visual focus encourages emotional as well as rational responses.

The potential applications for this technique are broad, ranging from depicting current brand identities, moods and feelings, or participants' aspirations in a marketplace, to exploring possible futures, for example: 'What money means to me', 'Brand X and Brand Y', 'My life'.

Collages are a great way to :

■ Get individual research participants thinking about particular concerns, hopes and aspirations, or alternatively about brands, packaging, advertising or a particular organization.
■ Get research participants to work together to draw out their individual views and work through them to create a composite picture. From

Husserl's perspective, we are creating 'a coalition of common perceptions of the world' (Mariampolski, 2001: 16).

Whether this exercise is carried out individually or in a group, the technique encourages participants to use their visual/aesthetic, tactile and emotional faculties as well as their intellect, and this fosters a wider perspective in their responses.

Participants are given a limited time to make their collage; 10 minutes is typical. This is partly a function of the time constraints of the research session, but it also prevents them becoming over-analytical and self-conscious. It means they have to 'get something together'.

With individual collages, the participant holds up the collage to the group and describes the representation and why he or she chose these images and words. What do they say about the theme the person is representing? With syndicate group collages, one person volunteers to present the material, aided by the rest of the team. The moderator encourages other participants to ask questions and build on the ideas portrayed. This exercise usually generates considerable excitement and engagement with the topic. It also produces material that, in a feedback session, can very effectively convey ideas to clients.

Psycho-drawing

Psycho-drawing uses the same principles as collage making, but the participant creates a drawing with coloured pencils and crayons. Participants may be asked to 'Draw how you feel about commuting to work' or 'What family means to you' or 'How you feel about banks'. The emphasis is on feelings, discouraging intellectual analysis and reassuring people that they don't need to be good at drawing. If participants are initially wary of the activity, the moderator might model the response required: for example, 'Here, this is how I feel about banks [drawing a big black squiggle with a crude face and down-turned mouth]. You may feel they are all sunshine and light...'

Participants are encouraged to fill the whole page of a large sheet of paper – there is a tendency to fold it in half so they have less space to cover – to use bold colours and shapes, and to draw rather than write. The exercise should take no more than 10 minutes. Each participant then holds up and elaborates on his or her drawing. The moderator needs to be curious and encouraging at this stage, as it can be a little daunting for participants to present their picture to the group.

Great. That looks really interesting... It sort of links in with Valerie's drawing. What is the stick man there in the corner? How does he fit in with it all... So how would you sum up the mood of the picture?

Psycho-drawings, because they tap into unfamiliar ways of accessing feelings, can be very cathartic, allowing participants to explore their feelings and make connections that had not previously occurred to them. These connections often trigger off responses in other participants, enabling the group to access areas that are generally below conscious awareness. Figure 9.8 shows one such example.

Figure 9.8 *My future in Canada*

Role-play

Role-play can be used to draw out the characteristics of a brand. For example, two participants are chosen. One is nominated as 'British Airways' and one 'Virgin Airlines'. Each participant is asked to talk to the group in the language and tone of voice of their nominated airline. The different styles of the two airlines are hot-housed and this sparks off conversation within the group as a whole. Differences surface as participants identify and articulate personal views that may have been obscure or half formed.

Role-play is also used to explore relationships between staff and customers in a service context. For instance, two participants work together, one taking the role of the bank manager and the other playing the part of a customer looking for a loan. The 'manager' may be briefed to act in a certain way, uninterested or helpful for example. How does the customer feel in this role? How does he or she want the manager to act? Enacting the situation in this way triggers emotions that to some extent replicate real life. These emotions can then be explored by the group.

Role-play does require a degree of confidence on the part of the moderator and it is important that he or she feels comfortable directing participants to act out scenes in this way.

WHEN TO USE PROJECTIVE TECHNIQUES

Projective techniques are useful in a wide variety of situations, for example:

■ to obtain fresh perspectives in heavily researched markets;
■ in new product/brand development or brand re-positioning;
■ in developing advertising strategy;
■ to evaluate courses/conferences when there is limited time and access to research participants;
■ to explore assumptions, relationships and expectations, for example in organizational research when there is a need to understand how individuals in different departments work together.

The range of techniques is extensive. Simple techniques can be incorporated into standard research approaches and used without pre-planning, and it is useful to have an armoury of simple projective techniques such as sentence completion and brand personification to hand, in case of need. More complex techniques, such as role-play need preparation, specific materials and training.

Projectives can be used pragmatically; that is, they can be introduced into a research session when the energy level is flagging and/or the discussion has become stale, repetitive or rhetorical – or simply to introduce a change in direction. An appropriately chosen projective technique can break or lighten the mood and help participants to re-engage with the research issues.

However, the primary use of projective techniques is to delve beneath the everyday, conscious mind, to access areas that are normally below conscious awareness and to tap into those associations, emotions, connections, beliefs and values that we do not normally have access to. By identifying and articulating content in these areas, we can incorporate rich seams of experience into our understanding of the research issues.

Projective techniques are most commonly, but not exclusively, used in group discussions, in part because the group effect means that there is less self-consciousness. If participants feel they are 'part of the crowd', they tend to be more relaxed about engaging in what may seem to be quite unusual activities, at least for adults.

GUIDELINES FOR USING PROJECTIVE TECHNIQUES

Projectives are tools to aid understanding not ends in themselves

Their purpose is to help researchers answer the research questions more fully, and judgement is needed in terms of their appropriateness in a particular research context. Sometimes a technique works well. Sometimes it doesn't. As with other forms of communication, if an approach doesn't work, then it needs to be abandoned and another tried.

Projective techniques are particularly useful in a group context

There is time for participants to relax and enjoy the process, in a comfortable environment. Research participants often enjoy the team work. When exploring brands, a group context is particularly helpful because brands are culturally defined, so it is easy to access shared meanings and cultural assumptions.

The materials produced from projective techniques are not the 'findings'

It is essential to explore with participants what their drawings, scrap-art and other creations mean, and why they have represented a brand or an organization in such a way. Projective techniques work most effectively and have greatest validity when research participants interpret the outcomes themselves. In their explanation of what they have produced, participants are making meaning of thoughts and feelings that were below conscious awareness, in their adaptive unconscious (Gladwell) or the unconscious (Freud). They are also forging links between logical and emotional content (Damasio).

Projective techniques need to be introduced at an appropriate stage in the research process

If projective techniques – especially those that participants might find challenging or embarrassing – are introduced too early in the research process, when participants are still settling into the group, they may be reluctant to join in. If introduced too late, participants may be flagging, having expended their energy and contemplating going home.

Ideally projective techniques should be introduced when the group is warmed up and enthused about the topic under discussion, but before too much discussion of the subject. This is particularly important for individual projectives. Ideally, individual perspectives will be shared before discussion is opened up to the group as a whole.

How the exercise is introduced is very important

To encourage participant involvement, the technique needs to be introduced appropriately. A simple explanation of what is required, delivered in a clear and confident manner, is required. Participants need to feel that what they are being asked to do is reasonable, makes sense and could be interesting.

Projective exercises are hard work; pacing the exercises is important

These exercises change the style and energy of the group. Often they speed up the process and increase involvement. Participants may need a quiet period afterwards to re-energize.

Different projective techniques work in different ways

Some techniques encourage participants to identify implicit structures, for example by using packaging to map the differences and similarities between brands and how they relate to one another. Other techniques present people with materials that they must react to, such as 'mood boards' or new confectionary to try, which leads to discussion. More complex tasks may involve disrupting the taken-for-granted world, which forces consumers to behave in different ways or explore new possibilities, for example by asking them to write a story from a different perspective, as a teenager or as a clothes manufacturer. These techniques can be particularly useful for challenging participants' habitual, often repeated, stories of their lives.

The researcher needs to be conscious of potential discomfort and embarrassment for certain participants

Commercial qualitative research should not make participants uneasy, even unintentionally. Researchers must be very aware of their language, tone of voice and manner when introducing the exercises, and vigilant for any signs that participants are not comfortable. If this does happen, participants should be allowed to opt out discreetly. This rarely happens. During 30 years of using projective techniques, I have never experienced anyone who became upset when asked to engage in these exercises. Typically, if the exercise is introduced as fun, where people just 'give it a go' and where there are no artistic expectations, the large majority really enjoy the task and quickly become so engrossed that it is difficult to get them to stop!

USING PROJECTIVE MATERIALS IN CLIENT FEEDBACK

A presentation that is one long series of PowerPoint charts can subdue the most eager of clients. Introducing drawings or photographs – or indeed any other materials – that have been directly produced by research participants can illuminate issues in a way that is often impossible for researchers to do on their own. When clients see and hold participant drawings, they often feel that they have direct access to consumers. This, in turn, helps them to understand rather than just hear what is being said by the researcher.

Material generated through projective techniques can therefore enable clients and creative teams to develop a more holistic understanding than would be possible by verbal input alone. Visual and auditory material – music, drawing, word associations, drama – can all provide a rich understanding of target markets and their relationships with brands and organizations.

Most importantly, weaving projective materials into client feedback and explaining how these materials enable access to consumers' thoughts, feelings, fears and aspirations – much of which is normally below conscious awareness – reinforces the notion that human nature is complex. It is too easy to view consumers as one-dimensional brand users. To really understand people and markets, we need to understand the complexity, the way the conscious–unconscious, logical–emotional, individual–cultural all flow into one another.

10 Consumer input to idea generation and development

WHY USE CONSUMERS TO GENERATE NEW THINKING?

Working with consumers to generate ideas that may eventually lead to new product innovations used to be a contentious issue, especially within ad agencies. The view was that consumers can't be creative; they can only respond to concepts and ideas produced by other (presumably more creative) individuals. Or so the argument went. Thankfully this view has more or less died out. Consumers are now regarded as a perfectly valid – indeed invaluable – source of new ideas, so why not make the most of this resource? This view has grown in popularity, alongside evidence that creative research techniques exist that are proven aids to new product innovation (Puccio *et al*, 2006). Indeed, in some quarters, creativity has been heralded as the new logic. As advertising planner Mark Earls (2002: 152) puts it:

> Creative Age thinking is thinking that includes the people normally excluded from strategy. As such it is democratic rather than elitist. It is intuitive and creative. It is passionate and inventive. It is about doing, not just saying. It is smart rather than clever.

Equally, qualitative researchers have the skills and expertise to delve beneath the rational, to explore psychological needs and drives and to encourage creative thinking. It therefore seems natural that they should be in the forefront of new thinking and the development of new ideas, products and services. Urban and Hauser (2003) point out that new products derived from consumer-need studies account for a high proportion of successful technological innovations – and have done for decades. They offer the example of Ford in the mid-1960s, which identified the trend amongst teenagers and young adults to customize inexpensive vintage Fords with V8 engines. To meet this opportunity the company launched the 1964½ Mustang, which captured the hearts of a new generation of baby boomers just reaching driving age.

Harnessing creativity

Two very different routes have developed for tapping into consumer creativity:

- Creative forums, comprising hand-picked individuals who meet face to face and work together to generate new thinking around a particular area. These forums are set up and managed by professional qualitative research teams and have grown out of the long qualitative tradition of encouraging creativity and innovation in a structured way.
- Online communities that have developed on the back of the current climate of equal participation and collaboration between research participants, researchers and clients. These communities have been fostered by the rapid growth of web-based forums and enabled by an array of online collaborative tools that allow participants to jointly create new ideas and develop them.

These creative approaches work in very different ways. They are likely to attract different types of people and also to differ in the degree of control that the researcher can assume.

CREATIVE FORUMS

Research participants, particularly when they are selected on the basis of their creative abilities and willingness to employ them, and when they are well guided and facilitated, can be a wonderful source of new ideas. By using a variety of imaginative verbal and non-verbal techniques and creative problem-solving exercises, consumers can provide very different perspectives on markets and produce many novel ideas. Creative forums can last from three or four hours to a full day or they can take place over several days.

Many of the approaches used in creative forums are grounded in projective techniques. Therefore, it is recommended that this chapter is read in conjunction with Chapter 9.

What skills and experience should we look for?

This depends on the task and how long participants will be engaged in the process. The more time and creative commitment that is required of participants, the greater the involvement and care that is needed in their recruitment.

Participants must be 'creative' and, just as important, willing to exercise their creativity within the workshop. If they are being recruited for a half-day session, then a truncated version of the creative panel recruitment exercises (see below) may be used. Questions such as 'List as many uses as you can think of for a pane of glass in two minutes' or 'How many ideas can you think of when you marry a chair and a car wheel?', whilst apparently superficial, do give a rapid indication both of an individual's willingness to 'play along' and the fluency of their ideas.

If the prime purpose of the creative session is to generate new product ideas within quite specific constraints (eg floor coverings), then it is a good idea to include some people who have recently bought a carpet, wooden flooring or the like. If, on the other hand, the aim is to generate ideas with broader boundaries, as with the DIY study described below or a study aiming to create new financial services or products, then it may be more important to include as diverse a set of people as possible, although not so diverse that the participants cannot relate to one another.

Depending on the nature of the session, clients, designers, planners and/or 'creatives' might be included alongside consumers. They may contribute as participants, engaging in the discussions and creative exercises, or they may be introduced as creative facilitators, for instance sketching packaging, products or cartoons to represent the participants' verbal descriptions.

However, participants need to feel at ease with each other. Mixing participants from advertising agencies and client companies with consumers can be extremely useful because of the diverse nature of the input. It can also be disastrous, if consumers feel awkward or demeaned by their comparative lack of knowledge. It is the job of the facilitator to select all participants (including clients) carefully and to foster a sense of safety and equality whilst the session is in progress.

Campbell Keegan was commissioned by a DIY company to set up a year-long project, developing and running a panel of diverse individuals who would work on new ideas within the DIY market. We advertised in a local paper for people who considered themselves to be 'creative'. Those who replied were sent an explanatory letter and a series of tasks for completion. The tasks had minimal direction in their wording. For example, participants were asked to write their autobiography to date, including as many factual details as they thought appropriate. They were also given a collection of creative tasks, both verbal and visual.

The tasks served two functions. First, it weeded out the faint-hearted (it took three hours or more to complete the tasks). Second, it illustrated the creative ability of each individual. The object of the tasks was to understand the individual's approach to problem solving. Assessment was, inevitably, judgemental, although the questionnaires were evaluated using the following criteria:

■ the ability to develop and express ideas either verbally or figuratively;
■ originality/imagination;
■ humour;
■ the unexpected;
■ the crazy but possible, as opposed to the predictably probable.

After this initial screening, a second stage of screening work was carried out. Selected participants were invited to a creative workshop and were set a variety of tasks, from making a paper aeroplane, to working in a group to build a house from Lego, to inventing a new game. A team of observers watched and evaluated participants in terms of their output, how they worked as a team, and the roles they choose to play. From these progressive stages of screening, 12 participants who worked well together were selected and convened as a creative panel. They worked together for a year, identified lawn care as an area that offered potential, and generated ideas for a wide range of gardening products.

Setting up a creative panel is a business risk. Budget is committed to the venture with no guarantee that it will lead to a marketable product. However, generating just one successful idea could more than cover the costs.

The range of creative forums

Creative workshops (Holmes and Keegan, 1983: 345–77), which are intensive sessions lasting from half a day to a day, can achieve some of the same benefits as a panel over a shorter time span. Workshops may have 30 or more diverse participants, who work on a variety of tasks in a combination of large groups and 'break-out' groups, throughout the session.

Langmaid and Andrews (2003: 29) describe 'breakthrough zone events' in which between 50 and 500 people from the client organization and the general public meet and spend one or two days together. The aim is to enable employees to become more innovative and to create new products, brand extensions and services.

How to encourage people to create?

The purpose of a creative forum is to encourage spontaneity and creativity although, paradoxically, it needs structuring to achieve this. It is not simply 'a long group discussion' in which participants have a quick 'brainstorm' at the end of the group.

Here are a number of practical guidelines, developed by Sidney Parnes (1967: 62–90) and his colleagues, back in the 1960s and still relevant today.

- *Psychological safety*: Creativity is high risk. Exposing our ideas to others potentially opens us up to criticism and ridicule. Evaluation may feel uncomfortable. To foster creativity, emphasis is placed on building on other people's ideas rather than undermining them.
- *Psychological freedom*: Stepping outside social or cultural norms and breaking down hierarchies is important, as is avoiding imposing a structure in which participants feel they need to 'play the role' or give yes–no responses. Encouraging people to question preconceptions encourages creative thought.
- *Re-defining the problem*: This is the single most important task. Too often we focus on the solution, when the problem itself has not been properly explored. Problem definition is often the route to creative solutions, and approaching something from a new angle may suggest a potential solution. 'How can I stop eating cream cakes?' can be re-phrased as 'How can I get slimmer and fitter?' and in a hundred other ways. Repeated re-phrasing of the 'problem' can throw a whole new light on an area.
- *Changing the frame of reference*: Jogging ourselves or others out of 'tram-line' thinking, encouraging thinking that is different and makes new associations – often through the use of non-verbal and

non-logical techniques – encourages originality. For example, drawing is a good leveller. Watching a group of suited business managers scrabbling around on the floor looking for the right colour crayon to convey their feelings about plane travel is, in itself, interesting. More importantly, it allows them to metaphorically 'shed the suit'. Drawing can change the tone of a workshop and bring out fresh ideas that the participants can then develop further when describing their drawings.

■ *Generating many ideas*: Statistically, the more ideas that are generated, the greater the chances of finding a significant or useful one (Guilford, 1970).

■ *Incubation*: The unconscious process of mulling over a problem or situation whilst engaged in quite different activities – such as 'sleeping on it' – is not simply folklore. It is an important and often neglected aspect of problem solving. Incubation can be utilized through reconvened sessions (in which the same participants reconvene a week or two later). In the intervening time, new ideas may be incubated.

These guidelines are just as relevant for idea generation within marketing departments as they are for creative consumer forums. Internal management sessions that are run along these lines, including representatives from many departments within the organization, can be enormously fruitful, provided all the attendees are willing participants. It is expedient for the session to be run by an 'outsider'. It is also important that senior management is involved in the process, as participants, non-intrusive observers and/or in the planning and dissemination of ideas. Their support ensures that the process is taken seriously within the organization.

Facilitating a creative forum

The environment in which the creative forum is held is important. Mobiles should be off-bounds and there needs to be sufficient time for people to open up, develop ideas and refine them. Equally, the venue should be sufficiently spacious to enable people to spread out when carrying out the exercises, and break-out rooms are needed for syndicate groups. Two or more moderators are often used, to allow for changes in pace and for recuperation.

The structure of the workshop will vary according to the objectives, which may be broad – such as 'People have a need for novelty. How can we provide it within this particular market?' – or fairly narrow: 'Invent a unique savoury spread.' However, regardless of the creative question, the structure will usually comprise three stages:

1. Problem exploration and definition.
2. Idea generation and development.
3. Idea refinement and problem solution.

Problem exploration and definition

The first stage is concerned with exploring the problems that are generated by the participants themselves or introduced by the workshop leaders. Defining the problem in as many ways as possible – and breaking it down into its component parts – is the first stage in generating solutions. For example, in a workshop on indoor gardening, 'How do I stop my house plants from dying?' may be re-defined in scores of ways, for example:

■ How do I water my plants whilst on holiday?
■ How do I regulate the amount of water I give my plants?
■ How do I teach the cat to water the plants?
■ Where do I buy plastic plants?

These 'solutions' may be sensible or absurd, but they help define the 'real' problem or problems and provide pointers to the solution. Absurdity – or the ability to look at a situation in a novel or uncharacteristic way – is an important ingredient of a creative forum. Participants are encouraged to think 'laterally', using a wide variety of devices such as:

■ word association (see Chapter 9);
■ personal analogy – the participant describes how it feels to be a partic-ular object;
■ forced couplings – ideas generated by forcing together two incompat-ible objects or ideas;
■ writing stories;
■ psycho-drawing – drawings that illustrate thoughts and feelings.

The common theme throughout these activities is that they are unusual and force participants to think or act in an uncharacteristic and often illogical way. They encourage a frame of mind that will be receptive to the novel and the absurd. They can also act as a short period of incubation, a distraction from the main activity. Food and drink can also be usefully employed in this way.

Idea generation and development

Defining the problem sets the scene for the next stage, which is gen-erating potential solutions. If the aim is to generate as many different solutions as possible to a specific problem, then the activity may be loosely structured, as in brainstorming (spontaneously shared ideas and solutions).

Alternatively, an approach such as attribute listing might be employed. Here, the attributes of a product are systematically adapted, modified, magnified, reversed and so on. For instance, a tin of soup could be elongated, square, re-sealable or 'squashy'.

A more systematic approach such as synectics (a structured problem-solving approach) might also be used. Participants are encouraged to develop, refine, modify and maximize the potential of the ideas they produce.

A wide range of projective techniques, carried out on an individual or group basis, are generally employed. The purpose of these exercises is to encourage participants to:

- defer their normal judgement processes;
- build on their own ideas and those of other people;
- produce as many ideas as possible.

Idea refinement and problem solution

Sometimes it is important not only to generate ideas but also to get some measure of their importance. A system of clustering or crudely ranking 'good' ideas, in terms of the client's strategy, can indicate which ideas should be pursued. Participants may be asked to list ideas in order of preference or prioritize them as a group. Alternatively, or in addition, ideas may be further developed as part of standard market research with a specific target market.

A key issue when running creative forums is the importance of structure. Without careful consideration of the objectives, recruitment criteria, venue, leader roles and the structure of the session, there is a risk that the forum will lack direction. Free expression, creativity and idea generation need to be carefully 'held' within a clearly thought out format.

COMMUNICATING OUTCOMES FROM A CREATIVE FORUM

Feedback from creative forums needs to be carefully handled. The format of the client meeting – and the atmosphere in which it takes place – is just as important as it is for creative forums with consumers. The meeting with the client team needs to be a working session rather than a formal presentation of 'findings'. It is a pooling of ideas, a stimulus to further thinking and development within the company, that all sides can join in.

In an appropriate setting and atmosphere, the material generated in the creative forum can be enormously helpful in communicating difficult or subtle ideas. Researchers face two endemic challenges. The first is getting to grips with how consumers really think, feel and behave in relation to the research area. The second challenge is managing to communicate this in a way that is understood – and felt – by the client team. The materials generated by creative forums can help in both areas by:

■ *Helping communicate thoughts and feelings*: Enabling an understanding of people in a different and more holistic way than through conventional qualitative research. Creative forums generate a huge amount of consumer-generated material that can be used to communicate this understanding to the client company.
■ *Offering a fresh perspective on people's needs*: Because the focus is, initially, on problem definition, creative forums have a broader remit. They can highlight important areas within a market that were not previously considered, and this can lead to fresh insights.
■ *Providing specific ideas*: A large number of specific product or service suggestions can be triggered. Many of these will be untenable, but they indicate areas of interest. A child's desire for strawberry-flavoured fish fingers may not be a useful suggestion at face value, but it suggests underlying interest in novelty and visual excitement. Other ideas, though bizarre, may spark off more tangible ideas in the marketing or insight departments. Creativity can be contagious.

ONLINE CREATIVE COMMUNITIES

The explosion of global communications, fostered largely by digital media, has, according to 'top management thinker' Charles Leadbeater (2008), encouraged an:

> unparalleled wave of collaborative creativity as people from California to China devise ways to work together that are more democratic, productive and creative... The generation growing up with the web will not be content to remain spectators. They want to be players.

It may be too early to say whether Leadbeater's dream of creative democracy becomes reality, but the spirit of collaborative creativity has certainly impregnated qualitative research communities and has led to the development of online approaches to collaborative idea generation, including online communities.

Online communities, introduced in Chapter 6, are used in one of the research methodologies that has grown out of the 'the digital revolution'.

The methodology has attracted considerable interest as a forum for collaborative and co-creation projects with consumers. In essence, an online community is a group of people who have been provided with an online environment in which to interact with each other (including the client and researchers) about topics related to a research interest. Clients may want to tap into leading-edge consumers or innovators, to collaborate 'two-way' with consumers and/or to have a global panel of consumers available to 'bounce ideas off'.

Online communities as creative hubs

An online community has been described as a 'bazaar' that grows from the free flow of ideas as suppliers seek to meet the changing needs of their customers. It is a 'bottom-up' community. By contrast, traditional research methods can be compared to a cathedral, with strict central command structures (Raymond, 2001). The nature of this free-flowing, bottom-up community means that the participants can follow their own interests, decide what they want to work on and respond if they feel so inclined. It becomes a journey of discovery. As Cooke and Buckley (2008: 267–92) put it, 'It offers market researchers opportunities, as yet untapped, to co-create goods and services with our respondents and to have them react to our concepts in an increasingly less directed way.'

Some researchers (eg Robarts, 2008) advocate the creation of short-term online communities in which researchers can obtain continual feedback from participants, liaise with clients and put ideas back into live research, online.

Client companies are doing it for themselves

Direct interaction and collaboration between customers and client companies has already happened in some areas. For example, Del Monte decided to create a new breakfast food for dogs. They recruited a private community of customers called, 'I love my dog', who quickly reached a consensus that Del Monte would never have considered: the dog food should be bacon-and-egg flavoured. In 2007 Del Monte created Sausages Breakfast Bites (Phillips, 2008: 41–42).

Hallmark cards set up a group around humour, in which customers shared their views of what was 'funny'. This provided Hallmark with clear guidance on changing tastes in different customer segments (Phillips, 2008: 41–42).

Coca-Cola has launched a site aimed at opening dialogue with consumers (http://www.letsgettogether.co.uk/home) and Canon, the camera manufacturer, has created a Windows Live Space to form a community where people interested in photography could showcase photos – and learn more about new Canon products (Vogt and Knapman, 2008: 46–51).

Cooke and Buckley (2008: 267–92) describe the Lego website, which has turned its army of online users into a design team by simply allowing them to build models from over 500 Lego pieces. Meanwhile, Dell is using Second Life to allow people to build their own computer and even to buy the finished product if they wish. In 2007, Dell created 'IdeaStorm' – a concept that has been widely imitated – in which customers were asked to suggest what improvements they would make to Dell's products. Other visitors to IdeaStorm could assess the importance of these ideas, and promote them or demote them accordingly (Phillips, 2008: 41–42).

The development of online communities, which are not overtly research-led, and client initiatives that talk directly to their customers, does raise the question of whether these developments can really be called research, at least as we know it. Some researchers see these developments as the future of qualitative research. Others are concerned that they will lead to a compromise in standards.

Where next?

Online research communities are moving fast and it is not clear how they will develop. Vogt and Knapman (2008) predict that marketers will be forced to share control of brands with consumer networks where ideas and beliefs are shaped and shared, 'in the battle for consumers' advocacy and collaboration'. They also suggest that it will be commonplace to recruit consumer advocates whose role is to seed ideas within their respective networks. Consumers will increasingly be seen as 'friends of' rather than 'consumers of' a brand. Finally, Vogt and Knapman suggest that consumer contact via social networks will not replace all traditional forms of market research. However, they predict that certain research areas – particularly new product development, brand strategy or deliberative research – will move from a selective consultation (traditional research) towards unconstrained debate within social networks where the initial ideas or agendas are 'seeded' but not controlled by researchers. If they are right, this will represent a significant handover of power from researchers to consumers and clients. Time will tell.

11 Designing a qualitative research project

RESPONDING TO THE CLIENT BRIEF

Now that we have explored qualitative methodologies and their appropriateness for different research projects in more detail, it is time to return to the business of qualitative research and, specifically, to the research proposal. Regardless of whether or not the proposal is competitive, and irrespective of its level of formality, the proposal is the agency's opportunity to demonstrate its research thinking to the client and spell out the ways in which the researchers will approach the project. It can take many forms:

- If there is no formal briefing document, because the research was worked out between client and researcher in an informal meeting, phone call or through a short written document, then the agency proposal is simply a summary of what has been agreed, but will include specific detail on the sample and methodology, and spell out the timings and costs.
- If there has been a written brief from the client, then the proposal is usually a more formal document, which is expected to address each of the sections outlined in the brief.
- Where there is a competitive pitch, that is where two or more agencies have been asked to write a proposal for the same job, then the agency usually puts a considerable amount of time and thought into the proposal, in order to demonstrate its superior skills, experience and ingenuity.

The discussion below covers the most comprehensive type of proposal, but the basic structure will be the same regardless of the level of formality and detail in the document.

Discussing the brief with the client

Where a research proposal is required, it is good procedure, if at all possible, to meet with the client before writing the proposal. At one time this was standard practice, but time pressures and competing commitments mean that a briefing meeting before writing the proposal is now the exception rather than the rule. Researchers are often expected to respond to the written brief, possibly expanded by a phone call.

Qualitative research, as we are repeatedly told, is a 'people business'. It is important to meet our potential clients to get an idea of what is important to them as well as understanding any political issues within the organization or concerns about this particular project. At a face-to-face meeting we will often hear or sense things that would not be put down on paper. This helps us to pitch the proposal in the most appropriate way.

In particular, the lack of a face-to-face meeting at this stage prevents the researcher from openly discussing the objectives. An experienced researcher is well placed to ask questions – in the same non-directive way as with research participants – that encourage the client to clarify and sometimes re-think the focus of the research: the researcher has probably worked on a similar project and can provide useful input. Martin Callingham, a former Group Market Research Director at Whitbread, puts it more strongly. 'The single most critical feature of a research design is to discover what the problem is... The fact that there is confusion over why the research is being done is the major reason for research failing' (Callingham, 2004: 117).

STRUCTURING THE PROPOSAL

The researcher needs to write a thorough proposal that does not duplicate previous areas of research, if possible. It is useful to know what research the client has already carried out in the relevant area and incorporate this within the proposal. This does not mean that the previous research has to be taken at face value. We can be aware of it, and refer to it in the proposal, without being overly influenced by it.

There is a standard way of setting out a proposal, and there may also be a house style in the research agency that needs to be adhered to. It is sensible to respond to the client's structure, if possible, not least because it is familiar to him or her, and can more easily be compared with competitive proposals if necessary.

The traditional sections of a proposal may vary slightly in how they are ordered or described, but generally cover the following areas:

1. Background and objectives.
2. Research sample and methodology:
   - research approach/es (if appropriate);
   - sample considerations (if appropriate);
   - proposed methodology/ies;
   - proposed sample structure;
   - stimuli (if appropriate);
   - topic guide (if appropriate at this stage).
3. Timing.
4. Costs.
5. Company and personnel.
6. Terms and conditions.

Background and objectives

This section is sometimes more problematic than one might expect. Received wisdom says that the researcher should add something new to the background – new insights or new information – rather than just replicate the background section from the client's brief. In practice, the background provided may be very comprehensive and there is little point in expanding on this for the sake of it. If this is the case, then summarizing the background concisely and intelligently – and perhaps drawing out a couple of novel implications – may be a better option.

If, on the other hand, the background section is skimpy, some judiciously added information about the client or background to the market, gleaned from the client's website, a general Google search or personal research experience, can demonstrate thought and effort; it shows the researcher has not simply copied the background section word for word from the brief. Essentially, the client knows the background – it is there to inform the researcher not the client – so it is best to concentrate effort on the sections that follow.

Research sample and methodology

This is the key section and the area on which most time and effort needs to be expended. Essentially it addresses:

■ What target audience/s needs to be included in the research sample?
■ Which research approach or combination of approaches is most likely to provide understanding, direction and answers to the research question/s?

The research sample

The research sample comprises the group or groups of people who need to be included in the research design. The sample relates to the target audience/s that the client wants to address with its product, service or communications. They are not necessarily the client's current customers. Determining the most appropriate research sample is not always as straightforward as it might seem. Whilst the core groups to be included are often clear, there may be peripheral groups who could provide useful input but are excluded because of budget constraints. Equally, the researcher, when writing the proposal, may feel strongly that groups not identified by the client can contribute to the research, and so may recommend in the proposal that they should be included.

Here are some examples of research samples, ranging from quite small-scale projects with homogeneous target audiences to larger projects, in which the sub-samples are quite fragmented and the variables to be considered in the sample structure are more numerous.

For the launch of a new skin care product, where there is reasonable homogeneity in the targeting

- female purchasers of premium skin care brands (from a specified list);
- all regular users of skin care products;
- aged 30–50;
- upper social class.

For a project on after dinner mints, where the aim is to develop greater awareness and trial of a particular brand

- regular purchasers of after dinner mints;
- an even spread of Bendicks, After Eight and Matchmaker brand users;
- aged 30+ (reflecting the purchasers of after dinner mints);
- men and women;
- social class left open.

For a project on financial services, which involves re-structuring the way in which the company will market to its customers

- six life-stage sectors (single/unpartnered, young couples with no children, couples with young children, couples with teenage children, children left home, retired);
- split by high net worth, middle income, low income;
- self-employed versus employed;
- different levels of financial interest/involvement;

■ range of social class groups;
■ men and women;
■ with different financial products / savings / pension arrangements;
■ regional groupings.

The research sample offers an overview of the sub-groups that need to be included in the research. In essence, the more fragmented the audience that is being researched, the more sub-groups there are likely to be within the research sample. The way in which these sub-groups are included in the research structure will depend, to a large extent, on the research methodology that is to be employed. The methodology needs to be considered before the research structure is put together.

The research methodology

Deciding on the methodology that is most appropriate in terms of the research objectives, requires a detailed knowledge and experience of the pros and cons of different methodological approaches (see Chapters 6). The following types of question can help steer the decision on methodology, but there are no hard and fast rules. Each project needs to be looked at individually.

What is the nature of the research?

Are the research questions concerned with gaining understanding and information, or do they need to generate new ideas, concepts and / or advertising strategy? Gathering information and understanding are likely to involve qualitative interviewing and / or ethnographic approaches. Idea generation will probably require creative forums in which groups of people can work together, sparking off one another and building on each other's ideas.

Does the research situation need to be highly structured or unstructured – and to what extent can this be achieved?

Qualitative research can be viewed along a continuum. At one end, the researcher is actively managing the research process, for example when interviewing research participants face to face. At the other end of the continuum, we have 'naturally occurring data', where the researcher is observing but has very little direct impact on the situation. The researcher needs to assess which is the most appropriate route, given the research objectives. In some cases, it may be appropriate to combine these approaches to achieve multiple perspectives.

For instance, to explore the behaviour of football fans, observational studies carried out at football matches (naturally occurring data), might be combined with group discussions (actively managed) in order to achieve different perspectives on the same behaviour.

There may also be practical constraints that limit the methodological options. For example, when exploring attitudes and behaviour in relation to 'safe sex', it might be tricky to carry out observational studies; the researcher might have to rely on interviewing, or devise ingenious methods by which participants can quickly deliver data, such as mobile messaging, blogs or twitter.

If interviews are the chosen approach, what type of interviewing is appropriate?

Interviews can be carried out face to face, over the phone, by e-mail, web link or post. They may be individual, paired, in groups. Which is the best approach?

This is partly a question of logistics. Is it difficult to access people? Are there issues of confidentiality? Are participants likely to be geographically spread? Do the research issues involve gathering longitudinal data? If the answer to any of these questions is yes, then one-to-one interviews will probably be necessary. If, on the other hand, people can be easily accessed and convened and the subject is not 'sensitive', then some form of group interviewing is a possibility.

The other issue is, 'what is the best method for the task?' Complex and/or emotional issues, which require considerable delving, an awareness of body language, tone of voice, silences and hesitations – and perhaps the use of projective techniques – would be best dealt with face to face.

However, some younger audiences or 'techies' may be more comfortable with virtual interviews, particularly if this approach is compatible with the subject being researched, as in the case of software or iPhones.

Does the research call for a one-off research interaction, or does it need to happen over time?

Much qualitative research is one-off, in that research participants are involved in the research and, the next time, a fresh sample of participants is recruited. This is routinely done on the basis that people can become 'over-familiar' with the research process and so their responses are atypical. However, there are occasions when reconvened groups are useful or when participants might be asked to carry out some follow-up task and report back on a blog (see Chapter 6).

Can the research participant act as researcher?

Would it be useful if individual participants explored certain research issues on their own and then shared their understanding with the agency researcher and other participants, for example by visiting certain stores or websites before or after a group discussion, or keeping a diary of certain activities?

These are some of the issues that the researcher will need to consider when choosing the most appropriate methodologies. There will be others, related to the specific project.

Sample structure

The sample structure is the programme of research that knits together the sub-groups identified in the research sample with the proposed methodology, within the client's budget. It is usually the task of the research agency to put this together and it represents the core of the research proposal. It requires considerable time, thought and skill to work out how to develop a research approach and structure that best meet the client's objectives in the most cost-effective manner. This is not an area where there are templates, and each sample structure will differ. Perhaps the most effective way of showing how a sample structure can be put together is by illustration.

The client, a manufacturer of baby food, is developing a new advertising campaign for its baby food brand, aimed at mothers of babies aged three months to two years old. The overall target audience (mothers who buy baby food) is made up of a number of sub-groups. In order to develop an appropriate sample structure, the researcher would need to consider the following factors:

■ There has been much previous research highlighting the differences between first and second-time mothers. First-time mothers are more likely to be anxious, to 'do what they have been told' rather than trust their instincts. Mixing first and second-time mothers in the same research situation or mixing the findings from the two groups will therefore create distortion, so the two groups are best kept separate.

■ The feeding needs of babies change rapidly. Talking to mothers, especially first-time mothers, about their baby's future needs is likely to produce spurious findings; they tend to focus on the current needs of their baby. A two-month-old baby has very different needs from a six-month one, so it is important that mothers with babies of different ages are researched separately.

■ This is an area where socio-economic factors may influence attitudes towards baby feeding and, in particular, breast-feeding. It might be useful to separate mothers from different socio-economic groups.

■ Previous research has indicated that attitudes differ by area of the country, so it is important to ensure a regional spread.

■ The company wants to look at advertising ideas, so face-to-face interviewing is most appropriate. Should the interviewing be carried out as 'one to ones' or in groups and, if in groups, how many should be in each group and how long should the sessions last? What time of day is most convenient for mothers with young babies – who may also have older children?

■ Mothers with very young babies will probably want to bring their babies with them to the research session; some will be breast-feeding. They may want to have their baby in the room with them. If the babies are to be looked after in an adjoining room, then adequate child-care must be provided. It is likely that some babies will need their mothers, so allowances have to be made for regular disruption in the group.

These are just some of the obvious factors that would need to be considered for this particular project. We might also want to think about whether breast-fed babies should be separated from those who are bottle-fed, given that this is an important consideration for new mothers. Similarly, the age of the mother, whether or not she is working outside the home and her views on manufactured baby food may all be factors to consider when devising a sample structure. There is always a balance to be struck between devising a comprehensive sample and fitting the research within the budget.

The objective when putting together a sample structure is not to attempt to control all variables or to achieve totally homogeneity in the sub-groups within the sample; this would clearly be impossible. The aim is to be aware – as far as we can at this stage – of the variables that exist. This is particularly important with group discussions. An appropriate degree of overlap in, say, attitudes, life-stage or product usage generates group cohesion and encourages a productive, open discussion; equally however, too much homogeneity inhibits discussion that highlights differences in attitudes and behaviour.

Returning to our baby food project, taking the factors we have identified into account, a first stab at structuring a research sample structure, defining the sectors to be included in the sample, could be as follows:

- Separate first-time and second-time (or more) mothers.
- Group participants into four categories: those with babies under three months, three to six months, six months to a year, and one to two years.
- Have a spread of socio-economic levels.
- Cover at least three areas of the country.
- Ensure that there is a spectrum of working/non-working women, to reflect the population.

This is the starting point for developing a sample structure that incorporates these factors within the research methodology and gives an appropriate weighting to each. Group discussions would be a suitable methodology, so a simple sample structure, recommended to the client, could be:

Eight group discussions:			
Gap	**Status**	**Age of baby**	**Socio-economic class**
1.	1st time mothers	under 3 months	Lower/middle
2.	1st time mothers	3–6 months	Middle/higher
3.	1st time mothers	6–12 months	Lower/middle
4.	1st time mothers	1–2 years	Middle/higher
5.	2nd time mothers	under 3 months	Middle/higher
6.	2nd time mothers	3–6 months	Lower/middle
7.	2nd time mothers	6–12 months	Middle/higher
8.	2nd time mothers	1–2 years	Lower/middle

The groups would be conducted in three areas of the country, and within each group there would be a spectrum of working and non-working women. The aim in putting together this structure is to rotate the variables, so that we can to some extent avoid bias. For instance, if all the groups of first-time mothers were in one region of the country, it would not be possible to know whether differences in the sample were due to 'first-time-ness' or the region in which the research was conducted.

The client will probably be very familiar with the factors outlined and will have clearly defined its target market. Equally, the client is likely to have strong views on how the sample ought to reflect their current or future target audience. However, the researcher may also have input, based on previous work with this client, experience of this particular market and cultural changes that may affect attitudes, such as the move towards organic baby food or preparing food at home from organic ingredients. The researcher is also expert in terms of what will help or hinder the homogeneity of the sub-samples.

Clients will generally welcome researcher input on the research sample, and in fact the research agency's views and recommendations on these areas often provide the basis for selection of the winning research proposal.

Stimuli

The stimuli are any tools or materials that are used in the research, in order to aid the research process (see Chapter 8).

At the stage when the proposal is written, it is often not clear what precise stimuli will be needed and the researcher may not be expected to discuss stimulus development until after the project is formally commissioned. However, if the researcher has specific ideas about approaches or techniques, such as projective techniques, that he or she believes are particularly relevant, then these could be included.

Topic guide

Again, the detailed topic guide is generally written once the researchers have been thoroughly briefed on the project, although a draft guide, outlining key areas, may be included in the proposal.

Timing

The research agency is expected to provide a timing schedule that either matches that suggested by the client or modifies it to fit with fieldwork needs or the agency's other commitments. Obviously, if the agency cannot do the work within the specified time, this should have been discussed with the client before the agency started to write the proposal. Minor modifications, agreed with the client, may be acceptable.

Costs

These have to be clearly spelt out and either fit within the client's budget or, if they exceed it, the reasons for the higher costs have to be discussed. Generally, it is expected that costs for each stage of the research programme will be spelt out. Clients differ in the level of detail they expect.

Researchers cost their projects in different ways. Some work on the basis of a unit cost; for example a group discussion costs x, an individual depth interview costs y. However, in recent years, the proliferation of qualitative research methodologies has meant that it is difficult to sustain this costing system. Many researchers now charge by a mixture of direct costs – that is, those services and costs that they will have to pay for in order to complete the project (eg fieldwork costs, incentives for research participants, transcription of interview material, viewing facility hire, travel and accommodation costs, stimulus production and chart preparation) – combined with a set day rate that covers the time commitment.

Company and personnel

This section details the people who will be involved and the role they will play in the project, along with their past experience. It also outlines the prior experience the research company has within the area of research.

Terms and conditions

Terms and conditions (T&Cs) outline the expectations, assumptions and responsibilities of the research agency. T&Cs only become relevant when things go wrong, but 'things going wrong' – whether because of a misunderstanding between client and agency or because the research was not what the client wanted or expected in some way – can be hugely stressful and upsetting for both sides. The research agency needs to invest time in creating a comprehensive set of terms and conditions that will act as some sort of benchmark if things do go wrong.

12 Managing a qualitative research project

GETTING THE PROJECT OFF THE GROUND

The client phones. You've won the tender and the project has been given the go ahead. After the initial buzz of excitement, reality kicks in. The project needs to be planned and set in motion.

A research project is a complex mix of logistics and relationships. The practical issues have to be dealt with as thoroughly as possible. However, managing the relationships – with clients, co-researchers, research participants, ad agency and so on – is just as, if not more, important. The first part of this chapter deals with the practicalities and the second part addresses the relationship issues that are intrinsic to all projects.

DEALING WITH THE PRACTICALITIES

How the researcher goes about this will vary, depending on the nature of the project, its size, how many parties are involved and the timing. Each project is a 'one off'. Nonetheless, there are a number of standard areas that need to be addressed, so it is possible to draw up basic guidelines.

There may be amendments that the client wants to make to the sample or methodology. Often these have to be agreed and signed off before the project can really get underway. Then, the immediate issues to be considered are:

- *Timings*: Is a further client meeting needed in order to finalize details? When does the fieldwork need to be carried out to fit with the client's timing? How best can fieldwork fit around ongoing work commitments?

■ *Recruitment*: Will it be done in house or through an agency? What sort of recruitment is needed? Does time need to be allowed to develop stimuli? Do fieldwork sessions need to be staged to allow for revision of the stimuli as the fieldwork rolls out.

■ *Venues*: For projects involving interviewing, will the research sessions be held in a viewing facility, in a recruiter's house, in a hotel, the participant's home or office? If the study involves ethnographic techniques, what type of locations are needed? What are the logistical issues? Similarly, for digital media, resources need to be booked.

■ *Research team*: Who will make up the research team? Who will lead it? What are the researchers' availabilities?

■ *Outcomes*: What outputs is the client expecting and when (feedback sessions, presentation, report)?

RECRUITMENT

The basic principles of recruitment are the same regardless of the research methodology: there are certain target audiences that need to be identified and included in the study. However, different methodologies require different levels and types of involvement from research participants, and this needs to be considered at the recruitment stage.

Recruiting for interviewing methodologies

If the project involves interviewing as a methodology, then research participants will need to be pre-recruited (unless short, opportunistic interviews, eg in a retail outlet, are to be carried out). Recruitment is generally organized either by an in-house field manager/department or through one of a number of recruitment agencies to which the research agency will subcontract the task. In either case, a member of the field team will be responsible for organizing the recruitment of interviewees, in line with the research spec. The field team has a large number of recruiters on their books (often several hundred) and they will book a recruiter or team of recruiters located in each of the regions in which the fieldwork is to be carried out. The recruiter's job is to find people who fit the spec and are available at the interview times, and to make sure that they do turn up. This may mean reminding them by phone or arranging cabs to pick them up.

Each recruiter is sent a recruitment pack, which will include the research spec and copies of a screener or recruitment questionnaire.

Recruiters will use different methods to locate potential research partici-pants, depending on the requirements of the project. For instance, a project with mothers of children under 10 might involve recruiting at the school gates. To recruit owners of small businesses, the use of directories and making initial phone contact might prove more successful. In general, participants who attend the same session should not know each other (unless this is a specific aim); the object is to achieve a cross section of people who fit the specified research sample.

When potential participants are identified, the recruiter will take them through the screener. If they fit the spec and are able and willing to attend the research session, then they will be recruited. The participants are usually paid an incentive for attending the session. The amount varies in relation to the ease of recruitment.

The screener is used to check whether potential participants fit the spec, which might be quite straightforward. For instance, the main recruitment criteria for a new cereal project might be age, family status, social class and purchase of particular brands of cereal.

However, for an innovation project, recruitment might include open-ended creative questions and/or a broad age range. An exploratory study in which the client company wanted to understand consumers' relation-ships with money, and how these differ by age and life-stage, involved an age range of 17–70. In other studies, the aim might be to recruit opinion leaders or experts in their field.

Where participants are recruited from client lists, for instance existing customers of a finance or retail organization, the client company will generally inform its customers that they might be contacted by the research agency. This helps reassure potential participants that the research is legitimate.

Difficulties with recruitment

Recruiting participants for a research project, regardless of whether this is for a fairly straightforward study or a more esoteric one, is sometimes difficult, for a variety of reasons.

Timing is often short
Good recruitment takes time. Recruitment is increasingly being squeezed by the need for fast turn-around on projects. At the same time, recruit-ment criteria are getting more complex. Inevitably recruitment standards suffer. As an industry we have to decide whether speed or quality is more important. We cannot realistically have both.

There are too few people in the target audience

The client may specify a particular sub-group. However if it turns out that these people constitute less than 1 per cent of the general population, eg people who drink hot chocolate mixed with peanut butter every Saturday night, then it is unlikely that they can be found quickly and economically, or convened in a central location. It is important to establish the penetration of the proposed sample in the population as a whole, so as to make sure 'up front' that the sample is achievable.

Interviews are arranged at the client's rather than the participants' convenience

Often the client company want particular times to view research groups, especially on international projects when clients may be flying in from different countries. However, recruiting full-time workers for daytime groups mid-week, for instance, is simply not feasible. A compromise is needed to ensure that interviewing is scheduled at times that participants can attend.

Recruitment lists may be out of date

Where the penetration of particular samples within the general population is low, lists of potential interviewees and their contact details are sometimes provided by clients. In theory this is useful and should cut down on recruitment time. However, these lists need to be treated with caution. In general they have not been gathered for the purpose of recruitment but for some other reason, such as customer mailings or collating sales data. Details are often missing and the lists may be out of date. It is usually safer to assume that these lists are inadequate until proved otherwise, although they can sometimes bolster 'cold' recruitment.

People have complex lives

Sometimes we ask recruitment questions that are just plain silly. How many times have you bought Gold Blend coffee in the last six months? No sensible person could answer this accurately – there are many more important things to remember in life. Equally, vague questions such as 'What is your favourite brand of soap?' imply that the individual thinks in terms of 'a favourite', that he/she has one, that it remains constant over time, that he/she can remember the name... and so on. It is easy to lose touch with common sense and see consumers as an alien species. We are all 'consumers'. It is worth running these screening questions past ourselves. If we cannot readily answer the questions, then it is doubtful that those who are less 'marketing motivated' will bother to do so.

Questions can be intrusive

Would we want to confess to a complete stranger that we suffer from incontinence or that we eat three bars of chocolate a day (although we are obese), or that we are recently divorced? People will massage the truth, in order to feel more comfortable. Can we blame them?

We need to consider how people will interpret the question? Will they be embarrassed? Would it be better to recruit them in a different way? Online? Through support groups? Through GPs? Through colleagues or friends? We need to think creatively about the best way to find research participants as well as considering the best way to explore the research issues with them.

Recruitment standards

There is much discussion within the research industry about poor recruitment. In the UK it is considered good practice that research participants are excluded from being interviewed more than once every six months – and they must, of course, fit the recruitment specifications. Nonetheless, there are times when they are not 'on spec'. Recruiters may nudge the recruitment criteria or research participants may lie about their habits or attitudes. Occasionally this is deliberate deception by recruiters and research respondents, in order to increase throughput and income. Research agencies need to be constantly vigilance for recruitment fraud. However, inadequate recruitment is more often a function of the unreasonable demands placed on recruiters. Insufficient priority is given to recruitment and consequently too little time is allowed for it. Not delivering the interviewees, or delaying the fieldwork, is simply not an option – the viewing facility is booked, the client and researcher are lined up, decisions have to be made – so the recruiter does what is possible in the time.

Online recruitment

Another option, preferred in some countries, is pre-recruitment online to a general database. Participants are screened on a wide range of criteria and the data is stored, so that when a recruitment spec arrives half the work is already done. The recruitment agency has a pool of background data on each participant and can more easily match individuals with the recruitment spec. This recruitment method depends on participants having internet access and being active online. It is therefore only feasible in countries where there is heavy penetration of online usage. This method is likely to become increasingly popular, as demand for qualitative research grows whilst it simultaneously becomes more difficult to recruit research participants. However, it may be that some social groups, such as low-income, high-mobility individuals, will still be difficult to access in this way.

Recruitment for ethnographic studies

In addition to the issues discussed above, there are a number of specifics that relate to ethnographic studies. As Desai (2002: 37) points out, observation and ethnographic methods may require considerable time commitments from participants. The researcher enters the participant's life for hours or even months. This raises a number of issues between researcher and participant. Participants need to be carefully screened and selected to ensure that they are clear about the level of commitment and what is required of them. Privacy and ethical considerations need to be addressed during the recruitment process. Therefore, recruitment for ethnographic research is likely to require more involvement and management on the part of the research agency if it is to successfully access – and retain – the right participants.

Recruitment for digital medium studies

Perhaps surprisingly, online qualitative research methods have not proved to offer the cost savings that were originally envisaged, largely because of the additional costs involved in setting up the project (Desai, 2002: 107). Although one of the biggest advantages of online research is being able to bring together geographically dispersed populations, recruitment usually includes offline screening (Desai, 2002: 113) because this increases response rates significantly. Building online communities, for example, is difficult (Comley, 2008). It is early days and time will tell whether recruitment methods will develop that are both cost effective and reliable.

Guidelines for best practice in recruitment, developed jointly by the UK Association for Qualitative Research (AQR) and the UK Market Research Society (MRS), can be found at http://www.aqr.org.uk/refsection/recruitment-bestpract.shtml.

RESEARCH VENUES

The venue in which the research takes place inevitably has an influence on the ways in which people respond and what they are comfortable expressing. There are two somewhat contradictory trends in terms of venue choice. There is a move toward ethnography in the belief that, if we are interacting with people on their home ground, then the research is more authentic. Simultaneously there is greater use of viewing facilities – which arguably are less authentic – because of their greater convenience for clients.

Viewing facilities

Facilities have thrived because clients can observe the research through one-way mirrors whilst remaining invisible. Most facilities around the world are centrally located in large towns or cities. To different degrees they are technologically well equipped, so that groups can be video and audio recorded and/or web-streamed to other countries, if necessary. Meetings can be convened before and after the sessions, so clients have the space to discuss research outcomes immediately after the session has finished. Perhaps most importantly, clients can see for themselves how research participants talk about their products or services and respond to ideas, concepts or other materials that are being researched. Actually experiencing the research in this way can enable clients to feel what participants are expressing in a way that may be difficult if they are hearing about it second-hand in a research presentation.

Viewing of groups can therefore become quite seductive, but it has its downsides. It is easy for clients who are watching the group to believe that this is all there is to the research, ignoring the rigorous analysis and interpretation that is needed in order to fully understand what it all means. Viewed groups are different from non-viewed groups. Viewing changes the dynamic between the moderator and participants; there is more performance and more structure to the session, both of which can subtly change the emphasis and the outcomes.

The trend towards ethnography

The move towards ethnographic research (see Chapter 6) has resulted in more careful selection of research venues, in order to facilitate context-specific interaction. For many years depth interviews and discussion groups have been carried out in retail environments such as banks, supermarket 'accompanied shops', clothes shops or car showrooms, to enable participants to look at store displays or layout whilst they are being interviewed. Increasingly however, more imaginative venues are being used and, in addition, the research is likely to be less formally structured. The decision on the appropriate venue for a particular project needs to be taken in the light of the research methodology and the objectives of the research, so that all of these research elements support one another.

THE IMPORTANCE OF PLANNING

Getting to grips with the detail

Qualitative research is often frenetic: running to catch trains, participants who don't turn up, stimuli that don't arrive on time, too little time to prepare and not enough hours in the day. There is often a feeling of being out of control. In spite of this, it is really important to make time to get the detail right.

The briefing meeting is a good time to pin down the client team. What stimuli will be needed? Who will be providing them? How many sets will be needed? Where will they be delivered? At what time? There are probably more misunderstandings about stimulus materials than any other practical aspect of qualitative research. The researcher needs to familiarize themselves with the materials to be researched, so it's important to get them in good time.

It's obvious but... arriving late for fieldwork, when there is a client and a roomful of participants waiting impatiently, is one of the most stressful situations for a qualitative researcher. And then... is the audio and video equipment working? Are there spare batteries? Is the digital recorder turned on?

With groups or depth interviews, are the names and contact details for the research participants to hand? If not, how can they be contacted if they fail to show up? Who is responsible for bringing the participant incentives?

I offer these comments as one who has repeatedly sinned. I am still grateful, 20 years on, to Paul Edwards, then an ad agency planner, who travelled for three hours from London to Brighton with me to sit in on some group discussions I was running. I opened the art bag to discover that I had brought the stimuli for another project. Paul was extremely gracious and accepted my offer of dinner. He also travelled down to Brighton with me the following week to try again!

Updates

Some clients expect regular updates on the progress of a project, particularly if they are the end users and will be responsible for implementing the research outcomes. Researcher 'availability' is a high priority for these clients and it is usually better to be proactive and offer feedback spontaneously rather than be caught unprepared by a phone call. Other clients, especially if they are managing the process but not involved in implementing the outcomes, are happy for the researchers to 'get on with the job' and report back when it is completed. The first group become anxious if there is silence, the latter group may interpret regular contact as indicating a lack of confidence on the part of the researchers. It is best to establish up front what suits the particular client and agree on a schedule of contact.

Confirming in writing

It is important that the nuts and bolts of the research schedule are clearly communicated, in writing. Details such as the number of people in a group, what will happen if there are shortfalls or mis-recruitment and who will be moderating are best spelt out up front to avoid misunderstandings. Equally, specifying what is not included is sometimes important. In the course of the fieldwork, additions or changes to the research structure might be made. The researcher needs to make it clear, at the time, whether these 'extras' will incur additional costs.

MANAGING RELATIONSHIPS

Politics, panics and prophylactics

A research team, at its most basic, is a triangular relationship involving the client, the researcher and the research participant. In practice, however, it is rarely this basic. The triangle is often overlaid with other involved parties. The commissioning client (the primary contact for the research agency) may be located in the market research department. He or she may be buying research for an internal client who, in turn, may be reporting to a senior team or other group of stakeholders. The advertising or design agency staff may also be involved, because their ideas are to be researched. At the same time, the researcher will be liaising with the recruitment department in his or her own organization or an external agency, with the viewing facility and with transcribers, trying to ensure that the back up is timely and professional. Similarly, research participants have their own agendas: what they believe the research is really about, whether or not they feel comfortable answering certain questions, wondering who is behind that one-way mirror that everyone is ignoring. There are many different agendas circulating in a research project, most of which are covert. For the researcher, there is often a sense of entering the lion's den when, in innocence, he or she arrives for an initial briefing meeting with the client and encounters a line of inscrutable faces. As far as possible, the researcher needs to ascertain the real agendas before embarking on the project, whilst being aware that these agendas may well change during the course of the work.

The commissioning client often has the chief responsibility for choosing the research agency, so a lot hangs on his or her choice. This is a gate-keeper role, liaising between the various parties involved, all of whom need to be handled with tact and diplomacy. If the research 'goes wrong', the buck often stops at the door of the commissioning client. This can be a fraught role. Ideally, the researcher will appreciate the commissioning client's position and attempt to reduce the inherent anxiety, whilst at the same time maintaining the role of experienced but dispassionate researcher.

Working relationships throughout the project

The messiness of qualitative research

Qualitative research is, in a sense, anarchic. By definition, it is not tightly controlled. Research participants partially negotiate the agenda with the researcher by introducing topics that they consider important, and outcomes cannot be predicted. This can provoke considerable anxiety in client organizations, which is hardly surprising, given that careers, budgets and brand success may depend on successful brand launches or advertising campaigns. Clients worry. Will the research respondents behave themselves? Will the results support the marketing manager's hunch? Or the hugely expensive creative executions? Whose side is the researcher really on? Whilst clients often love the immersion in qualitative research and the spontaneity of it, they may at the same time feel the need to control the process. In effect, they may be wary of the very creative process that is likely to encourage a productive development of the project. Therefore, in spite of the allure of qualitative research, there is often a simultaneous push towards the reassurance and illusory certainties of a 'controlled' research environment.

Conflicting research models

Friction can surface in a variety of ways. A classic 'bone of contention' is the topic guide (often called the discussion guide). This is a tool used by the researcher to provide an interviewing structure. It is not a questionnaire. In the course of the group discussion, the researcher may change the order in which the topics are addressed, or extend discussion of some topics because interesting and unexpected conversations arise that are relevant to the research issues. An anxious client, however, may prefer the researcher to strictly adhere to the topic guide, because the client views it as a set of research issues to be systematically covered (Bayley, 2006). This can cause conflict between the researcher, who wants to interview in a way that he or she feels will be most productive, and the client, who fears that the research will be compromised and the important topics will not be covered.

Similarly, the client may ask the moderator, at the beginning of a group session, to ensure that the participants rank the ideas being tested or to rotate the ideas in a specific sequence and give each one equal exposure. It is easy for the moderator to feel personally criticized, to think that his or her competence in managing the group is being questioned. Equally, if the moderator does not comply, the client may feel that he or she has not understood the research brief.

These differences arise from conflicts between different models of research – a positivist versus an interpretivist model (see Chapter 3). Interpretivist models view research as a form of iterative learning, in which the researcher and participants jointly work on the research issues in a way that is improvisational and evolving. Positivist models assume an imposed structure and consistency of approach. If the researcher understands where the client's request is coming from (and so realizes that it is not an implied criticism), it is easier to enter into a dialogue with the client in order to clarify the research approach adopted and explain why it has been chosen. The two parties can then decide how to handle their different perspectives. In practice, most researchers adopt an eclectic approach in which both positivist and interpretivist elements are happily mixed in order to better address the research issues.

Conflicts due to the model of research used are particularly common in international research because of different cultural research norms. As Ereaut (2002: 13–14) puts it:

> The addition of an international dimension multiplies by a large factor the problems of cultural translation inherent in qualitative market research in general, necessitating more layers and points of mediation... Client needs and assumptions must be translated, literally and culturally, for local markets and local researchers.

Shifting roles

The extent to which the client is involved in the research process between set-up and presentation has changed over time. Historically, clients often had limited contact with the research process between the briefing stage and the presentation; the fieldwork was regarded as the researchers' territory. However, times have changed. Nowadays, the client is often actively involved in the fieldwork, as observer or participant, and is likely to have input into, or actively participate in, the research process as it goes along.

Viewing facilities have grown hand in hand with clients' interest in experiencing the research, not just hearing about it 'second-hand'. Ten or more clients can simultaneously view group discussions and discuss the content as the group progresses. Equally, ethnographic techniques have grown in popularity because they enable clients to become immersed in 'the consumers' worlds'. There is greater fluidity, both in terms of research methodologies and in terms of where the research expertise resides.

This blurring of consumer and client worlds is sometimes heralded as a new model of research in which there is increasing overlap between the different roles of research participants, researcher, client, ad agency and others, and a greater emphasis on collaborative research and co-creation. In this model, all parties can potentially contribute to all phases of the research. The traditional dividing line between the roles of consumer and client (in all its forms) becomes porous and the customers are actively involved, working with the client to develop products and services. Whilst there are moves in this direction, it is too early to know how far this will develop and whether co-creation approaches will be limited to certain product areas or certain target audiences.

The effect of viewing facilities on researcher–client relationships

A factor that has contributed to increased client involvement in the research process is the prevalence of viewing facilities. Historically, particularly in the UK, group discussions were conducted in a recruiter's home, located close to where the research participants lived. At most, one client was allowed to 'sit in' on a group discussion. The client was positioned outside the research circle and not permitted to interact with participants until the end of the group, when he or she might be invited by the moderator to ask questions. The underlying assumption was that the moderator ran the group in an unbiased way from a position of research expertise. Clients were not regarded as research experts and were thought to be inevitably biased by their inside knowledge of the market.

The United States and most other countries moved away from this home-based model much sooner than the UK, and adopted viewing facilities as the norm. However, home-based interviewing is still fairly common in the UK, because it is considered less contrived than a viewing facility and likely to generate more honest and authentic responses. Many UK qualitative researchers question the use of viewing facilities on a number of grounds. Participants are shipped away from home to an event in which they are encouraged to perform for the audience behind the mirror. The moderator also feels the need to cater for client expectations, diligently following the discussion guide to satisfy the clients for example, instead of pursuing interesting areas of inquiry. There is a tendency for inexperienced clients to accept the views that participants express at face value, without sufficient reflection or awareness of context. In particular, there is a temptation for clients to regard analysis and interpretation as unnecessary once they have direct experience of consumers.

Advertising development

As we discussed in Chapter 8, advertising development is a special case and perhaps the most contentious arena for qualitative research. Producing advertising of all types, but especially for TV, is extremely expensive. Mistakes are costly, and this generates a high level of anxiety amongst the development team. The researcher can easily find him or herself in the firing line.

Advertising development research involves, at the very least, participation by:

■ the client team – who may include brand / product managers, marketing managers and other senior managers, as well as the research / insight team;
■ the advertising agency – including planners (who map the research programme and liaise between the researchers and the account managers), the account managers (who deal with the business of the account) and the 'creatives' who develop the advertising ideas;
■ the researcher – or research team, if it is a larger project.

The ad agency has made a considerable investment of time, money and reputation, in producing advertising ideas. It may not want the ideas researched at all because it fears, with some justification, that consumers will not be able to adequately evaluate the ideas in their unfinished form. The agency certainly doesn't want the ideas 'thrown out' in the research.

However, the clients are anxious to produce a good advertising campaign and believe that research will help to minimize the risks; they want some assurance that they are 'on track' with the advertising, and consumer feedback, however incomplete, is a way of doing this.

The researchers, meanwhile, are trying to remain impartial, steering a course between these different agendas, being balanced, honest and constructive in their analysis and interpretation of consumer responses to the advertising ideas.

Much hangs on the outcome of the research and in this highly charged environment researchers can end up as 'piggy in the middle', damned by the ad agency if they dare to criticize any of the ideas, but duty bound to feed back the good, the bad and the ugly, because that is their job.

This role requires sensitivity and experience on the part of the researcher, both in terms of interpreting the reactions of consumers to the creative material and in communicating the understanding gained to the advertising agency and the client. As Gordon and Langmaid (1988: 8) point out, on no account should the qualitative research be positioned as a check on the creative team. The role of the research is to help develop better advertising.

In essence, the researcher needs to be constructive and not didactic. There is a lot of difference between slating creative ideas that researched 'badly' and looking at what can be learnt from the ideas, however 'bad'. Advertising development research, especially at the early stages, is exploratory, ongoing learning, not evaluation. Approached as a collaborative exercise between researchers, clients and ad agency, it is likely to lead to a more productive and less highly charged encounter.

In the final stages of advertising development research, the ad agency and client are heavily invested in the campaign, both financially and emotionally. There are likely to be many political undercurrents that the researcher is unaware of, so he or she needs to tread carefully, whilst ensuring the delivery of well-thought-out, balanced and useful recommendations, however unpleasant. Tactically, it is better to warn the client ahead of the presentation if the news is particularly bad, for instance if the strategy appears to be off-beam. There is also a need for realism. If the 'big idea' works and is on strategy, then the executional details may not matter.

Managing the research outcomes

Communicating the research outcomes to the client can be the culmination of the research project, when it all finally comes together. Alternatively it can be the OK Corral, in which covert power struggles suddenly erupt and the hapless researcher is gunned down in the crossfire. Whilst researchers cannot fully protect themselves against the bullets, judicious planning can help reduce the risk (see Chapter 14).

ETHICS

Ethics might seem a strange topic to include within a chapter on managing a qualitative project. However, the welfare of research participants and the confidentiality of participant data have long been enshrined within qualitative practice and codes of conduct around the world.

However changes in social patterns and in the nature of qualitative methodologies have meant that ethical codes have needed to be revised. Black and whites have turned grey.

It is common practice for research sessions to be filmed. The film may be edited and shown to staff within the client organization, to increase customer awareness, for training purposes or other uses. Research participants have to give permission for the video to be used in this way and the research agency must guarantee that the film will not be used for purposes that the participant has not sanctioned. However, with YouTube and other digital forums on which material can be easily disseminated, it is much more difficult for researchers to control what happens to the material. Strict measures are needed within the research agency to ensure that confidential materials remain confidential.

With the development of social networking sites, researchers face a quandary. Is this material 'private'? Can it be used for research purposes without the consent of the person who created it? Are blogs accessible to all?

Other questions have arisen in relation to deliberative research, in which participants are gradually educated about complex issues before being asked to evaluate them. The process of education, inevitably, creates bias that can be seen as prejudicing the research.

When the boundaries of research are blurred, for instance with participant researchers in ethnographic studies, ethical standards cannot so easily be defined beforehand but must be decided within the context and 'in the moment'.

These emerging techniques do raise issues that need to be continually addressed. For instance, recently revised UK Market Research Society guidelines state:

> The collection of personal data from social networks such as Facebook or MySpace must be done in accordance with the Data Protection Act 1998 and the MRS Code of Conduct, ie the processing of personal data may only occur with the informed consent of the individuals concerned (*MRS News*, November–December 2008).

13 The 'hidden' processes of analysis and interpretation

THE ROLE OF ANALYSIS AND INTERPRETATION

Analysis and interpretation (A&I) are the least talked about aspects of qualitative research. Often they are not given the time, attention and thought that they deserve, in spite of the fact that they are the 'heart' of qualitative research. This is mainly because A&I are 'out of sight'. Clients will be present at the briefing meeting prior to the fieldwork, at which the objectives, research structure and content are agreed. They may attend the fieldwork itself and will almost certainly be present at the presentation or debrief when the researchers communicate the research outcomes and the conclusions and recommendations. However, they are very unlikely to be present when the researchers analyse, interpret and make sense of the meaning of the research data and develop recommendations that will ultimately help the client's decision making.

Clients rarely question the way in which analysis is carried out, and it is often difficult for researchers to describe what is happening when they 'analyse raw data'. In fact, it is questionable whether there is such a thing as 'raw data' if you believe, as many qualitative researchers do, that we are 'interpreting' all the time during the research process – as in the rest of life – trying to make sense of what we are hearing, seeing and feeling, as the project progresses.

Part of the difficulty lies in the fact that analysis and interpretation are not only intellectual activities. They involve intuition, emotion, judgement, making use of past experience, forming connections between different bits of data, recognizing patterns, bringing together individual behaviours and attitudes to create larger themes or trends; A&I are intensely creative activities.

Arguably, the 'invisibility' of A&I is creating a slippery slope, particularly in today's time-poor culture. What cannot be seen is deemed not to exist. Take a hypothetical scenario. Clients are watching a group discussion through a one-way mirror. They hear what the research participants are saying and take this at face value because 'what you see is what you get'. They believe that they have found 'the answer'. What need for further time-consuming A&I, given business pressures? So the data alone becomes the answer and the A&I are redundant. This becomes the 'norm'. After a while, no one even realizes that there could be anything else; we forget that the data is capable of being transformed through A&I, that it can illuminate and inspire the client and provide direction and guidance that goes way beyond the scope of mere observation and description of research participants' attitudes and behaviour.

My personal view is that if we reach the stage where qualitative researchers are only moderators and data gatherers, then the heart of qualitative research has died. And, more pragmatically, clients will look elsewhere for inspiration. Understanding the contribution of A&I to good qualitative research is therefore essential for the healthy development of skilled qualitative researchers and for the industry as a whole – which means that the flames of A&I must be lit and fanned in each new generation of qualitative researchers.

The difficulty of articulating and writing about analysis and interpretation is reflected in the paucity of literature on the subject. To my knowledge, the only book that specifically addresses commercial qualitative analysis and interpretation is by Gill Ereaut, *Analysis and Interpretation in Qualitative Market Research* (Ereaut, 2002). For those who are interested in delving into this area in more detail, this book is strongly recommended. I have borrowed liberally from Gill's book in writing this chapter and also from Roddy Glen's chapter on analysis and interpretation in *Excellence in Advertising* (1996: 119–43), which is itself excellent. Both of these very experienced researchers have succeeded in making sense of much that we know and do intuitively as qualitative researchers but have not easily been able to articulate – and they have linked this understanding to relevant theory. So, what exactly goes on in A&I? Where do we start?

DIFFERENT MODELS OF ANALYSIS

There are, broadly, two models that can operate throughout a qualitative research project: the classical research model and the emergent model. Both are useful and they do not represent either–or scenarios. Crudely, you could explain the differences between the two as: the classical model is more concerned with structure and the stages of research and the emergent model is concerned with 'the relationship between concepts or ideas'; in other words, you either focus on the fieldwork and then the findings, or you focus on the ongoing research learning and the patterns that are emerging. Inevitably, elements of each model exist in all projects. For the sake of clarity, they are described separately.

The classical research model

This model views research as a linear, staged process (Figure 13.1). Once the research problem has been defined, then each stage is completed before the researcher moves on to the next one. Data are regarded a bit like 'things'. As researchers, we unearth and gather up the data as 'findings' that have been lying there waiting to be discovered. Then, when we have the data all neatly gathered, we can start sifting through, categorizing and organizing everything into a logical order. This will enable us to present a neat, articulate and structured presentation of 'conclusions and recommendations' to the client.

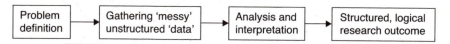

Figure 13.1 *The classical research model*

This model can be useful for new researchers to concentrate on, because it helps to delineate the different stages of the research process and create some sense of order out of the complexity of qualitative research. However, the model is not the reality; it is a sanitized, systemized version of reality. In order for the model to work, we have to create neat categories and then force people, brands, user-groups and so on into them. For instance, using this classical model, we might (fictionally) categorize Tesco shoppers as 'middle income, value oriented, sensible, down to earth', and Waitrose shoppers as 'up-market, quality oriented, foodies'. These are very useful marketing stereotypes, which provide direction for targeted marketing, but they are caricatures, not reality.

The emergent model

This model more accurately reflects the messiness of real life and the 'all-at-once-ness' of qualitative research (Imms and Ereaut, 2002: 8). In practice, human beings are frequently illogical and contradictory in their thinking. We do not think in straight lines. We make intuitive leaps.

Qualitative research, if it is to reflect the true nature of human beings, has to work with this 'messiness'. You could even say that it is precisely this messiness that is our strength; that it enables us to be creative and sometimes inspirational in our thinking.

Our brains are structured in such a way that we cannot just absorb data without influencing its content. The brain automatically makes meaning; that is its job. In practice, as thoughts and hypotheses spring into our minds, we may backtrack to re-evaluate and shift our previous thinking, then move forward, then back and so on. An emergent research process can be pictured as more of a spiral or a series of iterative loops, like a spring, rather than a series of clearly defined staging posts (Figure 13.2). The meaning emerges in this iterative process (Keegan, 2006: 668–71; 2009: 234–48).

In reality, all of the stages defined in the classical research model (problem definition, data gathering, analysis and interpretation) happen throughout the research process, rather than being sequential staging posts. It is virtually impossible not to move back and forth between different parts of the qualitative research process because this is how our brains work.

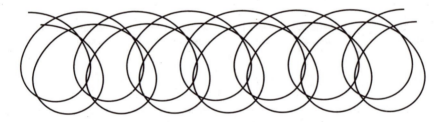

Ongoing thoughts, feelings, emotions (experience) – and also evaluation – shaping and being shaped by others and the environment. Knowledge or understanding evolving over time.

Figure 13.2 *The emergent model*

Emergence in action

Let's consider a couple of examples of this. When we first discuss the project with the commissioning client or the client team, thoughts from previous projects that were similar may jump into our minds unbidden. We may ask the client questions to clarify the research issues, and these might start a conversation that results in a re-think. It may shift the client's thinking, so that the research is defined in a slightly different way, or the emphasis within the different target audiences to be covered in the research might alter. This may have implications for the way in which the research is carried out, or how the topic areas are introduced.

Later, in a group discussion, say, we are interviewing research participants. We are aware of the overall research objectives and both consciously and unconsciously forming hunches or hypotheses, feeling confused or curious – all of which is part of the process of making meaning out of the ongoing conversations. Initial hypotheses are refined or give way to multi-faceted hypotheses as various early hunches or possibilities are tested and discarded. The initial stages of research are therefore invaluable in providing insight that helps to shape the gathering of further data.

> Initial group discussions with users of a mix of soap powder brands highlighted important differences between users of Brand A and Brand B. A working hypothesis emerged: that brand A loyalists were fairly relaxed about cleanliness and regarded dirt as synonymous with a healthy attitude towards family life. Brand B loyalists, on the other hand, saw dirt as 'the enemy', something to be dealt with efficiently and thoroughly. These initial hypotheses led to a decision to separate brand users in subsequent research, so that the hypotheses could be explored in more detail. The initial hypotheses were confirmed and this eventually led to different targeting for each brand user group.

Initial stages of research can also highlight problem areas and researchers have to decide how these problems can be addressed in later research stages.

> In the case study on 'Developing a customer-focused strategy' described in Chapter 5, we conducted workshop sessions with high-net-worth individuals, who were keen to portray an image of success. We tried – and found it very difficult – to get beneath the positive, upbeat surface that participants presented. However, we strongly suspected that there were anxieties lurking beneath the surface. After discussing this, my research

partner, Rosie, and I decided to be more forceful in the next workshops. We changed the structure of the sessions and asked participants to draw pictures of 'If everything went wrong'. This was an individual task, although conducted in a group context. The unfamiliar non-verbal activity (they were very comfortable with talking 'success') combined with a personal focus enabled us to break through into more personal areas and, as a result, to reveal a wealth of anxieties and fears of failure that illustrated the old axiom, 'The bigger you are, the harder you fall.'

These are examples of emergence in action. The researcher may use preliminary analysis to review the research questions and to provide focus for future fieldwork. The nature of the data gathered therefore evolves over time.

Emergence in conversation

Maybe this is all sounding too theoretical. Let's bring it back to a 'real life' situation. In this truncated, familiar, dialogue – a reconstruction of many research interviews – we can clearly see the ongoing, circular processes of moderation, evaluation and development that typically happen:

Participant: No, I don't like that [advertising concept].

Researcher: What is it you don't like about it?

Participant: Well, the woman, her manner. She's too… well too…

Researcher: Too what?

Participant: Too sexy. Too in-your-face.

Researcher: And what about the ad, as a whole, how does that strike you? What's happening there?

Participant: Well, she dominates it, so I don't like it.

Researcher: And if she was different…?

Participant: With a different woman, it would be different.

Researcher: In what way would it be different?

And so on….

This seemingly 'bread and butter' conversation is, in fact, the process of emergent A&I in action. The researcher and participant between them explore the parameters that might change the meaning of the advertising concept. The process is by no means accidental or undisciplined. Each utterance brings forth a response from the other person that slightly shifts the conversation (Mead, 1962: xxi). This response, in turn, elicits a further shift in direction and meaning in the conversation – and so on. Together, the researcher and participant construct a useful way forward (Keegan, 2008: 28–44). This is emergent inquiry, which is quite different from a process where 'data' is first gathered and then structured and presented as a body of fixed knowledge.

The point I am trying to make is that, in real life, A&I happens throughout all stages of the research process, from the time the researcher first picks up the phone and the client explains what the research is about until the project is completed, and arguably after this. A&I is a state of mind, a way of constantly reviewing and evaluating the research process, and for this reason I prefer the description 'qualitative thinking', because qualitative research seems too limiting. It is what the sociologist Judi Marshall (1999: 155–71) refers to as 'living life as inquiry'.

SPECIFIC STAGES OF ANALYSIS AND INTERPRETATION

Although A&I are integral to all stages of the qualitative research process and are, in fact, the heart of qualitative thinking, it is also true that, after the fieldwork and before the presentation, there is a stage when A&I are prioritized over other research activities. This is the stage when the researchers immerse themselves in the data: all the tangible outputs from the research (transcripts, notes, photos, drawings, diaries etc) and, of course, their own accumulated ideas, knowledge, hypotheses, opinions and feelings about the research questions. The task is to create meaning and structure that incorporate the research 'answers', provide conclusions and recommendations, and highlight the implications for the client.

Where to start? What to do with the mass of materials that have been produced? How is all of this data transformed into a client presentation that will be new, interesting, insightful and useful to the client and that he or she can use to build on existing knowledge?

Analysis and interpretation are often treated as one activity rather than two. As Ereaut (2002: 54) points out, the definitions are slippery and inconsistently used. Often the terms themselves are used interchangeably. It is possible, though, to make a loose distinction between, on the one hand, analysis as a process of 'sorting' data (transcripts of interviews, pictures, diary material etc) and looking for themes, and on the other hand interpretation, which is 'filling in the gaps': making links, observing patterns, creating overarching working models or theories. In practice, however, it is difficult to separate analysis and interpretation and deal with them sequentially. While the researcher is reading transcripts and searching for themes, almost inevitably certain insights will pop up out of nowhere or some interesting hypothesis will emerge.

'Sleeping on it' is not just an old wives tale. 'Incubation' is the process by which we can solve problems without consciously thinking about them. Insights or ideas 'well up' as if from nowhere. Parnes (1967: 38) gives the example of a little girl who had been trying for days to reinsert a cord belt into her pyjamas (this was written more than 40 years ago). One day, when getting ice cubes from the freezer she had an idea. She would wet the rope, make it into a circle and freeze it; then it would be easy to slide it through the opening in her pyjamas. I'm sure we can all contribute our own examples of incubation.

Getting to grips with A&I

For new researchers, data analysis and interpretation are often seen as the most enigmatic and daunting aspects of qualitative research. There are hours of tapes or pages of transcripts, there may be drawings, video, diaries, notes. It can seem overwhelming. On the other hand, no matter how much data one has, there is always the fear that there may not be anything of importance. Over time, as researchers become more experienced, they learn to 'trust the process'. Even when the fieldwork is finished and the experienced researcher still feels very unsure about the directions that are emerging, there is confidence that, with time, hard work and a dose of inspiration, 'the answers' will become clear.

In order to try to make the processes of A&I simpler and more comprehensible, they have been broken down into a number of stages, outlined below. This has been done to clarify the processes although, in reality, they do not exist in this tidy state. As discussed above, our brains move in mysterious ways and cannot always be corralled into a regimented approach!

A&I are intensely personal processes and, over time, researchers develop ways of doing them that work for them, as individuals or within their research group. Different researchers approach this stage in different ways; some adopt a very structured approach to analysing and coding data, whereas others regard it as an iterative process of making connections and forming hypotheses, in which they constantly return to the raw data to validate and develop their ideas.

In the early stages of learning to analyse and interpret data, it is probably useful to adopt a more structured approach, and from this an individual style will develop over time as a process of trial and error. Regardless of the qualitative research methodologies that are being used, the analysis involves a number of common features.

Gathering and organizing the data

Data takes many and various forms, which can include any combination of the following and many others as well:

- Audio or video recordings of interviews/discussions, which may have been transcribed, or lengthy ethnographic video recordings that need detailed coding.
- Notes or drawings made during ethnographic work or in the time between group discussions, or possibly notes made from follow-up phone interviews or e-mail contact.
- Visuals: these can be 'mood boards' produced by the client/ad agency and used to explore research areas; drawings made by research participants; or photos they have taken specifically for the research project or brought in from their photo albums; pages they have torn from magazines during the interview.
- Post-it notes, with comments participants have stuck on particular research stimuli.
- Video or written diaries, notes (eg on supermarkets participants have visited).
- Various projective materials that may be produced before, during or after the research sessions.
- E-mails, blogs, content from bulletin boards.

It is tempting, when a stage of the research – say two evening groups – has finished, for the researcher to gather up all the materials so he or she can get off home; materials can always be sorted in the morning. However, by morning it is difficult to remember who produced what. The researcher is faced with trying to reconstruct the previous night. Always tricky! It is essential that the researcher keeps the material generated from each sub-group in the sample separate, at least at the beginning of the analysis. It is worth planning ahead and labelling large plastic bags, for example 'Group 4, 25–34, Bradford'. At the end of the group, all the material goes into the bag and does not get muddled with material from the next group.

Recordings and transcripts

It is worth discussing audio recordings at this point because it is important to decide how these will be used. There are a number of options:

- The researcher may listen to the recordings and make partial or complete verbatim transcripts. At the same time, he or she may make notes in the margin: observations, thoughts, hypotheses, links with other interviews, emerging patterns.
- The recordings are sent out for full verbatim transcription and the researcher uses the texts for A&I. This means the recording quality has to be good and it also assumes that there is sufficient time for transcripts to be done (although nowadays transcription companies can often produce the texts overnight).
- Recordings can be listened to whilst reading a full verbatim text. This allows the researcher to re-experience the interview and make notes. The advantage of this approach is that it is multi-modal; the researcher can gain a greater appreciation of the 'non-verbal' part of the conversation, which is easy to underestimate when transcribing at the same time as listening. In practice, however, whilst this is the most thorough option, it is time and cost intensive and so it is rarely possible.

Pressures on researchers' time mean that few qualitative researchers are able to listen to all the recordings, and they usually work from a mixture of recordings, transcripts and the notes that they made during – or preferably immediately after – the interview. It is good practice to make notes, because they can capture the mood or spirit of the research session, which will help bring transcripts to life. They can also capture half-formed hypotheses, questions, confusion that can be picked up and explored in future sessions; these thoughts or ideas can quickly slip away as the researcher launches into the next session.

Ideally researchers should listen to at least some of the actual recordings. Re-living the conversation in a 'passive' mode (in the sense of not having to steer the interview, worry about covering content, maintain rapport etc) is quite a different experience from the 'active' mode of moderation. The researcher hears different things: the tone of voice, the expressions, the silences, the interaction, the excitement or the boredom. This non-verbal communication tells us as much as the words but, of course, it is missed in the verbal-only transcript. I am often surprised at the differences in take-out whilst running the group and when listening to the recording afterwards. A group that seemed relatively unexciting in the doing, can reveal subtle depths on re-listening. Sometimes the participants may have just been quiet, but focused on the topic. On the other hand, lively, fun groups that I enjoyed moderating can seem full of wisecracks and irrelevances on re-listening. At the end of the day, the enjoyment of the moderator and participants is a bonus, but it is largely irrelevant to the aims of the study.

Glen (1996: 119–43) suggests that the researcher should select recordings to listen to in which the views expressed were puzzling, and also those that were rich in comments and were particularly stimulating. He also urges caution to ensure that more vividly recalled data do not bias the outcomes, and points out that listening back to the recording has the added benefit of re-stimulating the thoughts that the researcher had during the original interview, which have often been lost afterwards.

Some researchers prefer to use video recordings to work from if these are available, because they provide some of the visual nuances of body language, which allow the researcher to get a fuller picture of the interactions within the group.

Whichever way the researcher chooses to use the audio or visual recordings, he or she will usually end up with a pile of transcripts and notes. This will also be true for much research that is not interview based. Ethnographic projects will be filmed, coded and notes taken, diary material needs to be analysed, pictures need to be interpreted by research participants and researchers so that they can feed into overall research findings.

Flagging up, making links and forming hypotheses

The fieldwork – or the particular stage of fieldwork – is completed, raw data have been gathered, so where do we go from here? Roddy Glen (1996: 119–43) identifies two principal problems:

- *Functional*: What to do with all the materials that have been accumulated during the fieldwork stages. How do you break down all the data and digest it?
- *Interpretative*: How to decide what it means. What to take literally and what to believe. How to decide what it all adds up to. And how then to relate it back to the structures the client can work with.

As Glen points out, 'there is no magic formula for coping with data, no unique prescription for success.' Each researcher has to develop his or her own way of working and this, in turn, will vary according to the nature of the project, the time available and the requirements of the client. During and after collecting data, researchers may have made notes of areas of interest; perhaps there are contradictions that emerge or areas of confusion.

Researchers often make a note of personal, conceptual or theoretical ideas that come to mind as they collect and start to analyse the data.

These may be hypotheses or similarities with other projects that the researcher has worked on. They may occur when writing up notes after observational work or when transcribing tapes. If more than one researcher is working on the project, then the researchers may compare notes or bounce ideas off one another and decide on areas to probe more carefully in the next stage of research and, subsequently, in the A&I.

A&I can be approached in a variety of ways, depending on the personal analytic habits of the researcher, the particular methodology being used and the theoretical position that the researcher adopts. At one extreme, amongst some academic researchers, the analysis of data can entail line-by-line coding of text in which researchers attempt to capture every nuance of language and tone. In conversational analysis, even the duration of pauses is measured and used as data (Puchta and Potter, 2004: 25–46).

Commercial qualitative researchers are more likely to adopt a holistic approach, which includes not just the words themselves but also attempts to understand the emotional content and the context within which the words are spoken. Researchers look for themes that will help them to understand how the participant or group of participants make sense of the particular area under discussion.

My personal method of A&I, evolved over 30 years, is fairly anarchic. With group discussions, I try to listen to all the recordings if there is time, and transcribe most of the content, adding thoughts, ideas and comments as I go along. With years of experience, I can do this quickly, Donald Duck style, as I speed up the playback and transcribe without pausing the recording. I find that, in the process of listening, selectively transcribing and jotting down thoughts, ideas and queries, the research questions start to answer themselves. Without my conscious involvement, themes 'pop up', rough structures form and representations that may eventually become themes or presentation charts come to mind. As they emerge, I roughly capture them and scribble notes alongside the transcript. I have learnt from experience to treasure these gifts from the unconscious. They frequently hold the key to understanding an important element of the research 'answer', although often I do not recognize their importance until later.

When the transcription is complete, I will construct a very crude set of what look like presentation charts. I always start by typing in the objectives of the research, in order to keep me on the straight and narrow. Then I construct a rough sequence of charts, from global issues (trends, frameworks for the particular market, participants' overriding beliefs about the research topic, cultural norms) to specifics (response to the new product or service) through to the research conclusions and recommendations. I do not worry at this stage about whether or not the content of these charts is accurate – it is too early to know. I am trying to preserve the ideas, in case they prove useful, and also to provide a rough structure to work within. If there are areas where I have no clue, then I will put in a chart with a heading (if I have one), but leave the chart blank. When Rosie, my research partner, and I sit down to make sense of all this, each with our rough 'presentations', we spark off one another, embellishing each other's thoughts, challenging them, feeding in supporting ideas, getting rid of themes that are inappropriate and returning to the transcripts to validate our hypotheses. This may take three or four hours. At this stage, exhausted, one of us will agree to put it all together into a draft presentation. We will then work on this, separately and jointly, until we are both satisfied that it is 'right'. It is very much an emergent approach to A&I, which works for us, perhaps because we have a long history of working together.

A structured approach to analysis

Roddy Glen suggests a more structured approach, which is probably a safer way to start. This involves the researcher devising a way of beginning to distil the content. This can be a quite simple system of comments and marks written in the margins of the transcripts, which can save time at later stages. It is crucial to regularly refer back to the objectives to ensure that these are constantly borne in mind when conducting A&I, as these form the agreed framework that must 'contain' the conclusions and recommendations. This process is one of immersion in the research data, but it is also the first stage of pulling out themes and patterns that will form the skeleton of the presentation, for instance recurring views or behaviours, minority viewpoints, a changing cultural climate, areas of concern. Glen offers the following example of the codes that might be used:

+ve	= positive response;
−ve	= negative response;
Q	= good quote;
comp-	= comprehension problem;
ident	= identification/relevance;
cyn	= cynical response;
pt	= prompted response;
??	= puzzling item/response;
rat	= rational response;
emot	= emotional response;
t/o	= main message takeout;
sm	= secondary message.

In addition, more interpretive notes can be added in the margin relating to the specific research issues that were addressed, for instance: 'story implausible', 'character disliked', 'humour works'. Some researchers will jot down embryonic hypothesis at this stage, such as 'needs to clarify message', 'make character more human'. When this stage is complete, the researcher will have done the groundwork on which the research outcomes can be built.

At this point, many researchers, transfer the notes made on the transcripts (or from the tapes) on to a very large sheet of paper, which Glen calls 'the tablecloth'. Each sheet delineates the sample sub-groups (columns) and the areas of discussion (rows) (see Table 13.1). Content can be literal or interpretative. The grid is then marked, ideally using different coloured pencils, to highlight response patterns, attitudes, behavioural traits and comments that appear to support or negate several of the emerging hypotheses.

From this point, it is possible to gradually build up initial hypotheses and conceptual frameworks, re-working and amending them through disciplined circling back to the raw data and 'tablecloth' data, until rigorous and usable conclusions emerge.

Very broadly, the processes of A&I can be viewed as a combination of 'small theory' and 'big theory'. The first stage is developing small theory, described above and in the first stages of 'Making meaning', below. It involves immersing oneself in the data: trawling thoroughly through it – within the parameters set by the research objectives – looking at each sub-group separately, making notes, adding questions, looking for themes and beginning to understand the connections and possibilities. Effectively it is content analysis. Small theory – the disconnected hypotheses and ideas that this spawns – are a spin-off from this content

Table 13.1 *The 'tablecloth'*

Topic areas \ Cells	25–34 BC1 South	35–50 BC1 North	25–34 C2D North	35–50 C2D South
Sector appeal				
Brands aware (spontaneous)				
Brands used/ in repertoire				
Differences between brands				
Brand A -- personality				
Brand B – personality				
Etcetera				

analysis. This is just the start. It forms the basis for the next stage: big theory – making meaning of it all in terms of the research objectives.

Moving beyond the data

Although there are occasions when the client simply wants a description of research participants' responses to the research issues, in general this is not enough. Description falls into the realm of reportage as opposed to interpreted findings, and focuses on specifics rather than drawing out more useful general themes that illustrate the relationship between consumers and the material being researched. In the 'lipstick' example below, the research objectives required an explanation of consumer responses and an evaluation of the appropriateness or otherwise of the advertising campaign. It is not enough to describe people's responses. The client wants to know if the campaign is likely to work with the defined target audience and, if so, what needs to be done to the campaign to maximize its effectiveness.

An agency is researching the development of a press advertising campaign for a new brand of lipstick. Research participants say that they dislike the ad. The researcher needs to understand why they have responded in this way; is this is a genuinely felt response (rather than say, irritation at cosmetic advertising in general)? What level of intensity is their 'dislike'? Is it to do with the style of the execution? Would some minor alteration change their response? Did one vociferous participant set the tone and the others follow? Was it an 'order effect' (ie they particularly liked the previous press ad shown)? These questions all relate to 'small theory'.

The researcher must then 'hover above the small theory' and go beyond it. Assuming that the participants do indeed dislike the ad, the researcher must ask, 'Does it matter?' There are lots of examples of ads that research participants do not like but that nonetheless do a good job for the brand because they demand attention, provoke controversy and raise the emotional temperature. Dislike of the ad is ultimately irrelevant. It is the reason for the dislike that will have a significant effect on the recommendations that the researcher will make to the client. The real question is: 'What does all this mean in terms of the client's proposed strategy?'

This is the stage that new researchers generally find most nerve-racking. Collating the data may be time consuming and frustrating, but it is also comforting and familiar. Making meaning is the stage when the researcher needs to let go of the data, interpret what respondents said (or did not say) and make sense of it all. Roddy Glen (1996: 119–43) describes this process as hovering above the data, once it is collated, ordered and differentiated:

> The ability to make intuitive leaps with confidence, once the data patterns have been assimilated, is a crucial part of the interpretative process and one that takes time and experience to develop. In interpreting qualitative data in this way, you should be courageous. You should trust yourself and believe in your own experience.

Making meaning

Qualitative research is all about meaning. Meaning is ascribed by people to things; things do not have inherent meaning, and the meaning exists because we construct it on the basis of our cultural knowledge and past experience. We know that the piece of rope strung across the garden is a clothes line; we know that the bright light in the sky is the sun; we know that sharp ringing noise is the door bell, because of our shared cultural experience. However, not all meaning is culturally determined. It is more difficult to establish the individual meanings that people place on things because these meanings are shaped by each individual's personal history. Simply analysing what people say does not always deliver the answer for a number of reasons, which Gordon and Langmaid (1988: 138) outline. Research participants:

■ are often inarticulate;
■ may be ambivalent, defensive or self-contradictory;
■ have not thought about why they believe what they do, or why they act in a particular way;
■ may not want to admit to others or themselves how they feel or behave;
■ bring beliefs about advertising and manufacturing to the qualitative interview that affect what they say they feel or do;
■ feel pressurized, intimidated or simply uncomfortable in the interview situation and environment.

In a group situation, it may be difficult to establish the true meaning of the research participants' relationship with the subject being researched because of the effect of group dynamics. Participants may 'follow a leader', become defensive or over-compliant, fight for leadership and adopt a critical stance. It is a truism that 'people don't always say what they mean or mean what they say.'

An experienced researcher will have an understanding of group dynamics, sensitivity to the group process and an awareness of body language, which enables him or her to interpret – to some extent – what the research participant really means. Over time, researchers also develop sensitivity to the conventions and taboos of various product fields, especially if they work in these fields frequently, which helps them to understand the real meaning of the communication.

In addition, as Gordon and Langmaid (1988: 139) stress, qualitative research is not a completely separate activity from the rest of life. In our 'normal' life we make sense of other people's conversations, behaviour, expressed and unexpressed feelings every day. We know when someone is interested or uninterested, bored or curious, by their body language. We interpret what is said in terms of the context. We are conscious of contradictions and inconsistencies. We note tone of voice. We listen carefully and make intelligent judgements about what is said or not said. Much of the 'making meaning' of qualitative research is a result of developing and honing these human skills to the point where they become finely attuned to the nuances of human communication.

Our job, as meaning makers, is described by Glen (1996) as:

> to build up a picture of each individual, and of how they affect and are affected by the interview situation. We then try to understand how they each view the things they are asked to consider (market, brand, advertising, packaging, propositions, etc) and to gauge the levels of enthusiasm, commitment, and sincerity with which these views are held. What do they seem involved with? What do they block? What 'language' do they use? How honest are they being? How consistent are they being? When are they being ironic or disingenuous, and when to take them literally?

The differences between normal meaning making and that which takes place in qualitative research is that, in the latter case, the meaning has a purpose that goes beyond simply understanding what is said. Qualitative research is concerned with the relationship between consumers and things. The task of qualitative researchers is to spotlight people's relationships with different things, so that our clients – who own or make those things – can better understand their meaning to consumers. This, in turn, enables researchers and clients to attempt to change the relationship between consumers and particular things.

For instance, take Coca-Cola, an instantly recognizable brand. It has a number of familiar brand attributes, positive and negative: young, funky,

American, lively, global, high sugar content, 'bad for you' and so on, which are very well established. These attributes can both support and undermine consumers' relationship with the brand. The importance of these attributes can also shift over time. For instance, the company might decide to downplay the 'Americanism' of the brand, because it is regarded as a deterrent to purchase in some markets. They might emphasize the global nature of the brand instead. If successful, this would mean that consumers perceive Coca-Cola in a different way and, ideally, develop a different relationship with the brand that would encourage them to buy it. The meaning of the Coca-Cola brand would have shifted.

Developing 'big theory' in terms of the research objectives

Once we have a clearer idea of the meaning that research participants attribute to the topics we are discussing (and it is important to re-emphasize that these stages are not neatly differentiated, as I have attempted to do here), we must ask, 'What conclusions can we, as qualitative researchers, draw in relation to "big theory" (overarching models of the market/area) and what are the implications in terms of the research objectives?'

We need to move beyond research participants' individual and collective verbal, emotional and physiological responses. This stage requires intuitive and imaginative interpretation, in which the researcher 'fills in the gaps', creating models or structures that help to explain the broader picture of consumer relationships with 'things' to clients.

In order to make these judgements, the researcher will draw on past experience. Most practitioners work in a wide variety of product fields. A process of cross-fertilization occurs, so that what has been learnt in a particular product field or with specific research problems can be very helpful in understanding what conclusions can be drawn in a different product field. The common denominator is people themselves and the researcher's understanding of human nature and behaviour.

THEORETICAL FRAMEWORKS

Theoretical frameworks can provide very useful models for illustrating and explaining how research participants relate to one another or to things. Some of these frameworks are well established and can easily be incorporated within qualitative research analysis. Other frameworks that help to encapsulate the relationships that exist within a particular market or system can be developed from scratch. In using these models, we are deliberately cutting through the messiness and confusion of real life that we discussed earlier, and creating a simplified and stylized picture in order to better communicate ideas, structures and theories.

Transactional Analysis

Transactional Analysis (TA) is an established model that is easy to understand (at a basic level), simple to use and can illustrate different human interactions. TA can be understood as three 'ego states', each of which represents one of the following aspects of our psyche: Parent, Adult, Child (Figure 13.3). They may be used singly or in combination (Berne, 1964: 28–32).

Put simply, these three ego states 'talk' to one another 'inside the individual's head'. The parent acts responsibly, likes to be in charge, rebukes where necessary. The adult is rational, in control. The child enjoys having fun or seeking gratification. To understand the dynamics, you just have to imagine the internal debate that goes on about eating that last chocolate éclair, as the internal parent and child fight for dominance: 'Yes, I will. No you won't. Yes I will.' Equally, these ego states come into play when we relate to others. For instance, we may adopt a particular stance, which can 'force' the other person to adopt a complementary position. If I lecture a colleague for being late for work (ie adopt a parental ego state), he might become resentful and sullen (moving into a child-like state) or he might calmly explain that his wife was ill and he had to drop her off at the doctor (adopting an adult state). Ego states can become stuck, so that they form recurring patterns. This often happens in one-to-one relationships (eg the henpecked husband and the bossy wife), but it can also happen in organizations or even in our relationships with brands. For instance, we might resent banks, because we feel they interact with us as if we were children, and then we act in a child-like way with them (unsanctioned overdrafts, overspending on our credit card).

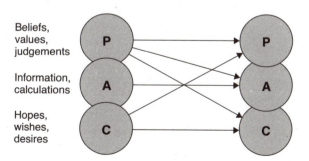

Figure 13.3 *Basic Transactional Analysis model*

TA in action

The case history below illustrates how TA was used to clearly differentiate two conflicting models of working within an up-market art gallery.

Senior managers in an art gallery chain wanted to review future strategy and, in particular, the way in which they worked with artists. A comprehensive qualitative research project was carried out by Campbell Keegan with a range of stakeholders. The element of the project that we will focus on below is the way in which the gallery staff, the artists, artist organizations, government bodies and the general public all related to one another. Over the course of the project, it became apparent that two quite distinct models of relationship existed.

As shown in Figure 13.4, The art aficionado model, some of the managers who ran the art gallery believed that their primary role was to support budding artists. Essentially, these managers adopted a parental role, including funding the artists 'up front'. However, some of the artists reacted in a child-like manner.

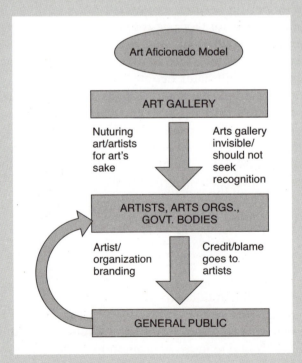

Figure 13.4 *The art aficionado model*

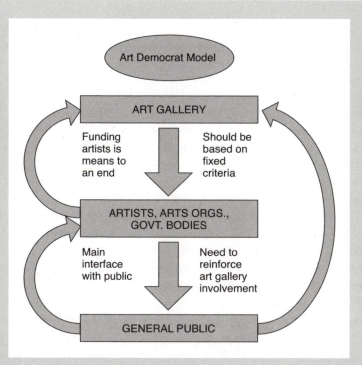

Figure 13.5 *The art democrat model*

Often the work that had been promised did not materialize or arrived late. There were no sanctions on the artists when this happened and the gallery often lost money. The artists who did succeed took credit for their own success with the general public whilst the gallery remained unrecognized. This model was generally good for the artists and provided some satisfaction for the managers, but was not particularly good for the long-term financial success of the gallery.

In Figure 13.5, The art democrat model, artists were given targets and delivery dates and there were sanctions if these were not met. Funding the artist was mutually beneficial to the artists and the gallery (the gallery and artist were jointly promoted). It was an adult-to-adult relationship and a more commercially viable model. Investment in artists was based on a judgement of their future contribution to the gallery. Equally, when artists were successful they were expected to contribute, both financially and in terms of promotion, to the gallery, so that both sides gained.

These two models of operation co-existed within the gallery culture and caused confusion and frustration, as they knocked up against each other. However, because it was a complex operation and even individuals did not consistently adopt one model of behaviour or another, it was difficult for the gallery management to identify where the problem lay. When, following the research study, the two models were presented to the gallery management team side by side, there was immediate recognition. There was an 'Ah-ha' moment, as the executive team suddenly understood why they felt they were 'swimming in treacle' much of the time.

The recognition of these conflicting models in operation – and the highlighting of the different TA ego-state relationships – allowed the management team to make a conscious decision about future strategy for the gallery. They decided to adopt a consistent art democrat model because this was more likely to achieve future commercial success. There was a period of uncertainty and unrest in the gallery as those who disagreed with this strategy came to terms with it, but the model provided a degree of clarity that allowed the organization to move successfully forward.

Developing models from the research data

Other models, which can be quite simple, provide an overarching framework for understanding a market or changes within a market. These can be developed from scratch to illustrate a global picture of particular behaviours or to illustrate trends within a market. For instance, the model shown in Figure 13.6 was developed to provide an overview of a range of different potential meeting/eating occasions. This provided the context for exploring the potential for savoury snacks within the specific sectors.

Equally, the model on page 226 (Figure 13.7), which illustrates the paradigm shift from a 'certain world' to a 'relative world', provided a backdrop for exploring the impact of fluctuating financial markets, changing employment patterns and social change on UK consumers. It was the 'broad picture' chart, which set the scene for more detailed discussion of high levels of anxiety amongst the UK population and how this affected consumer spending and saving.

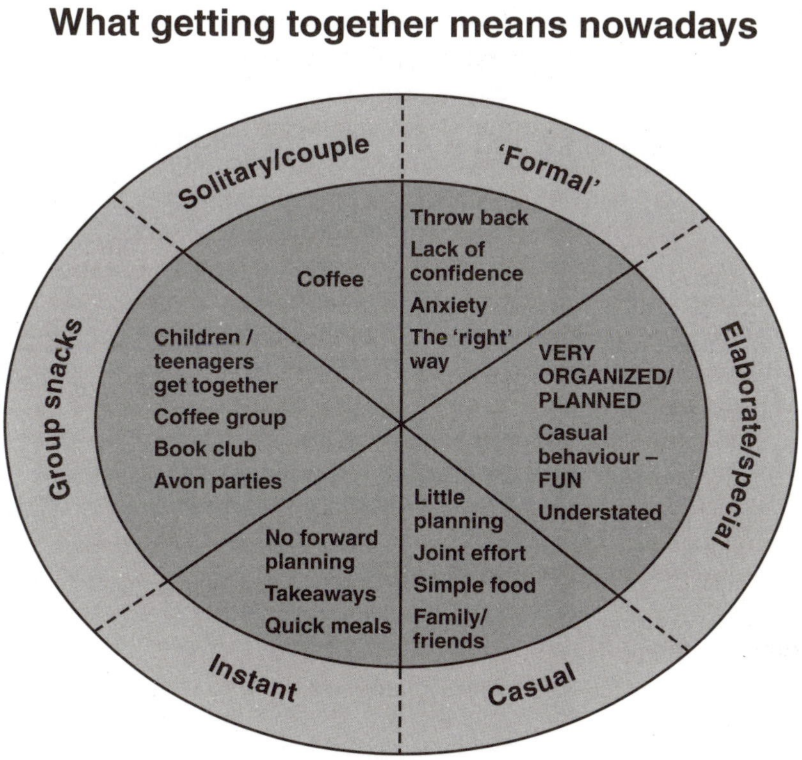

What getting together means nowadays

Figure 13.6 *Different meeting and eating occasions*

There are many ways in which these models can be constructed. The model in Figure 13.8 shows a spider map, based on consumer imagery of a (branded) milk drink. It illustrates the associations that consumers made with the brand. This model was later fed back into subsequent research as a visual prompt, to explore directions in which the brand might be developed in the future.

SATISFYING THE CLIENT AGENDA

At the end of the day, explaining how consumers relate to the world is not enough; the findings must be linked to the client agenda. Clients need to understand the ways in which consumers interpret the world as it relates to the client's products, services, brands, packaging, advertising, organization and so forth (in all its messiness, contradiction and complexity). Clients also need to know how they can best achieve their business or organizational goals through their understanding of consumers. This is

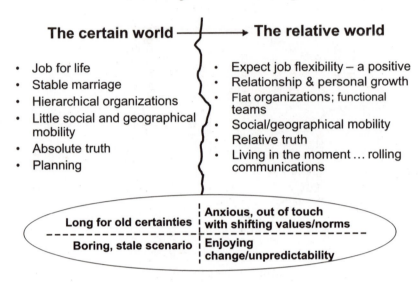

Figure 13.7 *From the certain to the relative world*

the purpose of commercial qualitative research, which must go beyond what people say, beyond what they mean, to develop conceptual frameworks, such as those illustrated above, that slot into the client's view of the world and enable them to see the research issues in a different way and/or a way that enables them to move forward and make appropriate business decisions.

The importance of experience

The best way to learn how to 'do' A&I really well is to hang around experienced qualitative researchers, watch what they do and, ideally, join them in the process. With A&I, as with driving, we can only learn so much by reading about it. The skill comes from doing it just as, for an experienced driver, the ability to drive is in the muscles as much as in the head. As I have stressed throughout this chapter, A&I is an ongoing process. In fact, I am often conscious, in the 'live' environment of the presentation when the adrenalin is flowing, that I am still making connections, still developing conceptual frameworks, responding to client questions that take the conversation and the thinking further.

Milka Imagery

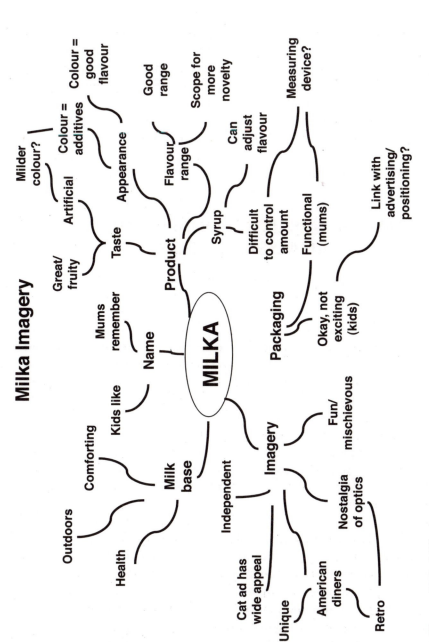

Figure 13.8 *Milka imagery*

Equally, learning as much as possible about how markets and organizations work – by watching advertising, examining packaging, observing customer service situations – is vital. As observers of consumer society and as consumers ourselves, we can learn a great deal by simply reflecting on our own reactions to the world around us. How do we evaluate products and brands? What makes a good consumer experience? What, precisely was it that made us feel welcome at our local curry house? Why exactly did we feel irritation when we phoned the energy supplier – was it the wait for an answer? What was said? The tone of voice? The lack of any result? Through familiarizing ourselves with the range of responses (practical and emotional) that are triggered by different types of human interaction – and the triggers themselves – we will be very well placed to intuitively recognize many consumer responses to similar situations.

COMPUTER-ASSISTED QUALITATIVE DATA ANALYSIS (CAQDAS)

At this point it is, perhaps, relevant to introduce CAQDAS, as a development that may have more relevance for commercial qualitative researchers in the future than at present. CAQDAS packages allow raw data to be sorted and categorized. For instance, text retrievers can highlight certain words or phrases in files, acting like Post-it notes. Code-and-retrieve can divide text into segments by theme or category and these can be placed in 'bins'. Code-based theory builders can allow graphic links between codes; for instance, taste, texture and colour could be subcategories of 'reasons for drinking the brand'.

CAQDAS is fairly widely used in academic qualitative analysis. Ereaut (2002: 127–39), quoting Nigel Fielding, an academic expert in the field, estimates that CAQDAS is used in 25–30 per cent of academic qualitative analyses. By contrast, CAQDAS is hardly ever seen within commercial qualitative analysis.

Why is it that commercial researchers have avoided using CAQDAS? Ereaut offers two explanations. First, she suggests that it may be due to a general antipathy to the use of computers in qualitative analysis, because they are associated with numbers/counting rather than ideas and thinking. They appear to be incompatible with creativity and sensitivity in interpretation, an impression exacerbated by computer terminology such as 'textbase managers' and 'conceptual network builders'.

Second, and perhaps more of an issue, is the fit between CAQDAS packages and commercial researchers' analysis needs. Ereaut (2002) highlights a number of reservations expressed by experienced researchers, including the centrality of 'code-and-retrieve' software, which assumes that categorization is always the starting point for qualitative analysis. There are concerns that this can lead to 'mechanistic' analysis, 'counting' of responses and overemphasis on the verbal – all of which could be counterproductive to good interpretive thinking. In the UK, in particular, emergent, holistic qualitative approaches to research are often adopted and these may sit uneasily with an overemphasis on coding and categorization.

There is little evidence that CAQDAS packages are being assessed more favourably by commercial qualitative researchers as they become more sophisticated, or that they are assuming a role within commercial analysis. Until packages move away from the code-and-retrieve model and offer a contribution to qualitative analysis as researchers practise it, it is unlikely that they will make major inroads into commercial practice.

14 Communicating qualitative research outcomes

The delivery of qualitative research outcomes or, more precisely, the way in which the researchers share their thoughts, ideas, hypotheses, learning, conclusions and recommendations with the client – in whatever format is appropriate – is critical to their acceptance and adoption.

As with analysis and interpretation (A&I), which is ongoing throughout the research process, communication with the client is likely to be continuous and there may well be informal feedback: phone calls, e-mails, interim meetings and, of course, client involvement in the fieldwork itself. This means that clients are likely, to varying degrees, to be familiar with the research content and this may affect the way in which the delivery session is handled.

There are three key areas to be considering when delivering research outcomes:

- *The content*: how the research narrative is constructed.
- *The delivery method*: the format in which the content is communicated.
- *The delivery style*: how effectively the research outcomes are communicated.

To some extent, these factors impinge on one another. For example, exploratory research might be best delivered in a workshop format, in which the team can use the session to further develop its thinking. On the other hand evaluative research, delivered to senior management, might require a formal 'PowerPoint' presentation.

Equally, an audience that is being introduced to the project for the first time at the feedback session will need more background information than if they had been actively involved in the process.

For convenience, I have used the term presentation generically in this chapter, to include all types of feedback unless I specify otherwise.

CONSTRUCTING THE RESEARCH NARRATIVE

Qualitative research presentations are always, essentially, a story: the movement of a narrative that makes sense to its recipients and gradually leads them to a logical conclusion that is both relevant, plausible and useful. This narrative is critical for the comprehension and acceptance of the research outcomes. A disjointed, unconnected set of findings will be difficult for clients to absorb and will lack credibility. If the researchers can find no obvious narrative in the research data, then they need to revisit their analysis and re-structure it in such a way that a story is created. They need to fill in the gaps, make more connections and develop overriding frameworks that make sense of disconnected ideas.

However, any old story will not do. The story needs to be constructed from the research data and it needs be anchored in two ways: it needs to be grounded in the research objectives and focused on the research outcomes (Lillis, 2002: 71).

The process of developing the story, as with all aspects of the research, starts at the beginning of the project and continues throughout the research process, but it is intensified in the A&I stage through the way in which we group our observations, the headings we choose in order to structure the data and the early narrative structure. Lillis talks about the importance of maintaining the balance between ongoing interpretations and keeping an open mind. 'Early storyline construction functions almost organically, developing and altering, with the input of further analysis and thought' (Lillis, 2002: 70). Different storylines can be 'tried out' for fit, and at some point the researchers will recognize a storyline that best fits with the data.

An essential skill that needs to be developed is knowing what to include and what to omit. Qualitative research produces a huge amount of data. Much of it is very interesting, but it may not be important in terms of the research objectives. The questions that need to be asked are: How relevant are these data? How do they support the story? In what way do they move thinking on? How do they fit with the research objectives?

On occasion, issues arise in the course of the research that are outside the original brief but have an important impact on the research issues. These need to be addressed, acknowledging that they are 'off side' but that they nonetheless add insight or understanding. Equally, objectives may evolve during the course of the project, and it is important to acknowledge this in the presentation and talk about how this has impacted on the outcomes.

Whilst the research objectives act as an anchor to ensure that the researchers stay 'on track', they are not a structure to be slavishly followed. Objectives are often presented as a list of information requirements that define broad areas, for example to understand women's relationship with dieting and weight loss; this is a complex, multi-faceted arena, which cannot be understood from a single perspective or in a linear way. The research objectives define the area, not the way in which it needs to be understood or the way in which feedback needs to be structured.

Reflecting on the story

Throughout the preparation of the research narrative, but especially when putting together the conclusions and recommendations section, researchers need to constantly reflect on the validity, accuracy and honesty of their judgements and opinions. As a general rule, we need to be more alert to personal bias when researching topics that interest us, because this is where it is most likely to occur. It is important to be passionate about understanding the research issues and addressing the research objectives, but dispassionate in relation to the subject matter.

Broadly, there are three screening stages that need to be applied:

- Is this feasible in terms of what the client can do?
  There is no point in making unrealistic recommendations. Rather, they should be framed in the context of the client's capabilities (Lillis, 2002: 72).
- Is my judgement sound?
  Can I honestly make this statement on the basis of the research data? How can I justify it? Could it be interpreted in another way? Do I need to go back and re-visit the data? How does this fit with my previous interpretations? And so on.
- To what extent might the research context have influenced the outcomes?
  Did the group situation produce hot-housed responses? Did participants change their behaviour as a consequence of being observed?

Did keeping a diary over-sensitize participants to issues that would usually be ignored?

The nature of the research objectives and the type of project will also influence the way in which the outcomes are put together. Geraldine Lillis offers a useful guide on the implications of different types of project for the outcomes that emerge, as shown in the box below (Lillis, 2002: 75).

The influence of project type on output delivery

Project type	Output implications	Specific issues
Broad market studies	Produce a wealth of detail	Content: Who needs to know what, when and in how much detail Delivery: Often several debriefs/presentations Detailed written output may be needed Crucial need to 'manage' data
Strategy development	Need to bring consumer 'alive'	Use consumer language
Executional guidance	Political minefield – be sensitive	Avoid adjudication Avoid painting by numbers
Qualitative pre-testing	Need to be concise and focused	Fast turnaround Stick to the brief!
NPD	Emphasis is on the positive and progressive	Interactive workshops Be visual
Evaluative and tactical	Don't assume it is straightforward/non-political	Be unambiguous

Reproduced by permission of SAGE Publications, London, Los Angeles, New Delhi, Singapore and Washington DC from Lillis, G. *Delivering Results in Qualitative Market Research* copyright (© Lillis, 2002)

Structuring the narrative

There is no definitive way of structuring a qualitative research narrative. However, there are certain basic principles that can be applied.

Crafting the storyline

This has already been discussed. The most important points to remember is that the storyline will probably not mirror the objectives (although it will answer them) nor will it follow the path of the discussion guide (although it will cover these areas).

Targeting appropriately

Clients spend time and effort targeting their products and services. We need to do the same, to ensure that the hard work we have put into the project is not wasted and that the client gets the maximum value from the research. This means making the outcomes comprehensible and fit to be acted upon. It may be useful to discuss the proposed structure with the commissioning client, to clarify what the audience wants and expects from the research (this may have moved on since commissioning).

A clear focus

As discussed, the narrative needs to lead to the conclusions and recommendations. Any content that is not contributing to this end should be discarded.

This is actually too bald a statement because, with exploratory research for instance, there may not be such focused goals and there is a risk of over-simplifying complex markets by omitting something that does not 'fit'. However, it is a reasonable default position – the researcher needs to question why an interesting but 'off narrative' section should be included in the presentation.

Broad to specific or specific to broad

It is common for the narrative to start broad, with the views, attitudes and beliefs of the target audience and then gradually home in on the specific research issues. This is a useful structure in that it provides an overarching context in which clients can locate specific research issues and make sense of the detail. This approach is particularly helpful for exploratory research because it encourages the audience to make their own internal connections with the research outcomes during the process, and also to explore ideas in the wider context of cultural and market changes.

An alternative approach is to start with the detail, for example the response to a specific advertising treatment, and then draw back to explain why participants responded in this way. This can be particularly useful in advertising development research, in which the strongest ideas are often discussed first in order to reduce audience anxiety.

The structure chosen will depend on the nature of the project, the audience needs, the level of anxiety about the project and how comfortable the researcher feels with the approach. Although either approach can be effective, what generally work less well is swinging back and forth between a broad and specific structure.

DELIVERING THE RESEARCH OUTCOMES

There are many options for feeding back research outcomes to client groups, both formal and informal, written and spoken. Informal feedback often happens during the course of the project, through e-mails and phone conversations, or immediately after the fieldwork. Formal, structured feedback generally happens after the A&I.

The delivery method differs by country. In the UK, the outcomes of most qualitative projects are communicated to the commissioning organization as a structured presentation (also called a debrief), supported by a printout of the presentation charts and other relevant documents. In the presentation, the researcher leads the client team from the objectives through the contextual issues and then focuses on the specific research issues (or conversely from the specifics to the general) and on to the conclusions and recommendations. Subsequently, a full written report might be required, but this is much less common nowadays, largely because feedback is acted on quickly and the report may be redundant by the time it is finished. The exception is some government-sponsored research where research reports need to be made available to the general public online.

Workshops are increasingly taking the place of formal presentations, especially for exploratory projects. These involve a more informal, interactional approach in which the research feedback is discussed and developed by the workshop participants. Workshops can also be useful:

- after a formal presentation, when participants have had time to absorb the feedback and are starting to consider the implications for their particular area of responsibility;
- to help client groups absorb and translate the research outcomes in relation to their specific work needs;
- when clients have been actively involved in the research process, are familiar with some of the themes that have emerged, and need to

progress their thinking and practical application of the research outcomes further.

In the United States similar terms for feedback to the client are used with quite different meanings. The term 'debrief' describes a short informal discussion of the researchers' top-line impressions, typically carried out 'on the road' immediately after each of the group sessions and prior to any formal process of transcription or structured analysis. Many US projects do not include a presentation stage although they often include reports: narratives of the fieldwork experience, with or without further analyses and recommendations (Imms and Ereaut, 2002: 108).

PREPARING FOR AND GIVING THE PRESENTATION

The chameleon role of the qualitative researcher

Strong communication skills are essential in qualitative research. The client needs usable outcomes that can bring about some sort of change in the thinking and/or actions of the client organization. The successful qualitative researcher knows how to deliver the research outcomes in a way that helps to fulfil the business objectives of the commissioning client. He or she needs to:

> [maintain] a constant balance between methodological purism and results oriented pragmatism, between the roles of disinterested researcher/ analyst and committed client agent/business partner (Lillis, 2002: 1).

Qualitative researchers are, by nature, chameleons. They need to be in order to communicate with a huge range of people from very different backgrounds. They must also be chameleons in the presentation of research outcomes. The researcher is, on the one hand, 'the voice of the consumer'; he or she has an understanding of the consumer's world that must be communicated, as far as possible, to the clients. However, this understanding needs to be translated – through the researcher's professional experience, market analyses and interpretation – into strategy that is useful to the client organization. There is a tension between these two roles and it is essential that the researcher maintains a foot in each camp, so that the connection between consumer and company strategy is not lost. If the conversation moves into areas in which the consumer has been 'lost', then the researcher must pull the meeting back to ensure that consumer attitudes and needs are taken into account.

Planning the presentation

Forward planning

Finding out who will be there

Ideally the client contact will provide a list of attendees, their job roles and involvement with the project. It is useful to identify the most senior person present – the person who ultimately signs off the strategy.

What is the style of the meeting?

Is it informal, with just two or three people, or is everyone in the department invited? Often this can change between the set up and the actual day, so it's worth checking.

How much time has been allocated for the presentation?

The researcher needs to prepare the presentation to fit the time available. If it overruns, senior managers may have to leave for another meeting just as the researcher starts on the conclusions and recommendations.

Is there a laptop/projector already set up?

If a laptop or projector is to be used, it is useful for the researchers to e-mail the presentation to the client so it is loaded up before they arrive. This reduces the stress of dealing with unfamiliar equipment. If the researchers are using their own equipment, it is important to arrive early to set it up before anyone else arrives in the room.

Does the client want hard copies of the charts/presentation notes?

Most clients are happy to have charts/presentation notes sent electronically, but if the researcher is asked to bring copies, it is best not to distribute these before the presentation; attendees will be tempted to turn to the end – and then they will stop listening to the researcher!

Keeping in touch with the client

It is useful to contact the commissioning client the day before the presentation, to give him or her a 'top line' so there are no surprises and anxiety is reduced. The client can also provide a last-minute update on attendees and any relevant politics.

On the day

What to wear

Whether we like it or not, how we dress affects the way people see us. We need to consider the audience and the impression we want to create. A meeting at an ad agency will require different dress from a visit to a client in the city. As the supplier, it is probably better to err on the side of being slightly over-dressed rather than too casual.

Introductions

It is good practice for the researcher to try to get everyone's names and to write them down. Non-verbal cues used in research sessions are just as relevant in this context; by smiling and making eye contact with individuals in the audience, the researcher becomes 'a person' rather than just 'the presenter', and this encourages the audience to be receptive and supportive.

Good housekeeping

The basic structure of the presentation needs to cover:

■ Stating the objectives:
  Some people at the meeting may not be familiar with the research objectives or stimuli. It is useful to outline these, without labouring them, in order to focus everyone's thinking.
■ Summarizing the research methodology:
  Again, this may be unfamiliar to some of the people present and needs to be briefly outlined.
■ Confirming the timing:
  The presentation is just one element in people's day and it is important to set the parameters.
  'I'm going to talk for about 45 minutes, then we'll have questions.' Or, 'We've got an hour, so if people want to ask questions as we go along, that's fine.' It is useful to establish the format with the commissioning client before the meeting.
■ Providing an overview:
  In that familiar maxim: 'Tell people what you are going to tell them. Tell them. Then tell them what you've told them.' In a complex presentation, it is useful to give a slightly more detailed overview of the structure that will be adopted.
■ Standing in other people's shoes:
  The researcher needs to understand the beliefs, concerns and hopes of the audience, as far as possible. This will help him or her to shape the presentation in such a way as to increase the chances of it being heard and acted upon.
  For instance, the creative who developed the ad campaign may be sitting in the audience. S/he is feeling anxious, defensive. Was the advertising OK? Brilliant? Did it bomb out? Meanwhile, the researcher is laboriously covering the background 'attitudes and

behaviour'. By the time the researcher gets round to talking about the advertising, the creative is irritated, frustrated and likely to take this out on the hapless researcher, especially if the news is not good. It is better to put people out of their misery in this situation. A quick summary at the beginning of the presentation will remove the uncertainty, allowing people to relax and absorb what is being said.

'One of the executions was very good in meeting the communication objectives, the other two were less successful. I'm going to talk about the two least successful ones first and briefly. There are good elements within them that could maybe be incorporated into the successful one. I'm going to talk about the successful one in more detail and look at how it can be developed.'

■ Beware of teaching the client to suck eggs:
When researching a subject area that is unfamiliar to us, it is easy to become over enthusiastic. The researcher needs to keep a cool head and an open mind. The subject may be new and exciting to us, but the client may have sat through numerous presentations that cover the same ground, and can become irritated by 'excessive coverage' of background areas. It is worth checking on the amount of background that is needed in the particular project.

■ Monitoring the mood:
It is important for the researcher to be alert to the mood in the room. The apparently passive audience is anything but passive; people are continually evaluating what the researcher is saying, referring to their previous knowledge, gauging how plausible he or she is and whether what is being said makes sense to them.

Are people looking bored? Are they sitting with arms and legs crossed? Looking out of the window? It is tempting for the researcher to ignore this and hope that he or she can get to the end of the presentation without challenge. But we ignore these signs at our peril because it is likely that this mood will intensify, so that when someone finally speaks up, their tone will be more extreme because they are pent up. Worse still, no one will say anything, but the company will never use the researcher again. It is usually best to deal with tension as it arises. If the researcher senses resistance to some of the content, it is best to invite interaction: 'Does that make sense to you?' 'What are your feelings about this?' 'Does this fit with previous research?' Dialogue will enable the researcher and clients to explore differences in perception, which may lead to further understanding of the research issues.

■ Presenting research as learning:
Presenting good news is easy. Everyone wants to hear it. Presenting bad news is less easy and needs to be carefully handled. I am not suggesting that the researcher should hide or dilute negative findings.

Bad news has to be told. However, the way in which negative outcomes are communicated plays a large part in whether or not they will be accepted and acted upon – and it is the researcher's job to convey feedback that is useful and forms a basis for action.

All research is a process of exploratory learning. Learning what does not work can be as important as learning what does. Where negatives or weaknesses have to be communicated, they need to be couched in terms of learning, where possible. For example; 'The fragrance is viewed as sophisticated, womanly, for someone quite confident and self-assured, but this packaging is seen as quite girly, flowery. There's a dissonance here. It's important to reinforce the existing positioning, rather than dilute it.'

■ Using all the senses:

We discussed how different people favour different senses in Chapter 7. Some people are more visual, others more auditory or kinaesthetic. Ideally the presentation would include a range of sensory styles. 'Changing senses' can also ensure that everyone is paying attention. After 30–45 minutes with no audience participation, even the most dedicated attendees will be starting to flag.

Playing video clips, showing the stimuli used, even a coffee break, can shift the mood and re-energize people. In particular, showing research participants' drawings or collages often has a quite electric effect. Clients get out of their seats, keen to study them, see what they mean. It feels as if the target audience are there in the room. I often photograph participants' drawings and collages and include these in the PowerPoint presentation, but I have started to bring the originals along to the presentation because they are raw, tangible, 'unprocessed' evidence of the research – and more interesting because of that.

The much-quoted 'death by PowerPoint' unfairly maligns PowerPoint; it is not PowerPoint that is at fault. PowerPoint does not excuse us, as qualitative researchers, from trying to make our presentations as interactive and creative as possible and from including the audience in the discussion. In fact it can even help us. Charts need to be simple, engaging and part of the ongoing narrative. They can also include projective materials; verbatim quotes, completed thought bubbles and consumer drawings to bring research issues to life.

■ Reinforcing the message:

As the end of the meeting approaches and adrenalin drops, there is a tendency for the researcher to tail off. It is important to maintain the momentum. The last 10 minutes are important. This is the time for tying up loose ends and reinforcing the key messages of the presentation. Summarizing and reinforcing the conclusions and recommendations will ensure that the audience leaves the meeting with the key themes top of mind.

SOME EXAMPLES OF PRESENTATION CHARTS

Clearly, the best way to understand how qualitative understanding can be effectively communicated is to see a qualitative researcher in action in a feedback session (presentation, workshop, informal chat) with their client. As I cannot deliver a live presentation in this context, I have included a few presentation charts to give a flavour of the way in which the researcher can introduce consumer language, thinking and psychology, illustrate target market attitudes and behaviour, encapsulate a research theme, illustrate market mapping and so on. Different research companies will have different styles of presentation.

Understanding the social context for entertaining at home

Sometimes introducing quotes from research participants – sparingly – conveys attitudes more convincingly than when mediated through the researcher.

How 'socializing' is changing

'No, not formal and stiff, but yes, authentic and elaborate. No minding your Ps and Qs. It's not pedestrian, or only for show. It's functional and appropriate. Big white napkins but no napkin rings. No Indian steel goblets with curry. Good red and white wine. No worrying about pudding first, or cheese. We all muck in – duck and dive. But yes, I do a huge amount of planning and preparation' (Fraser).

'I don't do formal, formal. We used to when I was married. It was sit down, couples and that was it' (Maureen).

Figure 14.1 *How participants view socializing*

Exploring perceptions of the fitness market

Before launching a new brand into the market place, it is important to clearly understand consumer attitudes within the sector.

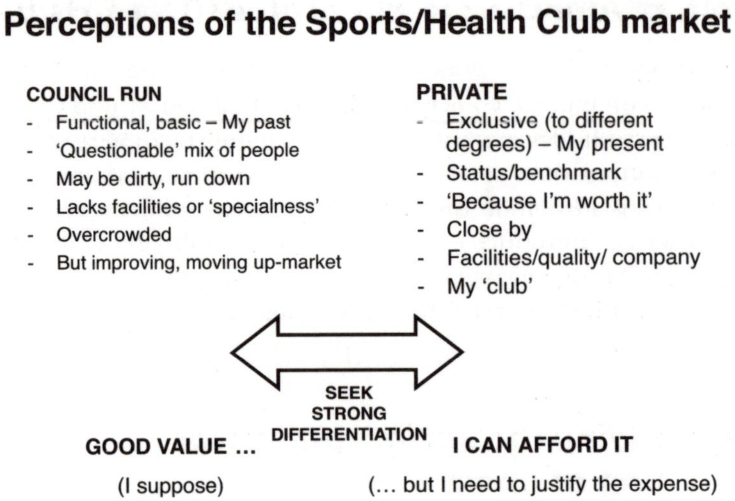

Perceptions of the Sports/Health Club market

COUNCIL RUN
- Functional, basic – My past
- 'Questionable' mix of people
- May be dirty, run down
- Lacks facilities or 'specialness'
- Overcrowded
- But improving, moving up-market

PRIVATE
- Exclusive (to different degrees) – My present
- Status/benchmark
- 'Because I'm worth it'
- Close by
- Facilities/quality/ company
- My 'club'

SEEK STRONG DIFFERENTIATION

GOOD VALUE ...   **I CAN AFFORD IT**

(I suppose)   (... but I need to justify the expense)

Figure 14.2 *Setting the context for positioning a new sports club*

Understanding how consumers categorize chocolate brands

This basic template can be a starting point for exploring the nuances of individual brands and where a new brand can be best positioned.

Brand positioning

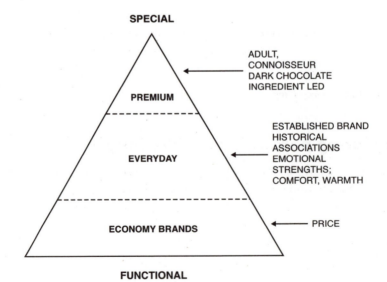

Figure 14.3 *Mapping chocolate brands*

Exploring young women's attitude towards body hair

These charts are part of an exploratory study aimed at understanding contemporary attitudes towards body hair amongst young women. This is a tricky area to explore, given the social taboos that exist and the rapid changes that take place in attitudes and behaviour during the teenage years.

The transition from girl to woman

	14 – 15	16 – 17	18 – 20	21 - 24	
Leaving Child-hood	• Changing body • Emotional upheaval • Fear of 'being different' • Strong feminine stereotyping • Comfort of girlfriends	• Socializing/ boys • 'On your own' • Knowing the rules • Establishing a 'style' • Celebrity following • School pressures	• Pressures of dealing with the outside world • Life choices • More comfortable with individual style • Grooming habits established	• Confidence in 'womanhood' • Pragmatism often strong • Convenience, quality, efficiency, are important • Priorities shift; work, partner, family • Time pressures	**Grown woman-hood**

Strong societal trend towards 'perfection'

Figure 14.4 *The context for developing a teen-targeted product*

Concerns of girls 16-17

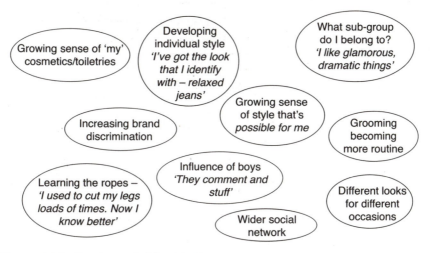

Figure 14.5 *Concerns of girls, 16–17*

How young women feel about removing bodily hair

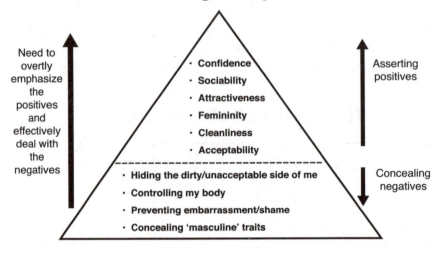

Hair Removal: Changes in perception by age

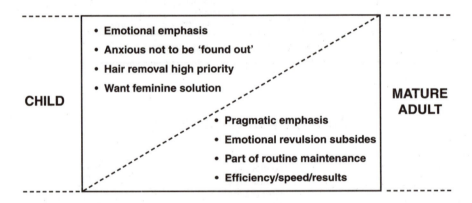

Figure 14.6 *Presenting an overview of the market*

15 Multi-country qualitative studies

THE GROWTH OF MULTI-COUNTRY STUDIES

Qualitative research projects are conducted worldwide, either initiated and conducted in one country, or as multi-country studies, coordinated from one lead country, with a commonality of research design. The five largest markets (based on total research spend) are the United States, UK, Germany, France and Japan, although emerging markets are expanding faster from a smaller base. Fourteen per cent of total global research spend in 2007 was on qualitative research (Esomar, 2008).

Multi-country studies, in which the same research structure and objectives are used to conduct linked projects in two or more countries, really took off in the late 1980s and grew throughout the 1990s. The birth of globalized marketing and the aim of global companies to sell their products and services worldwide meant that multinational studies were needed. At that time, the thinking was – largely – that the same products and services could be marketed worldwide, under the same names, packaging and advertising, and this would create efficiencies in production, delivery and advertising. As a result, fortunes were spent standardizing products across countries. For instance, Marathon, a well-loved chocolate bar in the UK, was re-named Snickers to the dismay of many loyalists, and the product formally known as Jif in Britain, Ireland, the Netherlands and Hong Kong was changed in 2001 to Cif in order to harmonize marketing and product inventories.

Brands by any other name

Brand names, in translation, however, were not always what they seemed. Many, possibly apocryphal, stories emerged. I cannot vouch for the accuracy of the following, borrowed from a blog by Terri Morrison and Wayne A Konaway (2006), but it conveys a flavour of the difficulties.

Pepsi had problems with Chinese when their slogan 'Come Alive with the Pepsi Generation' was translated for a Taiwanese billboard as 'Pepsi brings your ancestors back from the dead'. KFC (formerly known as Kentucky Fried Chicken) found that its 'Finger-Lickin' Good' slogan was translated into Chinese as the admonition 'Eat your fingers off'. When Ford Motor Co marketed the Pinto in Brazil, they discovered that 'pinto' was Brazilian slang for 'small penis'. Naturally, no man wanted to own a 'pinto', so Ford blithely changed the car's name to Corcel, which means 'horse' in Portuguese. The car reportedly sold well after that.

LOCAL OR GLOBAL?

With growing sophistication amongst multinationals, the blanket application of global marketing lost favour and, whilst the global strategy often remained, the way in which it was executed – the advertising, packaging, name and so on – were developed locally, to ensure that they reflected the culture of the particular country. However, fashions change, both within and across organizations, and there is a continuing state of flux. A multinational may go through a period when it 'gives power' to individual countries to develop appropriate advertising, but then the emphasis may swing back again to more centralized control. Inevitably this involves considerable political tension. A regional approach means that some regions cannot afford to employ specialist researchers, whilst others can support a whole team. Regional control also means that the research is 'closer to the customer'. However, the downside is that it is very difficult for the centre of the organization to get a global picture (Callingham, 2004: 47).

COORDINATING MULTI-COUNTRY STUDIES

How the industry is structured

Two broad approaches have emerged (Imms and Ereaut, 2002: 117).

Networks of independent qualitative agencies

These operate as semi-formal affiliations of agencies in different countries, which work together as and when one of the agencies is asked by a client to coordinate a multi-country project.

Global multinational research agencies

These large agencies have the resources to service clients' global needs, supplemented where necessary by local agencies.

Managing a multi-country study

Fiona Jack, an experienced international researcher, emphasizes that multi-country studies require a great deal of management and coordination to ensure that all the research agencies involved are completely briefed, that they have all the necessary materials, that there is consistency in the approach across all the countries, and that the research outcomes can be collated effectively (Jack, 2009, personal communication). The more countries that are involved, the greater the amount of work that is needed 'up front'.

Reinforcing the need for a high level of 'up-front' planning, Jane Gwillian and Gyorgy Pastor (quoted in Imms and Ereaut, 2002: 110) highlight six planning considerations for international research coordination:

- language and semantics;
- social habits and cultural mixes;
- legislation;
- differences in cultural norms and interpersonal relations;
- variations in market development;
- ways of doing research and the infrastructure of the research industry.

The lead agency

The most common approach to achieving synchronized planning across all of the countries involved is for a lead agency in one of the countries to act as the coordinator. This agency is directly responsible to the client and, once the project has been given the go-ahead, it takes on the task of briefing the agencies in the participating countries, writing the screener, the discussion guide and other research documents.

Traditionally a lead agency from the UK was often chosen, in part because much international work emanated from the United States and there was the advantage of a common language. However, the dominance of the UK is waning as multinational companies develop centres of excellence, particularly in European countries such as Italy, France and Germany. These centres often choose an agency on 'their patch' to take on the coordinating role.

A researcher from the lead agency will generally visit each of the agencies involved in the project in their home countries, to brief them face to face. This ensures that the local researchers are absolutely clear on the research requirements. The lead researcher will then stay over if the research is to be carried out immediately, or return in due course to the countries involved to observe the fieldwork. The aim is to achieve continuity and shared learning. However, with the high cost of travel and the researcher's time, and tighter budgets, briefing is increasingly carried out by phone or video conferencing. Equally, fieldwork, especially group discussions, can be web-streamed internationally, so it can be viewed by the lead agency in 'real time'.

ORGANIZING STIMULI

Delivering stimuli to a number of countries simultaneously, so that it arrives in time and in good condition, with its necessary transit or customs documents, is a feat in itself and, although this might seem to be a mundane task, it is essential to get it right. Fiona Jack describes the plight of her 25 vacuum cleaners, personally handed over to a courier company and destined for Hungary. Only 24 vacuum cleaners arrived and, as the shipment was incomplete, it could not be released by customs officials. The fieldwork had to be cancelled and the client, just arrived from Stockholm, flew straight back home.

The best option is to persuade the client to handle transportation of stimuli. Multinationals generally have the resources and the experienced 'on-the-ground' support to deal with the bureaucracy involved.

VIEWING FACILITIES

Clients are likely to choose group discussions for international projects because the structure, discussion topics and outputs are easier to standardize than they are with other methodologies, although increasingly clients are wanting a broader spectrum of approaches in multi-country studies (Jack, 2009, personal communication). Groups can be viewed and the content of the discussion can be simultaneously translated, which means that clients who cannot speak the local language can still experience the research at first hand.

Group discussions are conducted in viewing facilities throughout the world, and most large cities will have one or more such facilities (in large American and European cities there will usually be dozens). Although these can range from state-of-the-art, technologically sophisticated, roomy environments to cramped, poor-quality rooms with poor audio and visual aids, nonetheless they are available. The UK (and to some extent Australia) is different in that group sessions have traditionally been conducted in a recruiter's home, and this practice continues, although groups that are to be viewed are generally sited in facilities.

GROUP MODERATION

In the early days of multi-country studies, researchers from the lead agency might themselves conduct group discussions in another country. At that time, most studies only extended as far as Europe, so it was possible to get bilingual researchers relatively easily. Nowadays, however, researchers who are native to the country are usually employed. This is partly because of the vast range of languages that would need to be covered worldwide. More importantly, there is an acknowledgement that the researcher can only understand the nuances, slang, humour – all the aspects of culture that may influence participants' responses – if he or she lives in that culture.

An alternative is co-moderation, in which a moderator from the lead agency jointly runs the session with a local moderator. Sarah Davies regularly co-moderates groups in India and the local moderator interprets the cultural and social context. Davies emphasizes the importance of 'being there' and observing the cultural aspects that are so ingrained in the particular culture that a local moderator takes them for granted. They become 'rationally invisible' (Shotter, 1993: 60). Meanwhile, the 'outsider' can question the obvious (Davies, 2009, personal communication).

TRANSLATION

For clients who want to view the group, understanding the local language will usually present problems. They will not understand either the researcher or the research participants. Good simultaneous translation therefore becomes critical. If the translation is poor, then clients will believe that the group itself is being inadequately run. As Jack (2009, personal communication) emphasizes, the translator needs to have an excellent grasp not only of English but also of marketing in general, the specific research issues being explored and any political issues that are around. Ideally, he or she will be included in the briefing meeting, especially if the moderator who will be running the groups is not fluent in English. Familiarization with the stimuli before the groups start is essential, because it is impossible for the translator to inspect the stimuli as they are presented in the group, make sense of a cacophony of competing voices and translate accurately all at the same time.

ANALYSING AND COLLATING DATA

There are two schools of thought in terms of the way in which the data in a multi-country study are analysed, collated and shared with the client. Either the lead country adopts the role of 'controller', in which case the raw data (translated transcripts, drawings, diaries etc) are returned to the lead agency, which then analyses, interprets and prepares the presentation or other method of sharing the outcomes with the client. This way of working ensures a high degree of consistency and synchronicity of the data, but may lose the idiosyncratic perspectives of the individual countries.

The alternative approach is that the individual countries are given a greater degree of autonomy. Each country analyses and interprets its own data, incorporating local culture and conditions. However, the countries each follow a pre-prepared, structured template developed by the lead agency. The analysis process, categorizing and ordering of the data must fit within this template, so that analysis and recommendations from the different countries can be easily combined to provide an overall picture. Fiona Jack, who favours this approach, likes where possible to convene the researchers from different countries in a workshop after they have completed their analysis. In this way, areas of similarity and difference can be highlighted and cross-fertilization helps to synthesize outcomes and enhances the whole project.

Neither approach is better than the other. There is always a balance to be struck between comparable data that allow commonalities to be seen and data that are sufficiently culturally sensitive to provide an understanding of what makes each country distinctive and singular (Imms and Ereaut, 2002: 109). In part it depends on how much trust the research agency has in the overseas research agencies it is working with. Where there is an ongoing relationship and mutual respect, a more autonomous relationship is more common. Equally, with an unfamiliar agency in a country in which the lead agency has not previously worked, a controlling relationship might feel more comfortable.

VARIATIONS BETWEEN COUNTRIES

Cultures, habits and norms vary considerably from country to country and, just as when we are visiting a new country as a tourist, it is very important to try to gain some understanding of people's expectations and cultural behaviours in a research context.

For instance, in Japan it is not common to speak with people you do not know, so research participants will not naturally chat with one another whilst waiting to be interviewed. This means that there can be some awkwardness at the start of a group as it feels a very un-Japanese way of doing things.

In India there is a tendency for participants to be 'over positive', because they do not want to appear rude. It is important that the researcher is aware of this, so that research outputs can be viewed with the appropriate 'cultural lens' (Sarah Davies, 2008, personal communication).

However, it is easy to overstate the difficulties of carrying out qualitative research in more traditional countries. Jim Ryan, an experienced Middle East researcher, has conducted group discussions in Saudi Arabia with men on the topic of Viagra. He emphasizes the similarities with other countries, provided that certain local protocols are observed. For instance, the topic was introduced as 'sexual performance', although once the groups were up and running, the subject of 'erectile dysfunction' arose naturally (Ryan, 2005).

There are also some differences in group recruitment in Saudi Arabia, especially in relation to women. Recruiting friends and relatives through word of mouth is common, and it is normal for a female moderator to run female groups, which are held in a research participant's house, rather than a viewing lab (Ryan, 2009, personal communication).

References

Ayers, L (2008) Active listening, in *The Sage Encyclopedia of Qualitative Research Methods*, Vol 1, Sage, ed L M Given, pp 7–8, Sage, Los Angeles

Bayley, G (2006) *How do I Know What I Think until I Hear What I Say? Is it time to tear up the discussion guide?* Proceedings from the QRCA Conference Paper, Atlanta

Berger, P L and Luckmann, T (1967) *The Social Construction of Reality: A treatise in the sociology of knowledge*, Penguin, Harmondsworth

Berne, E (1964) *Games People Play: The psychology of human relationships*, Penguin Books, London

Burr, V (1995) *An Introduction to Social Constructionism*, Routledge, London

Callingham, M (2004) *Market Intelligence: How and why organisations use market research*, Kogan Page, London

Campbell, R (2008) *Are we Confusing New Qual 'Data' Sources with Analysis?* Proceedings from the AQR/QRCA International Conference, Barcelona

Cassell, C (2006) *Enhancing the Quality of Qualitative Research in the Work Psychology Field*, Proceedings of the Annual Division of Occupational Psychology Conference, Glasgow

Ceserani, J (2003) *Big Ideas: Putting the zest into creativity and innovation at Work*, Kogan Page, London

Chandler, J and Owen, M (2002) *Developing Brands with Qualitative Market Research*, Sage, London

Chrzanowska, J (2002) *Interviewing Groups and Individuals in Qualitative Market Research*, Sage, London

Comley, P (2008) Online research communities: a user guide, *International Journal of Market Research*, 50(5), pp 679–94

Cooke, M and Buckley, N (2008) Web 20 social networks and the future of market research, *International Journal of Market Research*, 50(2), pp 267–92

Damasio, A (2000) *The Feeling of What Happens*, Vintage, London de Groot, G (1986) *Deep, Dangerous or Just Plain Dotty*, Proceedings of the annual ESOMAR conference

Denzin, N J and Lincoln, Y (2005) Introduction: The discipline and practise of qualitative research in *The Sage Handbook of Qualitative Research* (3rd edn), ed N J Denzin and Y Lincoln, p 7, Sage, California

Desai, P (2002) *Methods beyond Interviewing in Qualitative Market Research*, Sage, London

Durkheim, E (1970) *Suicide: A study of sociology*, ed G Simpson, Routledge & Kegan Paul, London

Earls, M (2002) *Welcome to the Creative Age: Bananas, business and the death of marketing*, John Wiley, London

Ereaut, G (2002) *Analysis and Interpretation in Qualitative Market Research*, Sage, London

Esomar Industry Report (2008) *Global Market Research*, produced in cooperation with KMPG Advisory, Amsterdam

Freud, S (1970) Creative writers and day dreaming, in *Creativity*, ed P E Vernon, Penguin, London

Furnham, A (1999) *Body Language at Work*, Chartered Institute of Personnel and Development, London

Gladwell, M (2005) *Blink: The power of thinking without thinking*, Penguin, London

Glen, R (1996) Analysis and interpretation in qualitative research: a researcher's perspective, in *Excellence in Advertising: The IPA guide to best practice*, ed L Butterfield, pp 119–43, IPA/Butterworth Heinemann, Oxford

Goldsmith, R (1981) *Methodological Approaches to New Product Development*, Proceedings of the annual Market Research Conference

Gordon, W (1999) *Goodthinking: A guide to qualitative research*, Admap, Henley-on-Thames

Gordon, W and Langmaid, R (1988) *Qualitative Market Research: A practitioner's and buyer's guide*, Gower, Aldershot

Goudge, P (2006) *Employee Research: How to increase employee involvement through consultation*, Kogan Page, London

Guilford, J P (1970) Traits of creativity, in *Creativity*, ed P E Vernon, Penguin, London

Habermas, J (1974) *Theory and Practise*, Heinemann, London

Hague, P, Hague, N and Morgan, C A (2004) *Market Research in Practice*, Kogan Page, London

Harvey, M and Evans, M (2001) Semiotics: a window into competitor advertising, *Admap Magazine*, 418 (June)

Holmes, C and Keegan, S (1983) *Current and Developing Creative Research Methods in New Product Development*, Proceedings of the MRS Annual Conference, Brighton

Imms, M and Ereaut, G (2002) *An Introduction to Qualitative Market Research*, Sage, London

Keegan, S (2005) Qualitative research: the hidden persuader, *Organisations and People*, **12**(4), pp 11–17

Keegan, S (2006) Emerging from the cocoon of science, *The Psychologist*, **19**(11), pp 668–71

Keegan, S (2008) *Re-defining Qualitative Research Within a Business Context: Emergent inquiry: integrating research and business strategy*, VDM Verlag Dr Muller, Saarcrucken, Germany

Keegan, S (2009) 'Emergent inquiry': a practitioner's reflections on the development of qualitative research, *QMRIJ*, **12**(2), pp 234–48

Langmaid, R and Andrews M (2003) *Breakthrough Zone: Harnessing consumer creativity for business innovation*, John Wiley, London

Leadbeater, C (2008) *We-Think*, Profile Books, London

Lillis, G (2002) *Delivering Results in Qualitative Market Research*, Sage, London

Mariampolski, H (2001) *Qualitative Market Research: A comprehensive guide*, Sage, California

Marshall, J (1999) Living life as inquiry, *Systemic Practise and Action Research*, **12**(2), pp 155–71

Mead, G H (1962) *Mind, Self and Society*, University of Chicago Press, London

Morrison, and Konaway, W A [accessed 2006] Blog [Online] http://my.opera.com/kitkreuger/blog/2006/11/14/translation-problems-in-global-marketing

MRS News (2008), 44 (November–December)

Myers, J (1977) Marketing research is deficient in identifying deficiencies, *Journal of Marketing*, **41**(4)

Nancarrow, C, Spackman, N and Barker, A (2001), Informed eclecticism: a research paradigm for the twenty first century, *International Journal of Market Research*, **43**(1), pp 3–28

Nancarrow, C and Tinson, J (2006) Academic–practitioner symbiosis, *BPS Qualitative Methods in Psychology Newsletter*, 1

O'Connor, J and McDermott, I (1996) *Principles of NLP*, Harper Collins, London

Paley, J (2008) Positivism, in *The Sage Encyclopedia of Qualitative Research Methods*, ed L M Liven, pp 646–50, Sage, California

Parnes, S J (1967) *Creative Behaviour Guidebook*, Scribers, New York

Phillips, T (2008) Online Communities, *Research Magazine*, June, pp 41–42

Pike, R and Gordon, W (1997) *Carry on Round the 'U' Bend: An experimental comparison of three qualitative methodologies*, Proceedings of the ESOMAR Congress, Edinburgh

Pincott, G and Branthwaite, A (2000) *Nothing New Under the Sun,* proceedings of the Market Research Society Conference, London

Puccio, G J, Firestien, R L, Coyle, C and Masucci, C (2006) A review of the effectiveness of CPS training: a focus on workplace issues, *Harvard Review,* 15(1), pp 19–33

Puchta, C and Potter, J (2004) *Focus Group Practice,* Sage, London

Raymond, E S (2001) *The Cathedral and the Bazaar: Musings on Linux and Open Source by an accidental revolutionary,* O'Reilly Media, Inc, Sebastopol, CA

Robarts, G (2008) Graham Page, global director of innovations at Millward Brown, quoted in, The land of make believe, *Research Magazine,* July

Rogers, C R (1961) *On becoming a person: A therapist's view of psychotherapy,* Houghton Mifflin Company, Boston

Rogers, C R (1970) *Towards a Theory of Creativity* in *Creativity,* ed P E Vernon, Penguin, London

Roland, G (2003) *The Slag of All Semioticians,* Proceedings of the annual Market Research Society Conference

Ryan, J (2005) *Sensitive Subject in a Sensitive Market: Researching erectile dysfunction in Saudi Arabia,* proceedings of the Esomar Global Healthcare Conference, Paris

Salari, S [accessed 2009] [online] www.everydaylives.com

Seale, C (ed) (1998) *Researching Society and Culture,* Sage, London

Shah, I (1966) *The Exploits of the Incomparable Mulla Nasrudin,* Jonathan Cape, London

Shank, G (2008) in *The Sage Encyclopedia of Qualitative Research Methods,* Vol 2, ed L M Given, Sage, California

Shaw, P (2002) *Changing Conversations in Organisations,* Routledge, London

Shotter, J (1993) *Conversational Realities: Constructing life through language,* Sage, London

Smith, D V L (2007) *It's Not How Good You Are It's How Good You Want To Be! Are market researchers really up for 'reconstruction'?* Proceedings of the annual Market Research Society Annual Conference

Smith, D V L and Fletcher, J H (2001) *Inside Information: Making sense of marketing data,* John Wiley, Chichester

Smith, D V L and Fletcher, J H (2004) *The Art and Science of Interpreting Market Research Evidence,* John Wiley, Chichester

Tatar, J (2008) *Focus Groups on Second Life,* proceedings of the AQR-QRCA conference, Barcelona

Urban, G L and Hauser, J R [accessed 2003] *'Listening in' to find unmet customer needs and solutions* [online] http://www.mitedu/ hauser/ Papers/LI010303.pdf

Valentine, V (2002) *Repositioning Research: A new MR language model*, Proceedings of the Market Research Society annual conference, London

Valentine, V (2007) *Semiotics: What now, my love?* Proceedings of the Market Research Society annual conference

Vogt, C and Knapman, S (2008) The anatomy of social networks, *Market Leader*, Spring, pp 46–51

Walkowski, J (2001) *Online Qualitative Research for Motorola: Lessons learnt*, proceedings of the Association for Qualitative Research/Qualitative Research Consultants Association Conference, Paris

Wardle, J (2002) *Developing Advertising with Qualitative Market Research*, Sage, London

Whiting, M and Sagne, F (2005) *Windows on the World*, Proceedings of the Esomar, Innovate! Conference, Paris, February 2005

Willig, C (2001) *Introducing Qualitative Research in Psychology*, Open University Press, Berkshire

Wilson, T D (2002) *Strangers to Ourselves: Discovering the adaptive unconscious*, Belknap Press of Harvard University Press, Boston, MA

Zaltman, G (2003) *How Customers Think: Essential insights into the mind of the market*, Harvard Business School Press, Boston, MA

Index